ENCYCLOPEDIA
OF
WORLD
GEOGRAPHY

SECOND EDITION

ENCYCLOPEDIA
OF
WORLD
GEOGRAPHY

SECOND EDITION

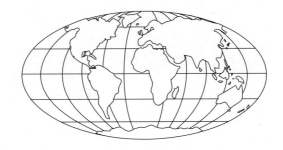

VOLUME FOURTEEN
Russia and
Northern Eurasia

Marshall Cavendish
New York · Toronto · Sydney

2002 Reference Edition

Marshall Cavendish Corporation
99 White Plains Road
Tarrytown, New York 10591-9001

www.marshallcavendish.com

AN ANDROMEDA BOOK

Planned and produced by
Andromeda Oxford Ltd
11–13 The Vineyard, Abingdon,
Oxfordshire OX14 3PX, England

www.andromeda.co.uk

Copyright © Andromeda Oxford Ltd
2002

**Library of Congress
Cataloging-in-Publication Data**

Encyclopedia of world geography /
[general advisory editor, Peter
Haggett].-- 2nd ed.
        p. cm.
    Includes bibliographical references
and index.
    ISBN 0-7614-7289-4 (set)
    ISBN 0-7614-7303-3 (v. 14)
    1. Geography--Encyclopedias.
I. Haggett, Peter.
    G133 .E48 2001
    910--dc21
                                        2001028437

Printed by: L.E.G.O. S.p.A., Vicenza,
Italy

06 05 04 03 02 01   6 5 4 3 2 1

This page: *Pre-1990 portraits of Marx,
Engels and Lenin in Winter Palace
Square, Leningrad (now St Petersburg)*

Title page: *A market stall in the
Caucasus*

CONTENTS

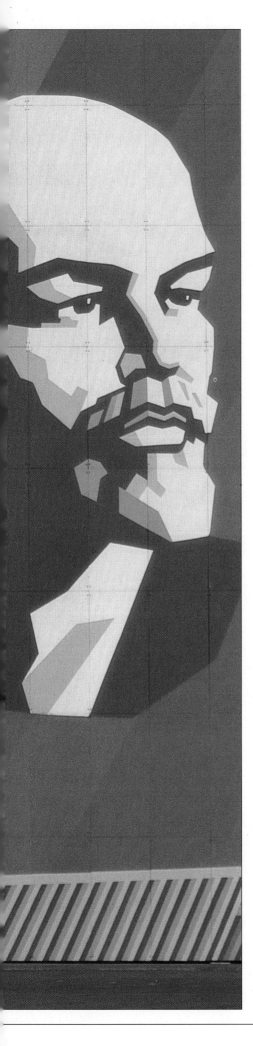

INTRODUCTION

Russia and Northern Eurasia

THE AREA COVERED BY RUSSIA AND NORTHERN Eurasia reaches a quarter of the way round the globe, extending west to east from the Carpathian mountains near the border with Poland and Romania to the volcanoes of Kamchatka, north of Japan. The sheer size of the region means that it encompasses spectacularly different landscapes. These are often the product of distinctive climate bands running laterally between the eastern and western borders. The bands are crossed from north to south only by the Urals – often taken as the boundary between Europe and Asia – and by three of the world's longest rivers all flowing into the Arctic Ocean.

The most northerly part of the region is an arctic environment of permafrost containing valuable mineral resources. South of the treeline is the central band where nearly a quarter of the world's forests lie. This area is the home of the Grizzly bear (or Eurasian brown bear), traditionally a symbol of Russia. Farther south again are the temperate grasslands and the black-earth farmlands of the steppes, one of the world's great grain-producing areas. These border the warm deserts of Mongolia (the Gobi), and of the Central Asian republics, which extend as far east as the Caspian and Aral Seas. High mountains such as the Pamir range and the Caucasus form the region's southern borders.

Three-quarters of this vast land area lies within one country, Russia, the largest in the world. Russian power, under the tsarist empire and later within the communist regime, controlled the region until the late 1980s. The many consequences of the recent collapse of the Soviet Union are shared by the diverse peoples of Northern Eurasia. The Soviet regime encompassed 126 different officially recognized nationalities though the majority are Slavic-speaking. Many of these peoples are now seeking a new identity, often aligning themselves with countries outside the region. The mainly Muslim Central Asian republics are turning to the rest of the Islamic world while the Baltic states look toward Scandinavia. Among their common problems are the environmental consequences of a period of rapid economic growth based on heavy industry, massive engineering projects and the exploitation of Northern Eurasia's vast resources. The Aral Sea, for example, has shrunk drastically, its wind-blown agrochemical residues poisoning local children. Even the remote permafrost zone bears the scars of largescale mining and the traffic that mining brought to the area.

North America

Central and South America

A	ALBANIA
AU	AUSTRIA
B	BELGIUM
BO	BOSNIA HERZEGOVINA
C	CROATIA
CZ	CZECH REPUBLIC
HUN	HUNGARY
M	MACEDONIA (FORMER YUGOSLAV REPUBLIC OF)
N	NETHERLANDS
R	RUSSIA
S	SLOVAKIA
SL	SLOVENIA
SW	SWITZERLAND
YU	YUGOSLAVIA

Europe

Asia

GREENLAND
(Denmark)

SVALBARD
(Norway)

ICELAND

RUSSIA

NORWAY

SWEDEN
FINLAND
ESTONIA
LATVIA
LITHUANIA

UNITED
KINGDOM
DENMARK
IRELAND

R
BELARUS

N
GERMANY
POLAND

LUXEMBOURG
CZ
UKRAINE

B
AU
S
HUN
MOLDOVA

FRANCE
SW
SL
C
ROMANIA

ANDORRA
BO
YU
M
AZERBAIJAN

ITALY
BULGARIA

PORTUGAL
SPAIN
GREECE
ARMENIA
TURKEY

GIBRALTAR
(UK)
MALTA
CYPRUS
SYRIA

TUNISIA
LEBANON
IRAQ

MOROCCO
ISRAEL

ALGERIA
LIBYA
EGYPT
JORDAN

WESTERN
SAHARA
(Morocco)

MAURITANIA
MALI
NIGER
CHAD

CAPE
VERDE

SENEGAL

MBIA
JINEA-
ISSAU
GUINEA
BURKINA
FASO
BENIN
NIGERIA

SIERRA LEONE
CÔTE
D'IVOIRE
TOGO
GHANA

LIBERIA
CENTRAL
AFRICAN
REPUBLIC

EQUATORIAL GUINEA
CAMEROON

SAO TOME
& PRINCIPE
GABON

REPUBLIC OF CONGO
DEMOCRATIC
REPUBLIC OF
CONGO
RWANDA
BURUNDI

CABINDA
(Angola)
TANZANIA

ANGOLA
ZAMBIA
MALAWI

NAMIBIA
ZIMBABWE
MOZAMBIQUE

BOTSWANA

SOUTH
AFRICA
SWAZILAND
LESOTHO

KAZAKHSTAN
MONGOLIA

NORTH
KOREA
SOUTH
KOREA
JAPAN

UZBEKISTAN
KYRGYZSTAN

TURKMENISTAN
TAJIKISTAN

CHINA

AFGHANISTAN
BHUTAN

KUWAIT
IRAN

QATAR
PAKISTAN
NEPAL

BAHRAIN
SAUDI
ARABIA
TAIWAN

UNITED ARAB
EMIRATES
OMAN
BANGLADESH

INDIA
MYANMAR
LAOS

ERITREA
NORTHERN
MARIANA
ISLANDS
(United States)

YEMEN
THAILAND
VIETNAM
PHILIPPINES

SUDAN
DJIBOUTI
GUAM
(United States)

ETHIOPIA
CAMBODIA

SOMALIA
SRI LANKA
PALAU
FEDERATED STATES
OF MICRONESIA

UGANDA
MALDIVES
BRUNEI
NAURU

KENYA
MALAYSIA

SEYCHELLES
SINGAPORE

COMOROS
INDONESIA
PAPUA
NEW GUINEA
SOLOMON
ISLANDS

MADAGASCAR
MAURITIUS

REUNION
(France)

VANUATU

NEW
CALEDONIA
(France)

AUSTRALIA

Africa

Australasia, Oceania and Antarctica

NEW
ZEALAND

Antarctica

1880

Russia and Northern Eurasia

COUNTRIES IN THE REGION

ESTONIA · LATVIA · LITHUANIA · MOLDOVA

BELARUS · UKRAINE · RUSSIA · GEORGIA

ARMENIA · AZERBAIJAN · TURKMENISTAN

UZBEKISTAN · TAJIKISTAN · KYRGYZSTAN

KAZAKHSTAN · MONGOLIA

height of land (meters)

5000
3000
2000
1000
500
200
0 (sea level)

■ capital city
● major town

▲ mountain peak
▼ depression

Domes of victory (*left*) The multicolored, onion-shaped cupolas of St Basil's Cathedral in Moscow have been a characteristic feature of the city skyline ever since they were built by Tsar Ivan IV in 1555. The cathedral commemorates his defeat of the Tartars – one of many peoples who have invaded Russia through the centuries.

Estonia

REPUBLIC OF ESTONIA

THE NORTHERNMOST OF THE THREE SMALL Baltic republics, Estonia lies on the eastern shore of the Baltic Sea, with Latvia to the south and Russia to the east. Finland lies to the north, across the Gulf of Finland. In 1991 Estonia regained its independence after half a century of Soviet rule that had never been officially recognized by some Western governments. The Estonian people, who speak a language similar to Finnish and share a common descent with them, have a strong cultural heritage that has survived many centuries of foreign domination.

NATIONAL DATA – ESTONIA	
Land area 45,100 sq km (17,400 sq mi)	
Climate cold temperate maritime	
Major physical features highest point: Munamägi 318 m (1,042 ft); largest lake: Lake Peipus (part) 3,548 sq km (1,370 sq mi)	
Population (2000 est.) 1,431,471	
Form of government multiparty republic with one legislative house	
Armed forces army 3,742; navy 344 air force 501	
Largest cities Tallinn (capital – 401,100); Tartu (98,400); Narva (72,100); Pärnu (52,200)	
Official language Estonian	
Ethnic composition Estonian 61.5%; Russian 30.3%; Ukrainian 3.2%; Belorussian 1.8%; Finnish 1.1%; others 2.1%	
Religious affiliations mainly Lutheran, with Eastern Orthodox and Baptist minorities	
Currency 1 Estonian kroon (EEk) = 100 cents	
Gross domestic product (1999) US $7.9 billion	
Gross domestic product per capita (1999) US $5,600	
Life expectancy at birth male 63 yr; female 74.5 yr	
Major resources bituminous shale, peat, amber, beef and dairy cattle, timber	

ENVIRONMENT

Estonia's low and undulating landscape bears the marks of extensive glacial activity. Notable features are the many islands off the coast including Hiiumaa and Saaremaa to the west (across the mouth of the Gulf of Riga), and Lake Peipus along the Russian border.

The climate is cool and northerly. Winds from the Baltic make the winters damp and raw, but provide relief from the much colder weather to the east. Although more than half the land is given over to pasture and fields, much of the natural vegetation remains. This includes mixed forest, with marsh and swamp in low-lying areas. Wildlife is still abundant in these parts, including deer and lynx.

SOCIETY

Estonians have inhabited this area for at least 2,000 years. Their first experience of foreign invasion came with the Vikings in the 9th century AD. In the 13th century Estonia came under the Christianizing influence of Germanic knights, who joined the Teutonic Order in 1237. German domination later gave way to Swedish and finally Russian rule in the 18th century. A growing awareness of Estonian culture and identity developed during the 19th century, and in 1918, following the upheavals of the Russian Revolution, the country at last became independent.

The new democratic regime proved fragile, however, and during World War II Estonia was little more than a pawn in the struggles between its more powerful neighbors. After being formally annexed by the Soviet Union in 1940 the country was under Nazi German occupation until 1944. The reimposition of communist rule after World War II brought with it enforced collectivization and an influx of Russian and Slav immigrants. In the late 1980s, however, the Soviet grip on the republic relaxed. Baltic nationalism revived, and independence came in 1991 following the breakup of the Soviet Union. Initially, the civil rights of nonethnic Estonians, who represent about 40 percent of the population, were reduced to favor the native population. However, the majority of the ethnic Russian population was able to vote in the 1995 elections.

Estonia has a strong cultural tradition, particularly distinctive in its music and literature. The Lutheran Church has a long history of choral singing, reflected in the music festivals held.

Wooded marshland and bog islands – such as these in the Endla State National Reserve – and boulder-strewn lowlands cover much of Estonia, the smallest of the Baltic states, making the land difficult to farm. Estonia also includes some 800 Baltic islands.

ECONOMY

Estonia had an efficient and prosperous economy, but still suffered much hardship after 1991, as other former Soviet Republics. By the early 2000s the transition to a market economy was showing signs of success and Estonia hoped to join the European Union in the near future.

Keeping livestock is the main agricultural activity, in particular raising beef and dairy cattle. Forest cover has been severely reduced in recent years and woodworking industries have suffered as a result, though a concerted reforestation program is now underway. The country has few natural mineral resources, apart from bituminous shale, which supplies power for the industrial sector and numerous byproducts for the chemical industry. Most other industries depend on imported raw materials.

Estonia has a well-developed communications infrastructure and a good welfare support network. There are some 40 Estonian newspapers, and since 1955 the republic has had its own Estonian-language television channel. Educational standards and literacy levels are high, and Estonia's 17th-century university at Tartu remains one of the great universities of the former Soviet Union.

Latvia

REPUBLIC OF LATVIA

L ATVIA IS A SMALL, NEWLY INDEPENDENT state that has much in common with the two neighboring republics of Estonia to the north and Lithuania to the south. Situated on the eastern shore of the Baltic Sea, it also shares borders with the former Soviet republics of Russia to the east and Belarus to the southeast.

ENVIRONMENT

The country has a long, sandy coastline that faces the Baltic to the west, while to the northwest, around the Gulf of Riga, it forms a broad arc with the capital, Riga, in the center. The landscape consists of undulating plains, rising in the east to a low plateau dotted with lakes and bogs. The cool, damp climate with moderate rainfall brings some very cold spells in winter. Oak and pine forests interspersed with pasture and meadows cover large areas of the country. The abundant wildlife includes foxes, lynx and squirrels, and the rare European beaver has been reintroduced to woodland areas.

SOCIETY

Like their Lithuanian neighbors, the Latvians (or Letts) are an ancient Baltic people. In the 13th century Latvia and Estonia came under the control of the German crusading order of the Livonian Knights. Latvia was later divided between Poland and Sweden, but by the end of the 18th century it had been absorbed into the vast Russian empire of Catherine the Great (1729–96).

The Russian Revolution of 1917 provided the opportunity for an upsurge in Baltic nationalism, and by 1920 Latvia was recognized as an independent nation. In 1940 Latvia was annexed as a constituent republic of the Soviet Union under the terms of the Nazi–Soviet Non-Aggression Pact. From 1941 until its reconquest by Soviet forces in 1944 Latvia was under German occupation.

A rapid industrialization program instituted in Latvia by the Soviets in the postwar period led to massive immigration into Latvia from other parts of the Soviet Union. The Latvians have, however, maintained a strong and vibrant culture and in 1988 their language replaced Russian as the official language; a prelude to independence from the Soviet Union, which was achieved in 1991. A liberalization of citizenship laws in 1998 eased the way for Russians to gain citizenship.

ECONOMY

Industrial production, once a major contributor to gross national product, was in decline for the first half of the 1990s. Once a leading Soviet producer of motor vehicles, consumer goods and telecommunications equipment, Latvia's main trading partner by the late 1990s was the EU. Latvia established free trade regimes with EFTA and the EU in 1996.

The capital city, Riga, has a long tradition as a seaport and trading center, and is one of the busiest of the Baltic cities. Elsewhere, the country is well served by rail, road and sea links, which have helped to encourage the growth of tourism. The welfare support network is highly developed. Educational standards are good and literacy levels high.

NATIONAL DATA – LATVIA			
Land area 64,500 sq km (24,900 sq mi)			

Climate		Temperatures		Annual
	Altitude m (ft)	January °C(°F)	July °C(°F)	precipitation mm (in)
Riga	3 (10)	–7 (19)	17 (62)	567 (22.3)

Major physical features highest point: Vidzeme 311 m (1,020 ft); longest river: Western Dvina = Daugava (part) 1,060 km (635 mi)

Population (2000 est.) 2,404,926

Form of government multiparty republic with one legislative house

Armed forces army 1,500; navy 1,000; air force 300

Largest cities Riga (capital – 779,600); Daugavpils (113,600); Liepāja (94,100); Jelgava (70,700)

Official language Latvian (Lettish)

Ethnic composition Latvian 55.3%; Russian 32.5%; Belorussian 4%; Ukrainian 2%; Polish 2.2%; Lithuanian 1.3%; Estonians 0.1%; Germans 0.1%

Religious affiliations mainly Lutheran, with Eastern Orthodox and Roman Catholic minorities

Currency 1 lats = 100 cents (from November 1993)

Gross domestic product (1999) US $9.8 billion

Gross domestic product per capita (1999) US $4,200

Life expectancy at birth male 62.4 yr; female 74.4 yr

Major resources amber, peat, limestone, gypsum, dairy produce, livestock, wheat, sugar beet, timber

Riga's 13th-century Doma cathedral dominates the Baltic city, which spans the Western Dvina river. The city was founded in 1201 by Bishop Albert I, whose crusaders, the Brothers of the Sword, Christianized the whole of Livonia (modern Latvia and southern Estonia).

Lithuania

LITHUANIAN REPUBLIC

L ITHUANIA LIES IN THE SOUTHEASTERN corner of the Baltic Sea, with Latvia to the north and Belarus to the east. To the southwest it shares borders with Poland and the Kaliningrad enclave that is part of the Russian Federation.

Although Lithuania is a small country now, in medieval times, as part of the Grand Duchy of Lithuania, it was one of the most powerful states in Eastern Europe. A strong sense of national identity going back some 2,000 years was vital to the struggle for independence from Soviet domination, which began in 1940 during World War II.

NATIONAL DATA – LITHUANIA	
Land area 65,200 sq km (25,200 sq mi)	
Climate temperate, transitional between maritime and continental	
Major physical features highest point: Juozapine 294 m (964 ft); longest river: Neman (part) 970 km (580 mi)	
Population (2000 est.) 3,620,756	
Form of government multiparty republic with one legislative house	
Armed forces army 4,300; navy 350; air force 250	
Largest cities Vilnius (capital – 577,800); Kaunas (411,600); Klaipeda (202,400); Siauliai (146,300); Panevezys (129,000)	
Official language Lithuanian	
Ethnic composition Lithuanian 80.1%; Russian 8.6%; Polish 7.7%; Belorussian 1.5%; others 2.1%	
Religious affiliations mainly Roman Catholic, with Lutheran and Reformed minorities	
Currency litas=100 cents (since June 1993)	
Gross domestic product (1999) US $17.3 billion	
Gross domestic product per capita (1999) US $4,800	
Life expectancy at birth male 64.3 yr; female 75.6 yr	
Major resources peat, petroleum, limestone, beef and dairy products, timber, tourism	

ENVIRONMENT

The terrain is mainly low-lying glaciated plains, with sand dunes along the coast and lake-strewn hills in the southeast. The marshy plains of the center are crossed by numerous rivers, including the Neman, which flows from the south into the Baltic Sea. The capital, Vilnius, is on the Vilnya river in the southwest.

Warm summers and cold winters, moderated by damp westerly winds from the Baltic, characterize the mainly continental climate; rainfall is highest in late summer. The plentiful natural vegetation ranges from forests of pine and oak to meadows and marshes. Wildlife includes wolves, badgers, wild boars and numerous birds.

SOCIETY

The Lithuanians, unlike their neighbors the Latvians, resisted conquest by the German crusading order of the Teutonic Knights in the 13th century and, as a result, were the last European people to be converted to Christianity. For 300 years the Lithuanians were united under the powerful rulers of the Gediminoviches dynasty, who established the Grand Duchy of Lithuania incorporating modern Lithuania, Belarus and western Ukraine. In the 15th century, alliance with Poland and later full union extended Lithuanian territory southeastward as far as the Black Sea. However, the expansionist aspirations of the nearby state of Muscovy were a constant threat. In the late 18th century Lithuania finally came under Russian domination, following the partition of Poland.

A precarious independence was gained in the aftermath of the Russian Revolution of 1917, but it was repeatedly threatened by border disputes with Poland. In 1940, under the terms of the Nazi-Soviet Non-Aggression Pact, Lithuania was annexed by the Soviet Union as a constituent republic but in 1941 the country was occupied by German forces. The expulsion of the Germans by the Soviet Army in 1944 reinstated the process of Sovietization.

With the collapse of central Soviet communist power in 1991, Lithuania finally won full independence. Lithuanian, which preserves more archaic features than almost any other language in Europe today, replaced Russian as the official language. The local cultural tradition was also kept alive during the Soviet era through music festivals and folk art.

Festive crowds (*above*) gather in Gediminas Square, Vilnius, capital of Lithuania, to celebrate their national identity. Lithuanians are mostly Roman Catholic, with a distinct language and culture. They finally became independent of the Soviet Union in 1991.

A Russian ship pulls in at the docks (*right*) in Lithuania's chief port, Klaipeda, a naval base on the Baltic coast linked to the Neman river by canal. Between December and March the sea freezes over and icebreakers are used to keep the port open.

Lithuania received far fewer Russian immigrants under Soviet rule than Latvia and Estonia, but it has always had a significantly large Polish community. Consequently it has maintained a strong Roman Catholic tradition.

ECONOMY

Lithuania's economy was disrupted by freedom from Soviet rule. By the late 1990s, 30 percent of exports were going to the EU and trade agreements were in place with neighboring countries. Growth was slow in the 1990s and inflation and unemployment rates remained high.

Agriculture, traditionally strong in meat and dairy farming, has diversified into grain and vegetable crops. Forestry provides local woodworking and other light manufacturing with raw materials. Mineral resources include some petroleum as well as limestone and other construction materials.

Railroads are gradually giving way to roads, as motor vehicles become the chief means of transportation. The Soviet regime encouraged the development of generous medical, welfare and educational facilities, but all three areas are now suffering from lack of resources.

БИЗОН

Belarus

REPUBLIC OF BELARUS

The former Soviet Republic of Belorussia, now officially known by its native Belorussian name of Belarus, stretches eastward from the borders of Poland to Russia. Ukraine lies to the south, and Lithuania and Latvia to the northwest. Often referred to as White Russia (a literal translation), the country has had a long history of domination by neighboring powers. In recent years it has also suffered significant land contamination and its people have been exposed to increased health risks, both associated with the after-effects of the Chernobyl nuclear disaster in Ukraine in 1986, when radioactive fallout was carried across the country.

ENVIRONMENT

The landscape of Belarus consists largely of rolling plains produced by ice-age glaciation. The north is crossed by a series of sandy hills and long ridges made up of glacial debris, while in the south the Pripyat and Dnieper rivers flow to Ukraine through marshlands that have been mostly drained for their fertile soils. A temperate climate, with moderate precipitation, varies between the more equable conditions of central Europe and the extremes of continental Russia.

A third of the land is covered by forests of birch, pine and fir in the north, and oak, ash, maple and beech farther south. In the west, the Belovezhskaya Pushcha – a remnant of the primeval forest that once covered much of Europe – stretches across the Polish frontier. Today it is a nature reserve maintained by both Belarus and Poland, rich in rare wildlife such as elk (moose), Wild boar and beaver. It also offers a refuge to the last of the European bison, descendants of zoo stocks introduced into the wild.

SOCIETY

The country was settled by eastern Slavic peoples about the 6th century AD. Gradually, their cluster of small princedoms came under the sovereignty of the Viking state of Rus, with its capital Kiev to the south. After the overthrow of Kiev in the 13th century, the area became part of the Grand Duchy of Lithuania, which, after two centuries of close alliance, finally entered a union with Poland in 1569.

In the 18th century, when Poland was repeatedly partitioned between Austria, Prussia and Russia, Belarus came under the jurisdiction of Russia and became a political and economic backwater. Under tsarist rule this area, together with Ukraine, became the homeland for most of Russia's Jewish population. Many knew it as the "Pale of Settlement". Forced to live within strictly defined areas, the Jews were also denied many of the basic freedoms of Russia's other subjects, including higher education and freedom of travel.

World War I left the country devastated, and the subsequent Russo-Polish War

Production line pottery (*right*) in a Minsk porcelain factory that produces teapots. Since being rebuilt after its near total destruction during World War II, Minsk has become a major manufacturing center producing a variety of products ranging from household goods, chemicals and foodstuffs to radios, trucks and tractors.

The Victory obelisk (*below*) in Minsk commemorates the dead of World War II, particularly almost the entire Jewish population. Minsk has been virtually rebuilt since 1944 when its recapture by the Russians left hardly a building standing. Its population has more than tripled in the past 40 years.

NATIONAL DATA – BELARUS	
Land area	207,600 sq km (80,200 sq mi)
Climate	temperate, transitional between maritime and continental
Major physical features	highest point: Dzerzhinsky 346 m (1,135 ft); longest river: Dnieper (part) 2,280 km (1,420 mi)
Population	(2000 est.) 10,366,719
Form of government	multiparty republic with one legislative house
Armed forces	army 52,500; air force 15,800
Largest cities	Minsk (capital – 1,751,300); Gomel (503,400); Mogilev (372,700); Vitebsk (356,000); Brest (293,000); Grodno (277,000)
Official languages	Belorussian, Russian
Ethnic composition	Belorussian 77.9%; Russian 13.2%; Polish 4.1%; Ukrainian 2.1%; others 2.7%
Religious affiliations	Eastern Orthodox and Eastern Catholic
Currency	1 ruble (Rub) = 100 kopecks
Gross domestic product	(1999) US $55.2 billion
Gross domestic product per capita	(1999) US $5,300
Life expectancy at birth	male 62.2 yr; female 73.9 yr
Major resources	coal, oil shale, petroleum, potash, limestone, metal ores, salt, dairy products, meat, grain, sugar

of 1919–21 resulted in Belarus being partitioned between Poland and the newly formed Soviet Union. At the outbreak of World War II, Soviet forces seized the Polish sector, which was then overrun by the Germans. The war years took a terrible toll on the population of Belarus; some 1.3 million people died, including most of the Jewish population. In addition, about 75 percent of all urban housing was destroyed, along with almost all of the country's industrial infrastructure. After long and bitter fighting, the Soviet Union took over the entire country, deporting its Polish population and establishing a nominally independent republic with a seat at the United Nations.

Increased freedoms in the late 1980s led to a resurgence of anti-Soviet feeling in Belorussia, culminating in the declaration of a fully independent republic of Belarus in September 1991.

ECONOMY

The economy of Belarus has always been closely linked to that of the Soviet Union. There was much hardship after 1991; the average inflation rate for 1990-96 was 715 percent. Belarus has resisted major change and opted for close economic and cultural ties with Russia. The traditional basis of the Belarussian economy is agriculture, which benefits from fertile soils and a favorable climate. The main crops are oats, rye and other grains, along with potatoes, a mainstay of the local diet, and sugar beet. Meat and dairy cattle are the main livestock. Forestry is significant, as are traditional beekeeping and fur-farming activities. However, all these activities, as well as the health of the people, have been severely affected by the consequences of contamination by the nuclear accident in 1986 at Chernobyl, in neighboring Ukraine.

Industry has increased in importance since the discovery of new mineral resources, including coal, oil shale, petroleum, potash, limestone, metal ores and enormous salt deposits. During the years of the Soviet regime, the Belarussian capital, Minsk, rebuilt its industrial sector to the extent that it became the industrial hub of the western Soviet Union. Today, manufactured goods range from heavy machinery to tools and instruments, furniture, textiles, television sets and electronics components.

Transportation is good, as the country is crossed by several major routes between Russia, the Ukraine and Central Europe. Its many lakes and waterways are also used to float timber to the factories. Welfare and education were highly developed under the Soviet regime. Literacy became virtually universal and education was free and compulsory between the ages of 7 and 17. For those who were able to continue into higher education, there were some 30 institutions to choose from. These good education facilities helped to sustain a strong Belarussian literary and musical heritage. In the years following World War II, the republic built up a conservatory of music, a state opera and ballet company and two state theaters as well as a number of folk music companies.

Ukraine

REPUBLIC OF UKRAINE

T HE EASTERN EUROPEAN REPUBLIC OF THE Ukraine lies on the northern side of the Black Sea, bordering Russia to the east and northeast, Belarus to the north, Poland, Slovakia and Hungary to the west, and Romania and Moldova to the southwest. The second most populous of the former Soviet republics (after Russia), it also ranks second in terms of its economic resources. Economic reforms following the collapse of the Soviet Union caused production to decline. Unemployment and hyperinflation were persistent problems in the late 1990s.

NATIONAL DATA – UKRAINE

Land area	603,700 sq km (233,100 sq mi)			
Climate		**Temperatures**		**Annual**
	Altitude m (ft)	January °C(°F)	July °C(°F)	precipitation mm (in)
Kiev	179 (587)	–6 (21)	20 (68)	554 (21.8)

Major physical features highest point: Hoverla 2,061 m (6,762 ft); longest river: Dnieper (part) 2,280 km (1,420 mi)

Population (2000 est.) 49,153,027

Form of government multiparty republic with one legislative house

Armed forces army 308,000; navy 16,000; air force 146,000

Largest cities Kiev (capital – 2,616,000); Kharkov (1,477,300); Dnepropetrovsk (1,089,000); Donetsk (1,033,800); Odessa (1,000,700); Zaporhizhya (840,400)

Official language Ukrainian

Ethnic composition Ukrainian 73.0%; Russian 22.0%; Jewish 1.0%; others 4.0%

Religious affiliations Eastern Catholic, Eastern Orthodox, Roman Catholic and Jewish

Currency hryvna=100 Kopiykas

Gross domestic product (1999) US $109.5 billion

Gross domestic product per capita (1999) US $2,200

Life expectancy at birth male 63.8 yr; female 73.7 yr

Major resources iron ore, coal, natural gas, oil, manganese, mercury, nickel, rock salt, dairy products, grain, meat, sugar beet, cotton, flax, tobacco, wine, forestry

ENVIRONMENT

Ukraine is famous for its steppe landscape: mile after mile of level, rolling terrain broken only by the Carpathian Mountains, which cross the far southwest between the Slovak and Romanian borders. Equally dramatic, though less high, are the Crimean Mountains that overlook the south coast of the Crimean Peninsula in the far south, dividing the northwestern part of the Black Sea from the smaller Sea of Azov.

Western Ukraine consists mainly of the Dnieper plateau. This low tableland, cut by deep valleys, descends to the Pripet marshes in the north, to the Dnieper river valley in the east and to broad coastal lowlands in the south. East of the Dnieper, the land rises once again to low hills along the northeastern border, and to the Azov Hills and the Donets Ridge in the southeast.

The climate varies from temperate continental in the northeast to Mediterranean on the south coast of the Crimea. Average January temperatures are below freezing point and precipitation is variable. The hot, dry summers of the southern Crimea have for a long time made it attractive to tourists.

Most of the forests are to be found in the south and southwest – in the Carpathian and Crimean Mountains. Farther north, mixed woodland alternates with bog and marshland, while a central band of woodland and steppe is largely given over to farmland. Some areas of virgin

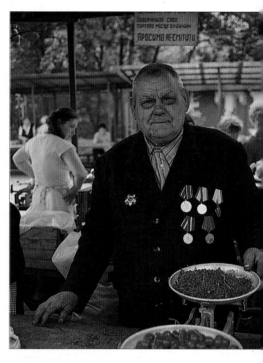

Berries and cherries are weighed by a proud, bemedaled veteran of World War II at a market stall in Kiev, the Ukrainian capital. Under Soviet rule, all food marketing was handled by the state; but today, small-scale private enterprise is making a return.

steppe in the south are designated as nature reserves, the oldest being Askaniya Nova, immediately north of the Crimean Peninsula. The south coast of the Crimea is renowned for its particularly lush vegetation of deciduous and evergreen grasses and exotic flowers and shrubs. Ukrainian wildlife is varied, including woodland animals – foxes, wildcats and Roe deer – and steppe-dwelling hamsters and jerboas.

The Ukrainian capital, Kiev, was once the heart of Kievan Rus, a trading empire founded in the 9th century AD by the Varangians – Viking adventurers from the north. This empire prospered until the 13th century, when it was overrun by Mongol and Tartar invaders from the east. In 1240 these invaders razed the city of Kiev to the ground. During the 14th century most of the area of modern Ukraine came under the sway of Poland and the expanding Lithuanian empire, while the south remained under Mongol control. In 1385 the Polish and Lithuanian crowns were united by the Union of Krayova and in 1569 the two countries entered a full political union.

As Poland-Lithuania pushed its frontier eastward, across the *ukraina*, or "borderlands", newly installed Polish landowners came into conflict with the Cossacks – Tartar warriors whom the Poles had originally recruited to defend their borders. In 1648 the Cossacks declared a semi-independent state, but faced with hostility from the Poles they turned

Architectural gems (*right*) A richly decorated church and bell-tower lie within the grounds of Kiev's Pecherskaya Lavra (Monastery of the Caves), founded in the 11th century. Catacombs below hold the body of the monk Nestor, an early Kievan chronicler.

Swirl of skirts (*below*) A colorful folk ensemble puts on an exciting display of popular Ukrainian dance and song. Ukraine has a vital cultural tradition, reflected especially in folk music, but also in classical music, the theater, literature and the cinema.

to Russia for support. In 1654 a union of Russia and the Ukraine was negotiated. This proved unacceptable to Poland, and a Russo–Polish war broke out, ending in 1667 with Kiev and territory east of the Dnieper being taken by Russia. In 1772 Poland was partitioned by Russia, Prussia and Austria, with the far west of the Ukraine going to Austria. By a second partition in 1793 areas to the west and south of Kiev went to Russia.

In the 19th century a Ukrainian nationalist movement was born; this enjoyed some success in the civil war that followed the Russian Revolutions of 1917. However, in 1922 the country became one of the four founder-republics of the Soviet Union. Although the 1920s saw a period of improved living conditions and the encouragement of the Ukrainian language, the situation changed dramatically in the 1930s. Stalin's policy of enforced collectivization of agriculture resulted in a terrible famine that claimed millions of lives. Harsh political repression followed, as Stalin systematically crushed the thriving Ukrainian national revival. In addition, millions died during World War II and much of the country's historic architecture and valuable art treasures were destroyed. After the war, Ukrainian territory in the far west was reunited under Soviet control. The expanded and influential Soviet Ukrainian Republic became a founder member of the United Nations, with its own seat.

Ukrainian nationalism, forced underground in the 1960s and 1970s, reemerged strongly in the late 1980s. Building a campaign on this new nationalism, the Rukh (or People's Movement) received powerful support in free elections held in March 1990. The attempted Soviet coup of August 1991 won no support in Ukraine, which declared independence only weeks later. In December 1991, the Ukraine joined the Commonwealth of Independent States, and began the long process of reshaping its political and economic structures as a fully independent multi-party democracy. Since then, there have been differences with the Russian Federation over former Soviet military installations, and over the future of the Crimea, which was transferred from Russia to Ukraine in 1954.

Out of more than a hundred nationalities represented in the Ukraine, the great majority are ethnic Ukrainians, and most of the others speak closely related Slavic languages such as Russian or Polish. Russians form the largest minority, notably in the Crimea, whose original Tartar population was deported to central Asia in 1944 amid much suffering. New-found religious freedoms have allowed historical differences to reemerge: Christians are divided between Eastern Orthodox in the east, Roman Catholics in the far west, and the majority Uniate or Eastern Catholics, who under 16th-century Polish rule acknowledged papal supremacy while retaining Eastern rites.

ECONOMY

A favorable climate, and the fertile *chernozem* or black soil of the steppe, made Ukraine the breadbasket of the former Soviet Union. At the height of production Ukraine was responsible for almost half of the Soviet Union's total agricultural output. The country is a major producer of grain, sugar beet, cotton, tobacco, wine, meat and dairy products. The Black Sea is an important source of fish, especially sturgeon for caviar.

Mineral resources include vast iron-ore reserves and the world's richest concentration of manganese-bearing ores. The Donets basin has large coal reserves, while oil is extracted near the Carpathians, in Crimea, and in the Donets area. The leading industries are the production of various metals and food processing. A large manufacturing sector also produces heavy machinery, chemicals and fertilizers. Most energy comes from fossil fuels, though a small proportion comes from hydroelectric installations that have been built along the Dnieper.

Chocks away at the launch of a ship built for a Greek company at a Ukrainian shipyard in Nikolayev on the Black Sea. Shipping is a major facet of Ukraine's economy: its ports handle cargo ships from around the world, as well as river-boats and passenger liners.

The program for nuclear power was halted after the disastrous reactor accident at Chernobyl, north of Kiev.

The railroad network is concentrated in the Donets and Dnieper industrial areas, and there are good highways connecting all the main population centers. Busy ports such as Odessa on the Black Sea and Zhdanov by the Sea of Azov handle ocean freight, while major rivers and canals provide links to Central Europe. Airports at Kiev and elsewhere offer flights to national and international destinations.

Health, welfare and education services were well developed under the Soviet regime, although the promise of 10 years of free education for all children has not yet been fully realized. The Ukraine has many large and prestigious institutions of higher learning, including the Academy of Sciences in Kiev.

Moldova

REPUBLIC OF MOLDOVA

M OLDOVA, THE FORMER SOVIET REPUBLIC of Moldavia, is a small country near the north coast of the Black Sea. It borders Romania to the west, and is otherwise surrounded by the Republic of Ukraine.

ENVIRONMENT

Moldova is a hilly country much of which lies between the river Prut, on its border with Romania, and the river Dniester, close to the Ukrainian frontier. It forms part of an ancient eroded plateau covered in rolling steppelands that is crisscrossed by deep valleys and ravines with heavily forested slopes. The climate is generally temperate with short, sharp winters and high rainfall in summer.

SOCIETY

Once known as Bessarabia, the land between the Prut and the Dniester has had a checkered history. The name "Moldova" dates from 1359, when the principality of that name was formed. However, Moldova was soon dominated by Hungary, Poland and, from the 16th century, by the Turkish Ottoman empire, which finally ceded part of it (Bessarabia) to Russia in 1812. In 1859, when the rest of Moldova united with Walachia to form Romania, Bessarabia was retained by Russia. But in 1918, when the Russian empire collapsed, its people chose to become part of Romania too, and the Dniester became the border with what later became the Soviet Union.

Rural life Wearing bright headscarves, two Moldovan housewives exchange news, while their compatriots relax on a bench. By culture and language, Moldovans are indistinguishable from Romanians, their western neighbors, from whom they parted politically in 1940.

During World War II Bessarabia changed hands more than once and in 1944 it was taken over by the Soviet Union. The Soviets quickly instituted a system aimed at erasing all historical links with Romania. The Russian (Cyrillic), alphabet was imposed on the Moldovan language, which is otherwise little different from Romanian. During the breakup of the Soviet Union in 1991, immigrant Ukrainians and Russians, who together outnumbered Moldovans in the east, opposed Moldovan moves toward closer ties with Romania by declaring a Trans-Dniestrian Moldovan Republic. Since 1992 a ceasefire has held and in 1994 the Moldovan government promised a high degree of autonomy. The idea of reunification with Romania was defeated in a referendum in 1994.

ECONOMY

Since Moldova has no mineral resources, agriculture is the mainstay of the economy. Sunflower seeds are an important crop, along with a variety of fruit, nuts, tobacco and vegetables. Much of the steppe has been turned over to growing wheat and other cereals. Food processing, engineering and the production of agricultural machinery also form a major part of the industrial sector. But it is in wine producing that Moldova has the greatest potential for international trade. The wine industry supplied the former Soviet Union annually with 320 million bottles of sparkling wine alone. Moldova is now developing the industry commercially.

A casualty of the old communist system of centralism, Moldova has now become heavily reliant on other members of the Commonwealth of Independent States, initially for medicine, petrol and electricity and now as trading partners, especially Russia. At the end of the last century, Moldova was struggling with negative economic growth, a balance of payments deficit and high inflation.

NATIONAL DATA – MOLDOVA	
Land area	33,700 sq km (13,000 sq mi)
Climate	moderately continental
Major physical features	highest point: Balaneshty 430 m (1,409 ft); longest river: Dniester (part) 1,420 km (880 mi)
Population	(2000 est.) 4,430,654
Form of government	multiparty parliamentary republic with one legislative house
Armed forces	army 9,800; air force 1,300
Largest cities	Kishinev (capital – 787,000); Tiraspol (216,700); Belty (180,800); Tighina (149,400)
Official language	Moldovan
Ethnic composition	Moldovan 64.5%; Ukrainian 13.8%; Russian 13.0%; Gagauz 3.5%; Jewish 1.5%; Bulgarian 2.0%; others 1.7%
Religious affiliations	Eastern Orthodox 98.5%; Jewish 1.5%
Currency	the leu (since 1994)
Gross domestic product	(1999) US $9.7 billion
Gross domestic product per capita	(1999) US $2,200
Life expectancy at birth	male 59.8 yr; female 69.2 yr
Major resources	lignite, phosphates, grapes/wine, tobacco, cereals, fruit and vegetables

Russia

RUSSIAN FEDERATION

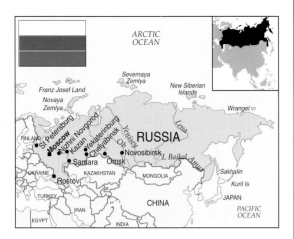

RUSSIA IS THE WORLD'S LARGEST COUNTRY, extending halfway round the globe. Much of this vast land is sparsely populated and has only limited natural resources. To the west Russia borders Finland, Norway, Estonia, Latvia and Belarus. The much longer southern frontier extends into central Asia and is shared with the Ukraine, Georgia, Azerbaijan, Kazakhstan, Mongolia, China and North Korea. To the north the country faces the Barents Sea and the East Siberian Sea, to the east the Sea of Okhotsk and to

NATIONAL DATA – RUSSIA

Land area 17,075,400 sq km (6,592,800 sq mi)

Climate	Altitude m (ft)	Temperatures January °C(°F)	July °C(°F)	Annual precipitation mm (in)
Moscow	156 (512)	–10 (14)	19 (66)	575 (22.6)
Sochi	31 (102)	7 (45)	23 (73)	1,451 (57.1)
Verkhoyansk	137 (449)	–47 (–53)	16 (61)	155 (6.1)

Major physical features highest point: Elbrus 5,633 m (18,481 ft); longest river: Yenisei 5,870 km (3,650 mi)

Population (2000 est.) 146,001,176

Form of government federal multiparty republic with two legislative houses

Armed forces army 420,000; navy 220,000; air force 300,000

Largest cities Moscow (capital – 8,389,700); St Petersburg (4,169,400); Novosibirsk (1,402,400); Nizhniy Novgorod (1,364,900); Yekaterinburg (1,272,900); Samara (1,168,000); Omsk (1,157,600); Kazan (1,108,000)

Official language Russian

Ethnic composition Russian 81.5%; Tatar 3.8%; Ukrainian 3.0%; Chuvash 1.2%; others 10.5%

Religious affiliations mainly Russian Orthodox, with Muslim and Buddhist minorities

Currency 1 ruble (R) = 100 kopecks

Gross domestic product (1999) US $620.3 billion

Gross domestic product per capita (1999) US $4,200

Life expectancy at birth male 60.6 yr; female 72.8 yr

Major resources oil, natural gas, coal, iron ore, platinum, copper, manganese, lead, zinc, tin, gold, silver, diamonds, timber, wheat, rye, barley, oats, flax, sugar beet, meat, milk, fisheries

the southeast the Sea of Japan. There is also a short outlet to the Gulf of Finland in the west, as well as coastal borders with the Black and Caspian Seas in the southwest of Russia.

Until dissolution in 1991, Russia was the powerbase of the Soviet Union. The breakup of communist structures has left a legacy of political unrest, fueling ethnic and national rivalries among Russia's disparate population.

ENVIRONMENT

Russia can be divided into five main areas: the East European Plain, extending from Russia's western borders with Europe to the Ural Mountains; the Ural Mountains themselves; the West Siberian Plain between the Urals and the Yenisei river; the Central Siberian Plateau – the land between the Yenisei and Lena rivers – and the remote mountainous areas of southern and eastern Siberia.

The land

The East European (or Russian) Plain occupies most of European Russia. In the far south it meets the massive barrier of the Caucasus, which defines the country's southernmost borders with Georgia and Azerbaijan. From here the plain extends northward in a broad swathe as far as the Barents Sea (part of the Arctic Ocean) and the plateaus of Karelia and the Kola Peninsula. At the heart of the plain and to the west of Moscow are the Valdai Hills, where several major rivers, including the Volga, Dnieper, and Western Dvina, have their sources. The plain meets a natural

Winter to spring (*above*) Brown water formed by melting snow creates swamplike conditions over vast areas of the country, as in this nature reserve near the Oka river in Ryazan province, southeast of Moscow, where mixed forest merges into wooded steppe.

The snowy bulk of Koryakskaya Sopka (*left*), a 3,456 m (11,337 ft) high volcano on the Kamchatka Peninsula in Russia's far northeast, rises above Petropavlovsk-Kamchatskiy. This is a geologically volatile area with 22 active volcanoes, as well as geysers and hot springs.

eastern barrier at the Ural Mountains: the traditional boundary between Europe and Asia. East of the Urals, the West Siberian Plain is a vast and sometimes marshy lowland covering some 2.5 million sq km (1 million sq mi) and crossed by two of the world's longest rivers, the Ob and the Yenisei.

Farther east, central Siberia is dominated by an extensive, irregular plateau, that contains several highland areas. It is bounded by higher mountains to the south, and to the east by the central Yakut lowland, formed from the Lena and Vilyui river basins. In the north the plateau is interrupted by the swampy lowlands of the Taymyr Depression, beyond which the Byrranga Mountains on the Taymyr Peninsula rise above the Arctic shoreline. Offshore are the rugged,

desolate islands of Severnaya Zemlya.

Ranges of fold mountains rise to the south of the Central Siberian Plateau. The westernmost of these is the Altai range, covered by permanent snowfields. Farther east, the Mongolian border region is crossed by mountain ranges interlaced with troughs and depressions. Northeast from the Eastern Sayan Mountains is the ancient Lake Baikal, the deepest lake in the world at around 1,620 m (5,310 ft).

East of Lake Baikal, and south of the river Lena, the mountains sweep eastward in an arc through southeastern Siberia to the northwestern shore of the Sea of Okhotsk. Farther southeast, the highlands of Sikhote-Alin look out across the Sea of Japan.

Northeastern Siberia is dominated by the Verkhoyansk, Cherskogo and Kolyma ranges, reaching to more than 3,000 m (10,000 ft). In the extreme northeast the mountainous Chukot peninsula faces Alaska across the Bering Sea.

In the northeastern corner of Russia the Koryak highlands extend into the mountainous backbone of the great Kamchatka

Peninsula, which divides the Bering Sea to the east from the Sea of Okhotsk to the west. The mountains continue southwest through the Kuril Islands to northern Japan, and from there northward again along Sakhalin island (notorious as a penal colony in the late tsarist and soviet period) off the western shore of the Sea of Okhotsk. This area is prone to earthquakes and volcanic eruptions.

Climate
Russia's climate is less varied than its vast size might suggest. Generally a cold, continental climate prevails, except in the far southwest near the Black Sea (which enjoys almost Mediterranean warmth) and in the extreme southeast near Vladivostok. Winters are severe, with temperatures sometimes falling as low as –70° C (–94° F) in northeastern Siberia. Average summer temperatures range from 8° C (46° F) on the Arctic coast to 20° C (70° F) in the valleys of the Caucasus.

Rainfall is moderate to low, and is often unreliable, especially in the interior. Notable exceptions include the areas bordering the Black Sea and the Caucasus, and the far southeastern coastal strip, which receive heavy monsoon rains during a humid summer season.

Plants
In northern coastal areas few plants other than mosses, lichens and grasses can survive, creating a characteristic tundra landscape. Farther south the tundra gives

way to vast tracts of forest known as the taiga. In the zone between the tundra and the taiga, there are larch forests in the east, birch and fir woodlands in the west.

In central parts of the East European Plain, and in vast regions of southeastern Russia, the natural cover is mixed forest. Southern parts of the East European and West Siberian Plains are covered in forest steppe. Farther south there are three main areas of semidesert; these border the Caspian Sea and the Caucasus Mountains in the southwest, and the Altai mountains in the south.

Animals

The northern coast is home to Arctic species such as Polar bears, Bearded seals and walruses, as well as gulls and loons. On the tundra, Arctic foxes and owls prey on Arctic hares and lemmings, while reindeer herds roam freely. Wildlife in the forests is more diverse. Elks (moose), reindeer, wolves, Brown bears, lynx, sables, squirrels, foxes and wolverines are found in the northern taiga.

The more southerly forests shelter Wild boar, mink and deer; Ussuri tigers inhabit the Primorski region in the far southeast. In the steppes, ground squirrels, jerboas and hamsters are hunted by Steppe polecats and Corsac foxes, while bird life includes falcons, cranes and eagles. In the Caucasus there are also many Mediterranean species.

SOCIETY

Throughout its long history Russia has been the crossroads of the Eurasian landmass. Under constant threat of invasion by nomadic horsemen from Asia for much of its early history, Russia built a vast transcontinental empire between the 16th and 19th centuries. Under the Soviet regime, built on the 1917 October Revolution, ethnic differences were forcibly submerged, to resurface in the 1990s.

History

From the 6th century AD, Finnic and Slavic peoples living in what is now western Russia became dominated by the Khazars, a group of Turkic and Iranian peoples who had migrated northward. The Khazars developed a prosperous empire including most of modern Ukraine and southern Russia, and in 737 established a new capital, Itil, near the mouth of the Volga on the Caspian Sea. Meanwhile, in the northwest, Viking explorers from Sweden pioneered a trade route from the Baltic to the Black Sea and Constantinople (modern Istanbul) by way of the Dnieper river. They founded first Novgorod in the north and then pressing south, established Kiev. Gradually the principal Slav peoples united around this city to form the powerful state of Kievan Rus. The Khazars were finally defeated in 965 by Grand Prince Svyatoslav of Kiev

Window on Europe (*above*) St Petersburg, seen here in an 18th-century engraving, was perhaps the greatest legacy left to Russia by Tsar Peter the Great. Founded in 1703 on a low and swampy site on the river Neva, it gave Russia an important outlet to the Baltic Sea.

Russia's imperial crest (*below*) – first adopted in Russia by Ivan the Great in the 15th century – is dominated by the double-headed eagle – a motif based on the Byzantine image of old and new Rome.

(d. 972). In 988 Svyatoslav's son Vladimir (c. 980–1015) was converted to Greek Orthodox Christianity. This event created close ties with the powerful Greek empire of Byzantium whose civilizing influence played a crucial role in shaping Russia's distinctive cultural identity.

The rule of Vladimir and his son Yaroslav the Wise (1019–54) saw the Kievan state's rise to prominence. But it was constantly plagued by attacks from its warlike neighbors in the south. In 1223 a new threat emerged from the east when Tartar Mongol horsemen advanced northward across the Caucasus. The Mongol progress across Russia was relentless, as they burned and sacked cities, slaughtered captives and exacted tribute. Novgorod in the northwest escaped the Mongol raids, but had to fend off attacks from the Swedes and the Germans in the west. The legendary Prince of Novgorod, Alexander Nevsky (c. 1220–63) eventually defeated his enemies in two great battles; one against the Swedes on the river Neva in 1240; and the other, against the Germans on the frozen Lake Peipus in 1242. By this time, however, the Mongols had reached Europe and established the Golden Horde empire, with its capital at Saray (near the Caspian Sea).

While eastern areas of the Kievan state remained under Mongol rule, the western parts were absorbed by Lithuania and Poland. However, the late 13th century witnessed the rise of a new and powerful state. When Alexander Nevsky's son, Daniel (1276–1304), became Prince of Moscow he founded a Muscovite dynasty, which ruled for the next three centuries until 1598. During this period Moscow rapidly expanded, in particular during the reign of Ivan III (Ivan the Great, 1440–1505) who finally ended his city's subjection to the Mongols in 1480. In 1472 he assumed the title of "Sovereign of all Russia" and adopted the emblem of the two-headed eagle. In 1547 his grandson Ivan IV (Ivan the Terrible, 1533–84) was crowned the first tsar of Russia.

The young tsar conquered the Tartar khanate of Khazan and began the great eastward expansion of the Russian empire, which took in Siberia and by 1649 reached the Pacific coast.

On the death of Ivan's son Fyodor I (1557–98), a Tartar noble, Boris Godunov (c. 1551–1605) who had been acting as regent, ruled as tsar. His reign was a period of intense upheaval in Russia known as the "Time of Troubles" (1595–1613); 18 years of civil war, famine, revolt and invasion by Poland, it ended when Michael Romanov (1596–1645) was elected tsar, founding the dynasty that went on to rule Russia until 1917.

Peter I (Peter the Great, 1672–1725), anxious to open up "a window on the west" and Europeanize his country, founded his new capital, St Petersburg,

The October Revolution: 1917

Russia's entry into World War I in 1914 at first stilled a rising tide of discontent with the tsar's reactionary government as all classes united against the German and Austro-Hungarian enemy. But the war went badly, casualties were heavy, defeats frequent and the economy crumbled under the strain.

On 10th March 1917 a shortage of bread led to strikes and riots in the capital. When the army joined the rioters, the tsar was forced to abdicate and the duma (parliament) was suspended. Power passed to two institutions: the Provisional Government, dominated by middle class "progressives", and the Petrograd Soviet of Workers' and Soldiers' Deputies, made up of a number of revolutionary workers' parties, including the Bolshevik Party. The two bodies shared power uneasily; democratic reforms were passed, but the war continued to go badly and the provisional government failed to address demands for land reform. Thus the provisional government alienated both right- and left-wing opinion. When, in July, the right-wing general Lavr Kornilov (1870–1918) attempted a military coup, the government was only saved by militant workers and its lack of real authority was exposed.

Only the Bolshevik Party, led by the formidable Marxist intellectual Vladimir Ilyich Ulyanov (1870–1924), codenamed Lenin, had consistently opposed the war and, campaigning under the emotive slogan "Peace, Bread and Land", it now began to gain

support. By September they controlled the Petrograd and Moscow soviets and began to plan their coup. The moment came on the evening of 4 November (24 October under the old Russian calendar) when Red Guards began to take control of Petrograd. The provisional government took refuge in the Winter Palace, which fell without a fight the following night. On 7 November Lenin announced that the soviet had seized power in the name of the working class and immediately issued decrees to end the war and commence land reform.

However, the revolution was by no means secure: the Bolsheviks were still a minority in the country as a whole and final victory came only after four years of bloody civil war.

Revolutionary orator Lenin, founder of the Russian Communist Party, addresses a crowd in Petrograd (now St Petersburg) in March 1917. Such events won support for the Bolsheviks and the October Revolution.

on the river Neva next to the Gulf of Finland. Through his military successes, the introduction of Western technology and by draconian government reforms, Peter turned Russia into a major European force. The country's expansion and Europeanization continued under the rule of the German-born empress Catherine II (Catherine the Great, 1729–96).

Much of the reign of Catherine's grandson Alexander I (1777–1825) was preoccupied by war with Napoleonic France. Russia's defeat of Napoleon gave the country heroic status, but Russian society remained feudal and its industrial backwardness was exposed in the Crimean War (1853–56). In 1861 Alexander II

(1818–81) abolished serfdom among the rural population, and attempted extensive social and administrative reforms. But dissatisfaction among the Russian intelligentsia grew, culminating in Alexander's assassination in 1881.

Under Alexander II Russia had conquered the Caucasus and Kazakhstan and penetrated deep into central Asia. By 1900 it controlled a vast empire of many nationalities extending to the borders of Persia, Afghanistan, India and China. After a disastrous war with Japan (1904–05), political unrest at home forced Tsar Nicholas II (1868–1918) to grant his people a *duma*, or parliament. The concessions proved to be too little, and too late.

The situation was exacerbated in 1914, when Russia plunged into World War I. Millions died in battle, the economy was overstretched and food supplies were soon seriously affected. In March 1917, after riots in St Petersburg (then called Petrograd), the tsar was forced to abdicate in favor of a provisional government. In November 1917 Vladimir Ilyich Lenin (1870–1924) at the head of the Bolshevik Party seized power in a remarkable coup that overthrew the provisional government. Lenin immediately withdrew Russia from World War I, and a devastating civil war (1918–22) ensued, which concluded in 1922 with the foundation of the Union of Soviet Socialist Republics.

After Lenin's death Joseph Stalin (1879–1953) won the power struggle for leadership, ruthlessly eliminating his rivals. In 1928 he inaugurated his first Five Year Plan: a period of intensive industrialization and the enforced collectivization of Russia's peasants. Agricultural production fell and a subsequent famine in the Ukraine in 1932 led to millions of deaths. Many of those who resisted Stalin's policies were either executed or deported to Siberian labor camps. In 1934 he embarked on the systematic elimination of all his political opponents leading to the Great Terror of 1936–38: estimates put the total deaths at some eight million.

In 1941, after the outbreak of World War II, an ill-prepared Soviet Union was invaded by Nazi Germany. The defeat of Germany was achieved by terrible sacrifice on the part of the Russian people and at a cost of more than 20 million lives. In the early postwar years a battle-scarred Soviet Union achieved considerable international power by establishing six satellite communist regimes in adjoining states of Eastern Europe. With the development of nuclear weapons and the race for military supremacy that accompanied it, the ensuing Cold War left the two great powers poised for mutual destruction. In 1962, under Soviet leader Nikita Khrushchev (1894–1971), war was narrowly averted after the United States and the Soviet Union contested the siting of Soviet nuclear missiles on the island of Cuba. Khrushchev's later efforts to improve relations with the West were cut short in 1964, when he was ousted by a collective Communist Party leadership that soon came to be dominated by Leonid Brezhnev (1906–82).

Unable to repair the growing rift between the Soviet Union and communist China, Brezhnev tried to establish a truce with the West. However, an increase

Church and state (*above*) Boris Yeltsin, the democratically elected president of the Russian Federation, greets the crowds after an Easter service celebration. Russian Orthodoxy was heavily suppressed throughout the communist era, though many of the magnificent churches were preserved out of a sense of national pride. Under Yeltsin's liberal regime the traditionally strong religious feeling of the Russian people resurfaced and the church found new vigor.

Walled for safety (*left*), the magnificent Trinity Monastery of St Sergius with its large Baroque refectory, in Sergiyev Posad, 70 km (43 mi) northeast of Moscow, offers a dramatic assembly of religious architecture. Founded in 1337–40 by Sergius of Radonezh (c. 1321–91), a dispossessed Moscow aristocrat who became a hermit – and later one of Russia's patron saints – the monastery has been a spiritual beacon of the Russian Orthodox Church for more than 650 years.

in religious and political persecution during the Brezhnev years, particularly of the Jews, continued to alienate Western sympathies, and the Soviet invasion of Afghanistan in 1980 prompted widespread international condemnation.

This state of affairs continued until Mikhail Gorbachev (b. 1931) became General Secretary of the Communist Party in March 1985. He introduced a new and radical style of leadership, aiming at a restructuring of government and the economy. In 1988 he withdrew Soviet troops from Afghanistan, and initiated arms' reduction talks with the West. At home, however, he faced a collapsing economy, growing industrial unrest and the resurgence of long suppressed national identities and ethnic conflicts in many parts of the Union.

In the late 1980s, as communist regimes began to topple throughout Eastern Europe, Gorbachev requested greater presidential powers in an attempt to prevent the break-up of the Union. Boris Yeltsin (b. 1931) and more radical reformers warned against a "new dictatorship". However, early in 1990 the Communist party effectively renounced its monopoly on power, and as support for the party dwindled, Yeltsin became president of the Russian Federation, the largest of the Soviet Union's constituent republics, in May 1990.

Meanwhile Gorbachev's diplomatic successes in the United States and Great Britain signaled the end of the Cold War, and new reductions in armaments. Although popular abroad, Gorbachev faced mounting unpopularity at home. As the constituent republics of the Union declared their independence, Gorbachev fought to maintain a degree of central authority in a new Union treaty, but in August 1991 a group of hard-line conservatives attempted to seize power.

Following mass demonstrations in Moscow and St Petersburg (then Leningrad), the coup collapsed after three days. Gorbachev, who had been under house arrest in the Crimea, returned to the capital, but his power had been overthrown by Yeltsin who had opposed the coup in Moscow. The failure of the coup confirmed that the Communist Party's

The Second Russian Revolution

In June 1990, following a highly successful Soviet–United States summit in Washington, the Western world celebrated the end of the Cold War between the two great power blocs. At the time, few Western politicians foresaw the growing instability within the Soviet Union itself.

During his presidency, Mikhail Gorbachev had fought hard to reform the Soviet system. The two Russian words *glasnost* (openness) and *perestroika* (restructuring) had become universally familiar as the expression of his vision of a more open society. But to achieve this goal Gorbachev had to walk a dangerous tightrope between the conservatives of the Communist Party and the new radical democrats. Despite all his efforts, ominous cracks appeared in the structure of the Union.

Just two months after the Washington summit, the Soviet republics of Armenia, Turkmenistan and Tajikistan declared their independence. Gorbachev struggled to preserve central authority by drafting a revised Union treaty to be voted on at a referendum.

However, Armenia, Georgia, Moldova and the Baltic republics refused to consider Gorbachev's treaty. Instead, Georgia, Latvia and Estonia voted for full independence from the Union. Meanwhile, a major food-supply crisis was fueling discontent in Russia and other regions.

On 19 August 1991, the day before the Union treaty was due to be signed, Radio Moscow announced that "ill health" prevented President Gorbachev from carrying out his duties. An eight-man "emergency committee" of communist hardliners took control, curbing demonstrations, strikes and the press. As tanks rumbled into Moscow, a crowd of protesters surrounded the Russian parliament building. At the forefront was the radical Boris Yeltsin, who condemned the coup, and called for a general strike.

Unwilling to turn their guns on the people, the army refused to obey the orders of the emergency committee, and without military backing the coup quickly collapsed. Gorbachev's policy of *glasnost* had borne unexpected fruit: an upsurge of support for the radicals broke the power of the Communist Party, and severed the remaining links of the Union.

authority was broken and the great monolith of the Soviet Union began to collapse. It was formally dissolved in December 1991, and 11 of its 15 constituent republics, including the Russian Federation, formed the Commonwealth of Independent States (CIS). Gorbachev had no option but to resign.

Yeltsin found the Russian parliament reluctant to embrace sweeping changes he proposed, and in 1993 armed conflict erupted when demonstrators seized the parliament building. Forces loyal to the president successfully aborted the attempted coup and a new parliament was elected later in the year under a new constitution, which gave the president greater powers. In the late 1990s, a state of continuing economic crisis was accompanied by a number of government corruption scandals. In 1999 Yeltsin, who had been suffering ill health, retired, naming Vladimir Putin as his successor. Putin was elected president in 2000.

Government

The Russian Federation has taken over many of the enterprises, resources and responsibilities of the Soviet Union. Perhaps the most dramatic change was the introduction of multiparty democracy at all levels of government, a process begun under Gorbachev's regime in 1989.

There are 10 autonomous areas, 49 provinces, 6 territories and 21 officially independent republics. The republics are highly autonomous and each elects its own president. Provinces and territories also elect their own governors.

People

The Russian Federation contains within its boundaries an enormous diversity of peoples. There are more than 60 different nationalities, who can be broadly divided into four main linguistic groups. The Indo-European group – those languages that developed in Europe and southern Asia – includes some 150 million Russian speakers, and accounts for the great majority of the population from the Baltic to the Pacific.

The other three language groups found in the region are the Finno-Ugric group, widely dispersed across the forest and tundra of the north and in the Balkans; the Turkic languages, which are spoken in southeastern Europe and Asia; and the Caucasian group encompassing the languages spoken in the west of the Caucasus Mountains, as well as Chechen, Ingush and Dagestanian languages spoken in the east of the Caucasus.

Waiting in line for food (*above*) at a mobile stall in the St Petersburg suburbs, where housewives gather to buy potatoes trucked in from a collective farm. In the early 1990s a fall in agricultural output, plus huge price rises, made daily living extremely hard.

The majority of Russians differ markedly from many of the non-Slav groups, in culture and religion as well as in language. Since the early 1990s here has been a tremendous resurgence in religious practice – considered reactionary and actively suppressed during most of the Soviet period – as the Russian people rediscover their spirituality. A strong Orthodox Christian tradition has survived within the Slavic communities, Baptists are numerous, and many ethnic and national groups have retained their own traditional religions; Islam among some of the Turkic peoples, and Buddhism among many of the Kalmyks and Buryats.

In wintry Siberia (*above*) a herd of domesticated reindeer are rounded up. Under Soviet rule the distribution of reindeer meat was collectivized, but herders were allowed to keep to the ancient custom of following the seasonal migration routes of the animals.

Cooperation in space (*below*) The American shuttle *Atlantis* and the Russian *Mir* docked together in 1995, allowing their crews to mingle; here, Russian cosmonauts Solovyev and Budarin smile at *Atlantis'* departing crew before the hatch closes it off again from *Mir*.

Transportation and communications

For the Russian economy to function at all, massive quantities of food and raw materials have to be carried over enormous distances. Since the abolition of central planning, distribution has been one of the greatest challenges facing economic reformers. Much needed foodstuffs are frequently left to rot in warehouses before they can be transported to the cities.

The heart of Russia's transportation system is the railroad network, which carries some three-quarters of all freight. Most track is in the west, especially around Moscow; the best-known link with the far east is the Trans-Siberian Railroad from Moscow to Vladivostok.

Surfaced roads cover six times the distance of the entire railroad system, but are less used. Most bulk freight is carried by rail or by water, and buses account for a high proportion of passenger traffic. Relatively few people own a car.

Foreign trade is chiefly conducted by a sophisticated merchant fleet. In the far north and east, shipping provides a lifeline between communities scattered along some 50,000 km (30,000 mi) of coastline. Although most harbors become icebound in winter, some, such as Murmansk, keep open all year. Airline services ensure year-round contact with the most isolated regions. An international airline flies to many major destinations.

Radio, television and the press are still adapting to the recent relaxation of censorship. Even before the breakup of the Soviet Union though, there was a more open approach to news reporting.

Welfare and education

Under Soviet rule, medical care was free throughout the Russian Federation. Although housing was inadequate and the standard of living relatively low, unemployment was practically nonexistent. The collapse of the Soviet system has thrown the old social welfare network into chaos. Russia now faces the same kind of social problems that have plagued the capitalist West: inflation, unemployment and a soaring crime rate.

Hyperinflation in the early 1990s brought a decline in living standards, and more and more Russians found themselves living below the poverty line. The welfare system is being reformed into an insurance-based system of benefits for sickness and unemployment and retirement pensions. Health and average life expectancy have declined and infant mortality has increased in the 1990s.

ECONOMY

Russia was the main driving force behind the economy of the former Soviet Union. Its rich deposits of minerals supplied heavy industry with raw materials, and its energy resources supplied power to the other republics and Eastern Europe.

In the 1990s Russia struggled to establish a modern market economy hampered by an entrenched bureaucracy and a dilapidated industrial base. Falling international oil prices and a failing currency led to a financial crisis in 1998 as a result of which the ruble was devalued and Russia defaulted on its international debt.

Agriculture

Wheat, barley, oats and rye form the major part of the agricultural sector, but the country cannot grow enough for its own needs. Only about a tenth of the land area is under cultivation, and most of this lies to the west of the Urals. The most suitable land for intensive livestock breeding, including beef and dairy cattle also lies in the west. Russia also has the world's largest reserves of timber.

The Russian fishing fleet, operating from the Arctic waters to the Pacific, is one of the biggest in the world and provides plentiful supplies of fish.

Industry

Heavy industry is the backbone of the Russian economy and draws on the country's enormous resources of raw materials. There are rich deposits of iron ore on the Kola Peninsula, in the Kursk Magnetic Anomaly near the Ukrainian border, and in Siberia. There are also major deposits of nonferrous metals in the Urals and Siberia including gold, copper, zinc and various rare metals.

In addition, Russia possesses vast energy reserves. There are huge coal fields in eastern Siberia, the Kuznetsk basin north of the Altai, and the Urals. Northwestern Siberia has the world's greatest reserves of oil and natural gas. The Volga and Yenisei rivers supply hydroelectric power to large stations nearby, and more hydroelectric plants are being built. The nuclear power program suffered a setback in 1986, when a major accident at Chernobyl in the Ukraine (then part of the Soviet Union) exposed safety problems in many installations.

Under the former Soviet system, Russia met most of the country's demands for industrial, agricultural and transportation equipment; few of these items were ever imported. But Russian-built machinery is only just now beginning to benefit from the microprocessor revolution.

Georgia

REPUBLIC OF GEORGIA

T HE REPUBLIC OF GEORGIA LIES AT THE eastern end of the Black Sea. To the north is the Russian Federation, to the southeast Azerbaijan and Armenia, and Turkey lies to the south. Its decision not to join the Commonwealth of Independent States after the breakup of the Soviet Union in 1991 was largely due to political and interethnic conflicts, but it also reflected the independent spirit of the nation. Membership was ratified in 1994.

ENVIRONMENT

Georgia is a country of mountains. The northern frontier with Russia runs along the massive mountain barrier of the Great Caucasus. These snowy peaks overlook the Black Sea in the northwest and have numerous spurs and secondary ranges cut by deep gorges. A central plateau called the Kartalinian Plain divides these mountains from a parallel range known as the Little Caucasus, whose lofty peaks and plateaus extend south into Turkey and Armenia. Farther east, beyond the capital, Tbilisi, the Kura river and its tributaries drain southeast into Azerbaijan through a series of upland valleys. The swampy plains of Kolkhida fringe the Black Sea coast.

The mountainous terrain produces a varied climate. Generally it is cold in the mountains in winter, with heavy snows, but the Great Caucasus also block still colder air coming from Russia to the north. Balmier winds from the Black Sea bring a damp, almost subtropical climate to the Kolkhida lowlands, whereas the eastern areas have much drier weather.

Much of Georgia is wooded, from sparse birch cover on the mountain slopes to dense broadleaf forests of beech, oak and chestnut at lower levels. In the drier east the forest gives way to grassland. Wildlife flourishes too, especially forest species such as roe deer, Caucasian deer, brown bears and wolves. Wild goats and their close relatives, tahrs, live in more mountainous areas.

SOCIETY

The Georgians pride themselves on a history that goes back to some of the earliest known records, and on a unique language with its own distinctive script. To the ancient Greeks, Georgia's western plain of Kolkhida was known as Colchis – the land whose fabled wealth inspired the legend of the Golden Fleece. Indeed, until recently sheepskins were still used to catch

Golden fields of corn lie within clear sight of the foothills and snow-capped peaks of the Caucasus Mountains in western Georgia. This region, with its almost subtropical climate, produces many agricultural products including tea, tobacco, flowers and wine.

Candles are lit during a service of commemoration. Christianity was adopted in Georgia in the early 4th century; the Georgian Orthodox Church (one of the world's oldest Christian communities) survives – with Christian Armenia – in a region dominated by Islam.

the gold dust in its rivers. After coming under the domination first of the Greeks and later of the Romans the country converted to Christianity in 330 AD. The Georgians have since retained their distinctive Orthodox faith, along with a strong sense of national identity, despite many centuries of domination by their powerful neighbors – the Persians and the Ottoman Turks.

By the 18th century Georgia had been fragmented into several principalities. Its rulers sought Russian help in their struggle for independence, but the Russian response was simply to take over the country piecemeal during the 19th century. At the end of the century Georgia was reunited – but under Russian rule. Despite this, the Georgians remained resistant to Russian influences. Under later more liberal-minded governors a renewed sense of national identity emerged, including an artistic revival and movements for social reform. One such Marxist-inspired group was joined in 1896 by a young Georgian called Joseph Dzhugashvili (1879–1953); in later years he became known to the world by his adopted name "Stalin" – meaning "steel".

Following the 1917 Russian Revolution, Georgia was established as an independent state. But in 1921, after a short occupation by the British, the Red Army invaded and declared a Soviet republic. Many nationalists, and even some communists, were murdered, and several peasant uprisings were brutally put down. During Stalin's purges of the 1930s still more Georgians were killed.

Glasnost (openness) in the 1980s gave Georgian nationalism a new voice that led in 1989 to a peaceful demonstration calling for independence. This was savagely crushed, but in April 1991, following a national referendum, the Georgian Supreme Soviet declared the country independent. Its chairman, the former dissident, Zviad Gamsakhurdia (1939–93) was elected president. A month later, however, his dictatorial methods provoked opposition, and soon afterward the country was plunged into armed conflict.

Early in 1992, after weeks of bloodshed, Gamsakhurdia was forced to flee the country. A new government was installed, under the former Soviet foreign minister Eduard Shevardnadze (b. 1928), himself a Georgian, who promised a return to stability. Gamsakhurdia returned to western Georgia in 1993 to ferment a rebellion which was only quelled with Russian help. Conflict with the self-declared Abkhazian Autonomous Republic in the northwest over its desire to secede from Georgia remains unresolved, Abkhazia again declaring independence in 1994. Shevardnadze was re-elected in November 1995.

ECONOMY

Georgia produces tea, citrus fruits, tobacco and fine wines; additional products include sugar beet and essential oils from

roses and other flowers. Sheep are the main livestock. The collectivization of agriculture had less impact here than in other former Soviet republics, so privately owned plots have flourished.

Georgia's rich mineral and energy resources encourage local industrial activity. There are deposits of coal, natural gas and peat, as well as fast-flowing rivers, ideal for generating hydroelectric power. Large manganese-ore deposits support most of the mining industry, but many other metals and minerals are also extracted. Tourism on the Black Sea coast has declined. Traditional industries have included steelworking, the construction of locomotives, engineering and chemicals. The richness of Georgian arts and culture can be seen in a long tradition of icon-painting and metalworking, embroidered textiles, and wood and stone carving. Its music and folkdancing are renowned.

Despite the rugged terrain, transportation is well developed, with links between the busy ports of Batumi and Poti and the densely populated hinterland. Healthcare and education in Georgia enjoy a high reputation among the former Soviet states. In particular, the widespread teaching of the ancient Georgian language helped the republic to retain a strong national identity and separate culture throughout the Soviet period.

NATIONAL DATA – GEORGIA

Land area 69,700 sq km (26,900 sq mi)

Climate	Altitude m (ft)	Temperatures January °C(°F)	July °C(°F)	Annual precipitation mm (in)
Tbilisi	490 (1,608)	3 (37)	25 (77)	462 (18.2)

Major physical features highest point: Shkhara 5,068 m (16,627 ft); longest river: Kura (part) 1,510 km (940 mi)

Population (2000 est.) 5,019,538

Form of government multiparty republic with one legislative house

Armed forces army 20,000; navy not available; air force 200

Largest cities Tbilisi (capital – 1,344,100); Kutaisi (264,000); Rustavi (178,500); Batumi (143,800)

Official language Georgian

Ethnic composition Georgian 70.1%; Armenian 8.1%; Russian 6.3%; Azeri 5.7%; Ossetian 3.0%; Abkhaz 1.8%; others 5.0%

Religious affiliations Georgian Orthodox 65.0%; Russian Orthodox 10.0%; Muslim 11.0%; Armenian Orthodox 8.0%; others 6.0%

Currency lari=100 tetri

Gross domestic product (1999) US $11.7 billion

Gross domestic product per capita (1999) US $2,300

Life expectancy at birth male 68.5 yr; female 76.8 yr

Major resources coal, natural gas, peat, manganese, other metal ores, timber, citrus fruit, tea, grapes (for wine), tourism

Armenia

REPUBLIC OF ARMENIA

MODERN ARMENIA IS A TINY, LANDLOCKED republic in the mountains to the south of the Caucasus. Its people are survivors of an ancient civilization that was once fought over by Mongols, Turks and Persians and of a nation that was all but destroyed. Armenia shares borders with Georgia to the north, Azerbaijan to the east, Iran and the Azerbaijani region of Nakhichevan to the south, and Turkey to the west. Armenia also claims the Armenian-populated enclave of Nagorno-Karabakh, which lies across its eastern frontier in Azerbaijan.

NATIONAL DATA – ARMENIA

Land area	29,800 sq km (11, 500 sq mi)		
Climate		**Temperatures**	**Annual**
	Altitude m (ft)	January °C(°F) July °C(°F)	precipitation mm (in)
Yerevan	990 (3,248)	−6 (22) 26 (78)	318 (12.5)

Major physical features highest point: Aragats 4,090 m (13,418 ft); longest river: Aras (part) 914 km (568 mi); largest lake: Lake Sevan 1,417 sq km (547 sq mi)

Population (2000 est.) 3,344,336

Form of government multiparty republic with one legislative house

Armed forces army 32,700

Largest cities Yerevan (capital – 1,278,700); Vanadzor (193,500); Kumayri (130,400)

Official language Armenian

Ethnic composition Armenian 93.0%; Azeri 3.0%; Russian 2.0%; others 2.0%

Religious affiliations Armenian Orthodox, with Armenian Catholic and Muslim minorities

Currency (since 1994) 1 dram = 100 luma

Gross domestic product (1999) US $9.9 billion

Gross domestic product per capita (1999) US $2,900

Life expectancy at birth male 67.2 yr; female 73.6 yr

Major resources copper, zinc, molybdenum, agriculture, grapes/wine, hydroelectric power

ENVIRONMENT

Armenia is occupied almost entirely by the mountains of the Little Caucasus, whose name belies their considerable height. The rugged landscape includes extinct volcanoes and high lava plateaus cut by deep ravines; frequent earthquakes show that mountain-building is still going on. The highest peak, Aragats at 4,090 m (13,418 ft), is in the northwest. Farther east is Lake Sevan, nearly 2,000 m (some 6,000 ft) above sea level. The Gegam mountain range to the west of the lake overlooks the capital, Yerevan, and the broad Ararat plain, which is crossed by the river Aras as it follows its southeasterly course along the borders with Turkey and, in the far south, Iran.

The country has a dry, continental climate; short, sharp winters and long, hot summers on the plains. The mountains are cooler, and winter conditions there are much harsher.

Steppe vegetation predominates, with drought-resistant grasses and sagebrush at lower altitudes, where jackals, wildcats and sometimes leopards are found. Oak woodlands in the southeastern forests merge with beechwoods in the more humid northeast. Here the animals include squirrels and brown bears. Alpine grassland on the higher slopes provides good summer grazing for wild goats and mouflons (wild sheep).

SOCIETY

The Armenians are descended from the various Indo-European peoples that inhabited the Ararat plain and surrounding areas from the 12th to the 6th century BC. Here, legend has it, Noah landed his ark after the Flood and founded the ancient city of Yerevan. The kingdom of Urartu (as Armenia was then known) flourished here between the 9th and 6th centuries BC, and became one of the most powerful states in the Middle East. In 520 BC the kingdom was conquered by the Persian empire, and then from 330 BC it was ruled by the Macedonian Alexander the Great (356–323 BC) and the Greek dynasty that succeeded him. Ultimately, Armenia fell under the dominion of Rome in 67 BC, becoming a buffer state between the Roman empire and the empire of Parthia – Rome's major rival for power in the east. When Armenia adopted Christianity in about 300 AD, it became a bulwark of Christianity in Asia.

In the centuries that followed, Armenia

struggled to retain its independence and cultural identity as it became a theater of war between the Persians, the Seljuk Turks and the Mongols. The population became scattered across the world, but nothing could destroy the strong sense of nationhood kept alive by the depth of its faith in the Armenian Church.

In the early 19th century, as the Russian empire advanced its frontiers across the Caucasus, the Armenians looked to the tsar for liberation from Persian and Turkish domination. By 1829 Russia had taken all the land now occupied by Armenia and Azerbaijan, except for western Armenia, which remained under Turkish rule. In subsequent decades there was a resurgence of Armenian culture, but following the Russo-Turkish War (1877–78) fear of Armenian nationalism led to repression in both Russian and Turkish Armenia. In 1915, during World War I, 1.75 million Armenians living in the western region ruled by Turkey were deported from their homes and c. 600,000 were massacred by the Turks. The establishment of the Soviet Republic of Armenia in 1920 prevented a Turkish takeover of the whole region and in 1921,

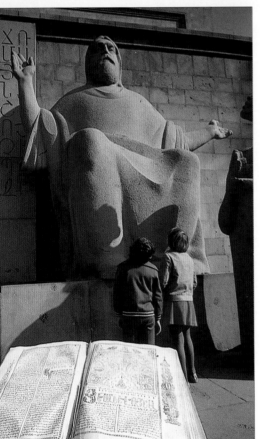

Spiritual home (*above*) The Armenian church of Khor Virap, in the shadow of Turkey's Mount Ararat, marks the site where the evangelist Gregory the Illuminator (257–332) was imprisoned by the pagan king Tiridates III, whom he later converted to Christianity.

Words in stone (*left*) Youngsters examine a statue of St Mesrob (c. 350–440), founder of the Armenian alphabet. It stands in front of the Matenaradan library, in Yerevan, whose archives hold a fine collection of ancient Armenian manuscripts, such as the one shown.

after the Russian Revolution and civil war (1917), the Bolsheviks gave the regions of Nagorno-Karabakh (which was mostly populated by Armenians) and Nakhichevan to Azerbaijan. The following year, Armenia and its neighbors Azerbaijan and Georgia were united in the Transcaucasian Soviet Federative Republic.

Armenia achieved separate status as a Soviet republic in 1936, but its territory did not include either Nagorno-Karabakh or Nakhichevan. This continued separation of ethnic Armenians from their native state created tensions between Armenia and Azerbaijan that the Soviet regime contained for many years until they erupted violently in the late 1980s.

Both republics achieved independence on the break-up of the Soviet Union and joined the Commonwealth of Independent States in 1991 and became a member of the UN in 1992. Conflict broke out again in Nagorno-Karabakh in 1992, with Armenian forces seizing much of the territory. A cease-fire ended the conflict in 1994, but sporadic violence continued. These troubles exacerbated the already acute problems of supply and distribution during the restructuring of the postcommunist economy and the introduction of multiparty democracy.

The vast majority of the republic's population are Armenians, who despite long periods of Muslim rule have retained their strong Christian tradition. They belong either to the Armenian Orthodox Church or to the much smaller Armenian Catholic Church, which is in communion with Rome. Some minority groups, such as Kurds, are Muslims.

ECONOMY

Agriculture is the main source of income, especially in irrigated areas of the Aras valley and around Yerevan. Here the crops include grapes, almonds, figs and olives. Apples, pears and cereals are grown on higher ground, while sheep and cattle are raised in the mountains.

In the second half of the 20th century the country industrialized rapidly, exploiting its valuable deposits of copper, zinc and molybdenum, and developing its capacity to generate hydroelectricity. The chief industries are mining, metallurgy, mechanical engineering and chemicals. Armenia also exports precision instruments and textiles, as well as quality brandies and wines.

In December 1988 a devastating earthquake destroyed many towns in northern Armenia and seriously affected its economic infrastructure. Numerous factories and power stations were lost and much of the country's financial resources had to be diverted to meet the immediate demands of humanitarian aid to earthquake victims. The disruption of power services, exacerbated by the continuing conflict with neighboring Azerbaijan, and a subsequent blockade on fuel imports caused much suffering for Armenia's population.

Several years later, in the early 1990s, factories and hospitals were still unheated, power cuts were routine and for increasingly longer periods each day. The government reopened its antiquated nuclear power plant at Metzanor, which had been closed since the 1988 earthquake, in an attempt to solve the country's fuel crisis.

Azerbaijan

REPUBLIC OF AZERBAIJAN

Lying on the west coast of the Caspian Sea, Azerbaijan occupies the southeast corner of Transcaucasia, with Russia to the north and Georgia to the northwest. Armenia is to the west and Iran to the south. Its territories include the autonomous oblast region of Nagorno-Karabakh in the southwest, which is also claimed by Armenia, and the autonomous republic of Nakhichevan, which lies farther southwest, beyond a strip of Armenian territory. It withdrew from the CIS in 1992 and rejoined in 1993, but is also making strong links with Turkey.

ENVIRONMENT

Northern Azerbaijan is dominated by the peaks of the Great Caucasus Mountains that extend southeastward, partly along the Russian border, as far as the capital and chief port, Baku. In the foothills of the Caucasus, the Kura river valley drops southeastward from the Georgian border, opening onto a broad floodplain that lies mainly below sea level. The mountains and plateaus of the Little Caucasus occupy Nakhichevan and western Azerbaijan, while in the far south the Talish Mountains on the Iranian border overlook the Caspian coastline.

In the lowlands the climate is dry and subtropical, with mild winters, long, hot summers and frequent droughts. Mountain areas that have a more continental climate experience cold winters with heavy snow; farther south it is wetter and more humid. The vegetation varies from steppe grassland in the drier lowlands to forests in the mountains and marshlands in the southeast. Wildlife includes leopards, gazelles and ground squirrels.

SOCIETY

The first people to inhabit Azerbaijan were Iranians, and for most of its long history Azerbaijan belonged to the Persian

Trapped innocent (*above*) A young girl from Nagorno-Karabakh – an Armenian Christian enclave in Azerbaijan – with straw brooms for sale. Like many thousands, she is caught by the fighting between Armenians and Azerbaijanis over the enclave's political status.

The waterfront of Baku (*right*) Azerbaijan's capital and major port on the west coast of the Caspian Sea. The city is heavily dependent on the nearby oil fields for its industry.

Olives from reclaimed land (*below*) Azerbaijani men and women clear weeds from a newly planted olive grove near Baku. The land they are tilling has been reclaimed partly from the desert and partly from an oil field that has ceased production.

NATIONAL DATA – AZERBAIJAN	
Land area	86,600 sq km (33,400 sq mi)
Climate	humid subtropical to dry continental
Major physical features	highest point: Bazar-Dyuzi 4,480 m (14,698 ft); lowest point: Caspian Sea –28 m (–92 ft); longest river: Kura (part) 1,510 km (940 mi)
Population	(2000 est.) 7,748,163
Form of government	multiparty republic with one legislative house
Armed forces	army 49,000; navy 3,000; air force 11,200
Largest cities	Baku (capital – 1,214,400); Gyandzha (299,300); Sumgait (277,300)
Official language	Azerbaijani
Ethnic composition	Azeri 82.0%; Russian 7.0%; Armenian 5.0%; others 6.0%
Religious affiliations	mainly Shi'ite Muslim, with Sunni Muslim and Armenian Christian minorities
Currency	manat=100 gyapiks
Gross domestic product	(1999) US $14 billion
Gross domestic product per capita	(1999) US $1,770
Life expectancy at birth	male 65.5 yr; female 74.1 yr
Major resources	petroleum, natural gas, iron ore, other metal ores, cotton, tobacco, grapes, fisheries

empire. Azerbaijanis themselves, many of whom live farther south in the Iranian province of the same name, are a people of Turkic origin who arrived with the 11th-century Seljuk invaders who conquered much of Asia Minor. Persians and Turks fought for control of Azerbaijan throughout the ensuing centuries until finally the Russians gained a foothold during the early 19th century. The Treaty of Turkmenchai in 1828 divided the country between Persia (which gained the south) and Russia (the north).

During the chaos that followed World War I and the Russian Revolutions of 1917, the Azerbaijanis set up an independent anti-Bolshevik republic, but were invaded first by Turkey and then, in 1922, by the Soviet Red Army. In the subsequent resistance to Soviet rule, many religious and political leaders were killed and collectivization of farmland was fiercely resisted by Azerbaijan's peasantry. For a brief period from 1922 it became part of the Soviet Transcaucasian Federation, but it was eventually incorporated into the Soviet Union as a constituent republic in 1936.

Today most of the inhabitants are Muslim Azerbaijanis. However, there is a sizable minority of Armenians, who are mainly Christian, concentrated in the Nagorno-Karabakh enclave. In 1988 a long-standing dispute with Armenia over this area erupted into widespread violence and resulted in the departure of thousands of Armenians from the country. When Azerbaijan and Armenia both achieved political independence on the dissolution of the Soviet Union in 1991, their conflict over Nagorno-Karabakh escalated into a war. A 1994 cease-fire brought temporary peace, but the status of the enclave remains unresolved. Azerbaijan has a 125-member parliament elected by majority vote and a directly elected president. There were several attempted coups in the 1990s and the political situation remains unstable.

ECONOMY

Azerbaijan has little arable land, but nevertheless is a major producer of cotton, tobacco, grapes and other fruit. The Caspian Sea is a ready source of fish, especially sturgeon for its highly-prized caviar, but this important industry is now threatened by severe pollution.

Other natural resources include metal ores, natural gas and vast reserves of oil, which is refined mostly in the Baku area. Baku once provided half the world's supply of oil, and the petroleum and chemical industries expanded rapidly around this area until it became the Soviet Union's fifth largest city. The burgeoning industrial sector is now extremely diversified, from chemicals and gasoline to textiles, and electrical and other consumer goods. A market-based economic reform program and increased oil production was encouraging foreign investment and boosting GDP growth rates in the late 1990s.

Transportation includes good railroads and an extensive road network. Shipping lines from the busy port of Baku serve Russian, central Asian and Iranian destinations. Free health, welfare and education services were well developed under the Soviet regime. Azerbaijan's strong intellectual tradition is shown in its prestigious scientific institutions.

Turkmenistan

REPUBLIC OF TURKMENISTAN

T HE DESERT REPUBLIC OF TURKMENISTAN IN south-central Asia extends southeast-ward from the eastern shore of the Caspian Sea to its frontier with Afghanistan. Kazakhstan and Uzbekistan lie to the north, and Iran to the south.

ENVIRONMENT

The land rises sharply in the west from below sea level on the Caspian shore to the Krasnovodsk plateau. Southeast of the plateau, the mountains of the Kopet Dag follow the Iranian border. The mountains are prone to earthquakes, but are flanked by a narrow belt of oases – the most popular area for settlement. The capital,

NATIONAL DATA – TURKMENISTAN	
Land area 488,100 sq km (188,500 sq mi)	
Climate continental	
Major physical features highest point: Firyuza 2,942 m (9,652 ft); longest river: Amu Darya (part) 2,539 km (1,578 mi)	
Population (2000 est.) 4,518,268	
Form of government multiparty republic with two legislative houses	
Armed forces Army:16,000; air force:3,000	
Largest cities Ashkhabad (capital – 613,400); Chardzhou (214,100)	
Official language Turkmenian	
Ethnic composition Turkmen 77%; Russian 6.7%; Uzbek 9.2%; Kazakh 2.0%; others 5.1%	
Religious affiliations mainly Sunni Muslim (87%)	
Currency manat=100 tenes (since 1994)	
Gross domestic product (1999) US $7.7 billion	
Gross domestic product per capita (1999) US $1,800	
Life expectancy at birth male 61.9 yr; female 68.9 yr	
Major resources petroleum, natural gas, coal, sulfur, cotton, wool, lead, zinc, copper, gold, fisheries	

Ashkhabad, formerly a lonely outpost of the Russian empire, is in this belt. The rest of Turkmenistan is mostly a feature-less wilderness; 80 percent of the country is covered by the bleak plains of the Kara Kum desert. Toward the Afghan frontier in the southeast, the land rises to meet other mountains in the far eastern corner.

The climate is generally arid with little rainfall, except in the southern oasis belt, and with hot summers and cold winters. Vegetation consists mainly of poplars and willows along the river banks, and sparse woodland in the Kopet Dag.

SOCIETY

Turkic nomads have roamed the deserts of central Asia since the 9th century AD. Today the Turkmen are mainly a Muslim people, probably descended from the Seljuk and Ottoman Turks.

The rivalry between individual Turk-men peoples was often intense. When Russian troops invaded the eastern shore of the Caspian Sea in 1869, they were able to turn these divisions to their advantage. Even so, it took 30 years and a major battle, in which 150,000 Turkmen were killed, before the region was finally ab-sorbed into Russian Turkistan. After the 1917 Russian Revolutions, British forces helped in the attempt to create an in-dependent Transcaspian state. When the British troops withdrew in 1920 the Soviet Red Army quickly seized control and in 1924 the Turkmen Soviet Socialist Repub-lic was proclaimed.

Under Soviet rule the Turkmens were united for the first time, but anti-Soviet guerrilla warfare continued into the 1930s. Aspirations toward self-determin-ation were not fulfilled until 1991, when the Soviet Union collapsed and Turkmenistan joined the Commonwealth of Independent States. Government remained under the autocratic control of President Niyazov (b. 1940), re-elected in 1994 and his former Communist Party.

ECONOMY

Turkmenistan's economy has been depen-dent on its cotton crop and also on sales of oil and gas. In the late 1990s it suffered from a reduced income as a result of the inability of its customers in the former Soviet Union to meet their oil bills. Foreign debt was increased by Russia's refusal to export Turkmen gas. Hope for economic growth in the future is centered on the construction of new pipelines through Iran and Turkey.

Advancing sand dunes in Turkmenistan's Kara Kum desert. Covering some 340,000 sq km (130,000 sq mi), the Kara Kum consists mainly of bleak plains and some farmland, with only a small area – less than 10 percent – containing the immense, crescent-shaped dunes.

Cotton and wheat account for two thirds of agricultural production. Maize, rice, silk and fruit are also important. Local sheep and camels provide wool and hides for making the region's famous Bokhara carpets and rugs.

Turkmenistan has rich mineral resources including lead, zinc, copper and gold. It possesses the world's fifth largest reserves of natural gas. In the late 1990s, Turkmenistan signed oil development agreements with several international oil companies. Other industries include engi-neering, cotton textiles and food process-ing. The growing road network is sup-ported by a major railroad link from the port of Krasnovodsk through Ashkhabad to the oases of the interior. The Kara-kumsky Canal, the world's longest irriga-tion and shipping canal runs parallel to the railroad.

The Soviet regime aimed at providing a comprehensive welfare and education system. Considerable improvements were made to the literacy levels of the popula-tion under the communist regime. Since independence the Turkmen language has been restored as the state language and the country's mosques and religious insti-tutions, long suppressed under Soviet rule, have been reopened.

Uzbekistan

REPUBLIC OF UZBEKISTAN

THE FORMER SOVIET REPUBLIC OF UZBEKISTAN lying amid the deserts of south-central Asia, was once crossed by the fabled silk road to China. It is bounded by Kazakhstan to the north, and Turkmenistan and Afghanistan to the south. In the east a complicated frontier separates Uzbekistan from Tajikistan and Kyrgyzstan.

ENVIRONMENT

The northwestern frontier crosses the undulating Ustyurt Plateau, east of which is the salty Aral Sea, with the broad Amu Darya (Oxus) river delta at its southern end. From here the vast, sandy desert of the Kyzyl Kum stretches as far as the foothills of the eastern mountains. In the extreme east, beyond the capital Tashkent and the Chatkal mountains, is the fertile Fergana basin.

Uzbekistan has a mostly semi-arid climate, with rainfall largely confined to the east. Typically, a short winter with severe frosts is followed by a long, intensely hot summer. Vegetation ranges from desert shrubs to woodland in the east.

SOCIETY

Although the Uzbek people are of Turkic origin, they took their name from the Mongol khan Öz Beg who ruled 1313–40, and who may have converted them to Islam. They moved southward into their present territory in the 15th century, establishing khanates on lands that had once belonged to the powerful Tartar conqueror Tamerlane (1336–1405).

In the late 19th century the area was conquered by Russia, but Uzbekistan's present boundaries only took shape in 1924, when it became a constituent republic of the Soviet Union.

Although Uzbeks form the majority of today's population, there are some 60 other ethnic groups – a cause of much conflict. After the Soviet Union's disintegration in 1991, Uzbekistan joined the new Commonwealth of Independent States as a fully independent republic. Despite a multiparty constitution, the former Communist Party led by President Karimov (b. 1938), and re-elected in 1995 until 2000, tolerates little opposition.

ECONOMY

Intensive irrigation has made Uzbekistan one of the world's largest cotton producers, but it has also reduced the flow of the Amu Darya, causing the level of the Aral Sea to fall dramatically, devastating the local fishing communities. Fruit and rice are cultivated in oasis areas, and some cereals are grown in the east.

Mineral resources include huge deposits of uranium, gold and various metal ores, as well as some coal, oil and natural gas. Oil and gas production was expanding in the late 1990s. Hydroelectricity supplements the power these produce. Major manufactures include farm machinery, textiles, chemicals and food products.

The road and rail networks are extensive, and Tashkent's international airport is an important refueling point for flights between Europe and southern Asia. The beautiful architecture of Uzbekistan's medieval Islamic cities – Samarkand, Bukhara and Kiva – is now a considerable attraction to tourists.

NATIONAL DATA – UZBEKISTAN				
Land area 447,400 sq km (172,700 sq mi)				
Climate	Altitude m (ft)	**Temperatures** January °C(°F)	July °C(°F)	**Annual precipitation** mm (in)
Tashkent	478 (1,569)	–2 (29)	26 (78)	375 (14.8)
Major physical features highest point: Beshtor Peak 4,299 m (14,104 ft); largest lake: Aral Sea (part) 66,500 sq km (25,700 sq mi)				
Population (2000 est.) 24,775,519				
Form of government multiparty republic with one legislative house				
Armed forces 45,000 (1994) army 35,000; air force 2,000				
Largest cities Tashkent (capital – 2,144,500); Namangan (413,600); Samarkand (371,000); Andijon (342,000); Bukhara (263,500)				
Official language Uzbek				
Ethnic composition Uzbek 71.4%; Russian 8.3%; Tatar 2.4%; Kazakh 4.1%; Tajik 4.7%; others 9.1%				
Religious affiliations mainly Sunni Muslim (88.0%)				
Currency soum=1,000 coupons (since 1994)				
Gross domestic product (1999) US $59.3 billion				
Gross domestic product per capita (1999) US $2,500				
Life expectancy at birth male 64.3 yr; female 70.7 yr				
Major resources natural gas, coal, uranium, gold, silver, copper, lead, zinc, tungsten, molybdenum, cotton, grain, livestock, agriculture				

No shortage of bread A trio of Uzbek market stall-holders keenly proffer their freshly made flat, round loaves to passersby. Bread, a staple part of the diet, is the traditional accompaniment to the typical Uzbek meal of rice, mutton and vegetables.

Tajikistan

REPUBLIC OF TAJIKISTAN

I N THE HIGHLANDS OF SOUTH-CENTRAL ASIA lies the small mountainous republic of Tajikistan, which shares borders with Afghanistan to the south and China to the east. To the north is Kyrgyzstan and to the northwest Uzbekistan.

ENVIRONMENT

Most of eastern Tajikistan, dominated by the icy wastes of the great Massif known as the Pamirs, is more than 3,000 m (10,000 ft) above sea level. The two highest mountains within the Commonwealth of Independent States are in this area. The highest, named Communism Peak in the Soviet era, rises to 7,495 m

A party of Tajik men prepare to celebrate the circumcision of a young boy – part of his initiation into the Islamic faith – in traditional style. Soviet suppression of religion was in practice greatly relaxed in the Central Asian republics.

(24,590 ft). In the north, other mountain ranges extend into Uzbekistan from Kyrgyzstan across Tajikistan, and north of these lies the fertile Fergana basin, famed for growing a variety of exotic fruits. In the southwest a number of rivers drain southward into the Amu Darya river.

The climate is continental, with cold winters, and long hot summers in the valleys; the higher mountains are markedly colder. Precipitation is largely confined to the high valleys bordering the Pamirs, from where water carries downstream to the much drier areas. Plant and animal life varies according to altitude.

SOCIETY

Most of the peoples of Central Asia have a language and culture strongly influenced by a history of Turkic invasion. The ethnic roots of the Tajiks, however, go back to ancient Persia, and the people speak a language that is Iranian rather than Turkic in origin. In the 16th century the area became part of the Bukhara emirate of the Mongol empire until it was overrun by Afghans in the mid 18th century. Although absorbed into the Russian empire in the 19th century, there was considerable resistance to Soviet domination in Tajikistan in the 1920s, and it did not become a constituent republic of the Soviet Union until 1929.

The population of Tajikistan is an ethnic mixture that includes Uzbeks, Russians and Tartars; the Tajiks themselves are a combination of several older ethnic groups. The years leading up to full independence in 1991 were overshadowed in Tajikistan, as in other parts of the crumbling Soviet Union, by ethnic unrest and violence. Political unrest escalated into civil war in 1992 with fighting between government forces and a coalition of Islamic and pro-democracy groups. Thousands died or were forced to flee before a UN-sponsored ceasefire was agreed in 1996. Further outbreaks of fighting occurred in 1997 and 1998.

ECONOMY

Agriculture in Tajikistan relies on extensive irrigation. Cotton is the chief crop, but cereals, rice and many kinds of fruit and nuts are also grown. There is also livestock farming mainly for the production of wool and meat. The country is rich in mineral resources, including iron ore, coal, oil and natural gas. Along with hydroelectricity (generated from the country's fast-flowing rivers), these fuels provide power for domestic consumers and for the factories that produce cotton textiles, clothing, carpets, food and machinery. Carpet making is still an important source of foreign revenue.

Transportation by road and railroad is adequate for local needs despite the difficult terrain. More remote districts maybe reached by air, and there are regular international flights to neighboring states. Tajikistan's towns have well developed health, welfare and education services, but these are much less developed in the widespread isolated rural areas.

NATIONAL DATA – TAJIKISTAN	
Land area	143,100 sq km (55,300 sq mi)
Climate	continental
Major physical features	highest point: Qullai Garmo 7,495 m (24,590 ft); longest rivers: Amu Darya (part) 2,539 km (1,578 mi), Vakhsh 800 km (497 mi)
Population	(2000 est.) 6,440,730
Form of government	multiparty republic with one legislative house
Armed forces	7,000, supported by 30,000 Russian troops
Largest cities	Dushanbe (capital – 691,600); Khudzhand (205,200)
Official language	Tajik
Ethnic composition	Tajik 64.9%; Uzbek 25.0%; Russian 3.5%; others 6.6%
Religious affiliations	mainly Sunni Muslim (80.0%)
Currency	1 Tajik ruble (R) = 100 kopecks
Gross domestic product	(1999) US $59.3 billion
Gross domestic product per capita	(1999) US $2,500
Life expectancy at birth	male 64.2 yr; female 70.2 yr
Major resources	lead, zinc, gold, uranium, iron ore, coal, oil, natural gas, hydroelectric power, cotton, wool, cattle

Kyrgyzstan

REPUBLIC OF KYRGYZSTAN

KYRGYZSTAN IS A MOUNTAINOUS REPUBLIC in central Asia. It has Kazakhstan on its northern frontier, Uzbekistan to the west, Tajikistan to the southwest and a long border with China to the southeast.

ENVIRONMENT

Kyrgyzstan is dominated by a massive mountain range, the Tien Shan, which extends the length of Kyrgyzstan's frontier with China from Pobedy Peak at 7,439 m (24,406 ft) in the east to the Alay mountains in the west, near the southwestern border with Tajikistan. The rest of Kyrgyzstan is largely made up of a series of parallel mountain ranges divided by deep river valleys and basins. The deepest basin is in the northeast, where the clear, waters of Lake Issyk-Kul are enclosed by a ring of snowy mountains. In the west, the central Fergana valley opens out into a broad basin, most of which lies within Uzbekistan.

The mountains bring plentiful water to an otherwise desert area. Their higher slopes are wet and cold, with heavy winter snowfall. In contrast, summers in the valleys and basins are hot and dry, but runoff and meltwater from the mountains make irrigation possible on a wide scale. Vegetation ranges from dry scrub and woodland in the valleys to alpine meadow on the higher slopes. Wildlife is plentiful in the mountains.

SOCIETY

The origins of the mainly Muslim Kyrgyz people are uncertain. Their Turkic language resembles the language spoken in neighboring Kazakhstan, and many believe that both groups arrived from the northeast in the 13th century, seeking refuge from Mongol invaders. The pastoral nomadic life of the indigenous population changed little over the ensuing centuries, until Russians colonized Kyrgyzstan in the 19th century. The area was subsequently annexed region by region, until in 1876 Kyrgyzstan was made part of Russian Turkistan. Much of the best land went to Russians, who settled in the low-lying, fertile regions. The ruthless enforcement of collectivization that followed the 1917 Russian Revolution irrevocably altered the traditional way of life of the Kyrgyz people. In 1924 the area became an autonomous oblast (region), and in 1936 was incorporated into the Soviet Union as the Kyrgyz Soviet Socialist Republic. But resistance to Soviet rule, carried out by local guerrilla groups or *basmachi*, continued into the 1930s.

Today the Kyrgyz account for little more than half the country's mixed population. The largest minority group, after the Russians, are the Uzbeks, who in 1990 were involved in violent clashes with the Kyrgyz as deepseated interracial tensions resurfaced with the relaxation of Soviet rule. The previous year the Kyrgyz had clashed with the Tajiks over a border dispute. In July 1991 the Kyrgyz Supreme Soviet instituted its own presidential government, and before the end of the year the newly independent republic of Kyrgyzstan joined the Commonwealth of Independent States. A revised constitution was adopted in 1994, with first elections in 1995 for the bicameral parliament.

ECONOMY

The main agricultural activity is livestock breeding, especially cattle, sheep and goats. The Kyrgyz, renowned for their horsemanship, use horses for rounding up and tending livestock. The country is self-sufficient in grain, and other crops include tobacco, cotton and poppy (the opium-producing species). Agriculture is highly mechanized, and makes use of extensive irrigation.

Industrial development has benefited from plentiful supplies of hydroelectricity and fossil fuels including coal, oil and natural gas. Industries are based on local resources and include food processing, weaving, textiles and manufacturing footwear. The mountainous terrain poses communication problems, mostly resolved through the development of the road network. Medical and educational facilities, made readily available under the old Soviet regime, include modern hospitals and welfare centers, schools and institutes of higher education.

A temple to the arts, the imposing opera house in Bishkek (formerly Frunze), capital of Kyrgyzstan. Founded as late as 1878, the city is built on a grid pattern, with wide tree-lined boulevards and parks. The large industrial quarter was developed in the 1960s.

NATIONAL DATA – KYRGYZSTAN

Land area	198,500 sq km (76,600 sq mi)
Climate	continental
Major physical features	highest point: Pobedy Peak 7,439 m (24,406 ft); longest river: Syr Darya (part) 2,200 km (1,370 mi)
Population	(2000 est.) 4,685,230
Form of government	multiparty republic with two legislative houses
Armed forces	army 12,000
Capital city	Bishkek (793,100)
Official language	Kyrgyzian
Ethnic composition	Kyrgyz 52.4%; Russian 21.5%; Uzbek 12.9%; Ukrainian 2.5%; Tatar 1.6%; others 9.1%
Religious affiliations	mainly Sunni Muslim with a Christian minority
Currency	som=100 tyiyn (since 1993)
Gross domestic product	(1999) US $10.3 billion
Gross domestic product per capita	(1999) US $2,300
Life expectancy at birth	male 63.3 yr; female 71.9 yr
Major resources	coal, oil, natural gas, gold, mercury, uranium, cattle, sheep, goats, tobacco, cotton, sugar beet, cereals, hydroelectric power

Kazakhstan

REPUBLIC OF KAZAKHSTAN

RUSSIA

KAZAKHSTAN

CHINA

THE REPUBLIC OF KAZAKHSTAN EXTENDS across central Asia from the Caspian Sea in the west to China in the east. It shares a long frontier with Russia to the north, and borders Turkmenistan, Uzbekistan and Kyrgyzstan to the south. After Russia, Kazakhstan is the second largest of the former Soviet republics, and one of the most influential members of the Commonwealth of Independent States. The capital was moved to Astana in 1998.

NATIONAL DATA – KAZAKHSTAN

Land area	2,717,300 sq km (1,049,200 sq mi)			
Climate		Temperatures		Annual
	Altitude m (ft)	January °C(°F)	July °C(°F)	precipitation mm (in)
Alma-Ata	775 (2,543)	–9 (15)	21 (70)	598 (23.5)

Major physical features	highest point: Khan-Tengri 6,398 m (20,991 ft); lowest point: Mangyshlak Depression –132 m (–433 ft); longest river: Irtysh (part) 4,400 km (2,760 mi)
Population	(2000 est.) 16,733,227
Form of government	multiparty republic with one legislative house
Armed forces	army 25,000; air force 15,000
Largest cities	Alma-Ata (1,059,600); Karaganda (429,200); Chimkent (367,800); Taraz (328,800); Oskemen (309,400); Pavlodar (300,000); Semey (268,200); Aktobe (254,200)
Official language	Kazakh
Ethnic composition	Kazakh 42.0%; Russian 38.0%; Ukrainian 5.4%; Tatar 2.0%; others 12.6%
Religious affiliations	Muslim 47.0%; Russian Orthodox 44.0%; Protestant 2.0%; others 7.0%
Currency	tenge=100 kiyn
Gross domestic product	(1999) US $54.4 billion
Gross domestic product per capita	(1999) US $3,200
Life expectancy at birth	male 62.8 yr; female 72.4 yr
Major resources	coal, oil, natural gas, iron ore, bauxite, copper, nickel, lead, gold, uranium, chromium, cereals, cotton

ENVIRONMENT

Kazakhstan's predominantly flat landscape is broken by several mountain ranges in the east and southeast on the borders with Russia, China and Kyrgyzstan. Most of eastern Kazakhstan is an eroded tableland characterized by shallow uplands, depressions and lakes. The west is lower-lying, with the northern basins of the Aral Sea in the center, and farther west beyond the Mugodzhary Hills, the Caspian Sea.

The country's climate is characterized by intense winter cold and summer heat. Precipitation levels are generally low. More than two-thirds of Kazakhstan is desert or semidesert. The central lakes are salty, as are the lowland marshes in the west, and in the center there are few permanent rivers. The grass steppelands in the north are the country's most fertile regions. Wildlife ranges from wolves and bears to gerbils and mole-voles that inhabit the steppes and the desert.

SOCIETY

Kazakhstan is named after the Kazakh peoples, Turkic-speaking nomads who established a powerful khanate in the region during the 15th and 16th centuries. In the 18th and 19th centuries their empire broke up and was gradually overrun by the Russians. From 1861 onward, newly emancipated Russian and Ukrainian peasants settled in the fertile northern steppes. Kazakh nationalism culminated in a bitter civil war in Kazakhstan after the 1917 Russian Revolutions. In 1936 it was incorporated as a Soviet republic.

The Soviet regime became increasingly repressive in the late 1930s when Kazakhstan's traditionally nomadic peoples were collectivized on huge cattle farms. Many fled to China and Afghanistan. In the 1950s and 1960s vast tracts of uncultivated territory were transformed into arable land. This was known as the "Virgin Lands" project; its longterm effect on the ecological balance was disastrous. The Soviet regime also set up sites in the desert for the Soviet space launching program and for nuclear weapons testing. With the relaxation of Soviet rule in the late 1980s, nationalist sentiments resurfaced. Kazakhstan's refusal to recognize

the Soviet coup of 1991 was a major reason for the Soviet Union's breakup. Kazakhstan regained its independence in December 1991. Elections in 1994 were declared invalid in 1995, after which President Nazarbaev (b. 1940) took power to rule by decree. Today's population includes almost as many ethnic Russians as Kazakhs, which creates tensions.

ECONOMY

Kazakhstan is extremely rich in mineral resources including iron ore, bauxite, copper and nickel. It has proven oil reserves of 2 billion tonnes, and the successful exploitation of these will make the country one of the biggest oil producers in the world in the 2000s.

In the late 1990s Kazakhstan signed agreements with China and with a number of international consortia to explore and develop oil and natural gas fields. This should help Kazakhstan out of the economic collapse it suffered after the breakup of the Soviet Union. Chemical production, metal smelting and the manufacturing of heavy machinery are important industries as well as the more recent electronics and pharmaceuticals.

Agriculture employs around one quarter of the population. The production of grain and cotton has now replaced the traditional cattle, sheep and horse breeding as the major activity.

A Kazakh shepherd Kazakhstan is home to some 200,000 nomadic shepherds and herdsmen, who, like the Tartars before them, pack their yurts (collapsible houses) on their horses and travel with the changing seasons to favorable pastures for their flocks.

Mongolia

REPUBLIC OF MONGOLIA

A burgundy-robed Buddhist monk in the monastery at Erdeni Dzuu in central Mongolia, southwest of the capital, Ulan Bator. Buddhism was introduced into Mongolia by Tibetan teachers in the 13th century at the request of Genghis Khan's grandson, Godan Khan.

MONGOLIA IS A VERY LARGE LANDLOCKED republic with China on its southern frontier and Russia to the north. It is sometimes known as Outer Mongolia, to distinguish it from Inner Mongolia, an Autonomous Region of China.

ENVIRONMENT

Most of the country is over 1,000 m (3,300 ft) above sea level. The highest peaks are in the Altai mountains, in the lofty central massif of the Hangayn range, and in the Hentiyn range, which runs northeast-ward from the capital, Ulan Bator. Much of the country is prone to earthquakes.

Nearly four-fifths of Mongolia is dry steppe grassland, and much of the rest is cold, arid desert. Most of the south is occupied by the Gobi, an area of stony desert and low mountain ranges. Forest, mostly on northern mountain slopes, covers less than one-tenth of the land. The winters are long and extremely cold, with snow in the higher mountains. Wildlife is plentiful. Lynx, bears and deer inhabit the northern regions, while the steppes support marmots and gazelles. The snow leopards of the Altai are becoming endangered.

SOCIETY

For thousands of years Mongolia was inhabited by nomadic peoples from central Asia and southern Siberia. In the 13th century they were united under the warrior Genghis Khan (c. 1162–1227). He and his successors established a vast empire that extended across China, much of central Asia and Russia. In 1368, however, the empire collapsed and Mongolia came under Chinese domination.

After the Russian Civil War (1918–22), the Chinese were eventually driven out of Outer Mongolia, and the Mongolian People's Republic was established in 1924. From its foundation, the Mongolian republic was closely tied to the Soviet Union. Its government was set up along Soviet lines, with only one political party. A new constitution, which introduced a multi-party 76 seat elected parliament and guaranteed freedom of speech, was approved in 1992 with first elections held later that year. A second free election was held in 1996 with the Democratic Union party winning, finally ending communist control of the country.

Most people in the republic are Mongols; the Kazakhs are the largest non-Mongol minority. Religious practice was suppressed for many years under the Soviet regime, but other cultural traditions have been kept alive.

ECONOMY

Mongolia's grasslands support a huge livestock population, including sheep, cattle, goats and horses. Crop farming is minimal. The forests provide some roundwood for fuel and for industry.

The country has large deposits of coal (the chief energy source) and fluorite, as well as copper, molybdenum and other metal ores. Most industries process raw materials. The principal exports are minerals and animal products; imports include machinery and a range of consumer goods. Most trade is with countries of the former Soviet Union.

The Trans-Mongolian Railway, linking Mongolia with Russia and China, is the country's major transportation route. There are few surfaced roads and camels are still used in the south. Ulan Bator has an international airport and offers internal flights to other cities.

The state provides free health, welfare and education services. Literacy levels are high, and most children receive schooling.

NATIONAL DATA – MONGOLIA			
Land area	1,566,500 sq km (604,800 sq mi)		

Climate		Temperatures		Annual
	Altitude m (ft)	January °C(°F)	July °C(°F)	precipitation mm (in)
Ulan Bator	1,337 (4,385)	−26 (−15)	16 (61)	209 (8.2)

Major physical features highest point: Hüyten (Nayramdal) Peak 4,374 m (14,350 ft); longest river: Selenga 1,000 km (620 mi)

Population (2000 est.) 2,650,952

Form of government multiparty republic with one legislative house

Armed forces army 20,000; air force 1,250

Capital city Ulan Bator (619,000)

Official language Khalkha Mongolian

Ethnic composition Khalkha Mongol 77.5%; Kazakh 5.3%; Dörbed Mongol 2.8%; Bayad 2.0%; Buryat Mongol 1.9%; Dariganga Mongol 1.5%; others 9.0%

Religious affiliations Shamanist, Buddhist, Muslim

Currency 1 tugrik (Tug) = 100 möngös

Gross domestic product (1999 est.) US $6.1 billion

Gross domestic product per capita (1999) US $2,320

Life expectancy at birth male 64.4 yr; female 67.3 yr

Major resources oil, coal, copper, tungsten, molybdenum, phosphates, tin, nickel, zinc, gold, livestock

REGIONAL PROFILES

Russia and Northern Eurasia

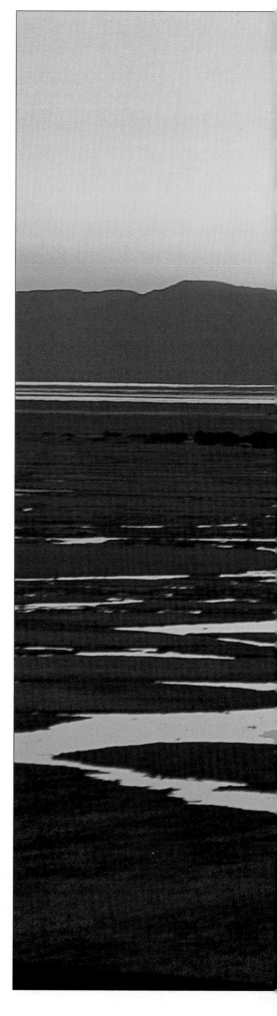

Lake Baikal, in southern Siberia

PHYSICAL GEOGRAPHY

Russia and the republics around it display geology on a grand scale. Extending a quarter of the way around the globe, the region contains within its boundaries an immense variety of landforms and climates – high peaks and low plains, flooding rivers and sandy deserts, subtropical beaches and permanently frozen ground. Over much of the region the sheer scale of the gradual change over great distances from one kind of environment to another gives rise to rather monotonous landscapes. High mountains ring the eastern and southern perimeter, forming a huge amphitheater whose auditorium stretches from the Baltic to the banks of the Yenisei, looking out over vast plains and low flat plateaus to the Arctic Ocean. To the southeast, beyond the mountains, lie grasslands and the desert expanses of Mongolia.

COUNTRIES IN THE REGION

Armenia, Azerbaijan, Belarus, Estonia, Georgia, Kazakhstan, Kyrgyzstan, Latvia, Lithuania, Moldova, Mongolia, Russia, Tajikistan, Turkmenistan, Ukraine, Uzbekistan

LAND

Area 23,967,200 sq km (9,251,339 sq mi), including largest country on Earth
Highest point Qullai Garmo, 7,495 m (24,590 ft)
Lowest point Mangyshlak Depression, –132 m (–433 ft)
Major features plains and plateaus of north, Ural Mountains, Caucasus Mountains, Pamirs and Altai ranges, Kara Kum, Kyzyl Kum and Gobi deserts, Arctic islands

WATER

Longest river Yenisei, 5,870 km (3,650 mi)
Largest basin Yenisei, 2,619,000 sq km (1,011,000 sq mi)
Highest average flow Yenisei, 18,000 cu m/sec (636,000 cu ft/sec)
Largest lake Caspian Sea, 371,000 sq km (143,240 sq mi), largest area of inland water in world; Lake Baikal is world's greatest in volume, at 22,000 cu km (5,500 cu mi) and maximum depth, at 1,620 m (5,184 ft)

CLIMATE

	Temperature °C (°F) January	July	Altitude m (ft)
Moscow	–10 (14)	19 (66)	51.2 (156)
Sochi	7 (45)	23 (73)	102 (31)
Krasnovodsk	2 (36)	28 (82)	292 (89)
Ulan Bator	–26 (–15)	16 (61)	4,385 (1,337)
Verkhoyansk	–47 (–53)	16 (61)	449 (137)
Vladivostok	–14 (7)	17 (63)	453 (138)

	Precipitation mm (in) January	July	Year
Moscow	31 (1.2)	74 (2.9)	575 (22.6)
Sochi	201 (7.9)	60 (2.4)	1,451 (57.1)
Krasnovodsk	11 (0.4)	2 (0.1)	92 (3.6)
Ulan Bator	1 (0.4)	76 (3.0)	209 (8.2)
Verhoyansk	7 (0.3)	33 (1.3)	155 (6.1)
Vladivostok	19 (0.7)	116 (4.6)	824 (32.4)

NATURAL HAZARDS

Earthquakes in Mongolia, southwest and northeast republics, drought, extreme cold, landslides and avalanches

THE ANCIENT FOUNDATIONS

The area that comprised the former Soviet Union is an immense plain encircled by high mountains along its borders to the east, south and southwest, and divided in two by the Ural Mountains. The plain has a foundation of ancient Precambrian crystalline rocks more than 600 million years old, which were worn down to a near-flat surface before being covered by sedimentary rocks. Lying on the Eurasian tectonic plate, they provide a stable base for the sedimentary rocks, which have retained their horizontal strata over large areas.

The basement rocks form two platforms. The Russian platform underlies the European part of the region – that is, as far east as the Ural Mountains and Ural river. The old rocks are seen at the surface only in the northeast and southeast. The Siberian platform covers a large part of Siberia, the land east of the Urals between the Arctic Ocean, the Kirgiz Steppe and the mountains along the southern border. It outcrops over a small area in the north and a much larger area in the south. Between these two platforms the basement rocks form a vast, shallow basin (geosyncline) that filled with sedimentary rocks during the Paleozoic era, 590–248 million years ago. These were raised up to form the Ural Mountains when the platforms moved closer together about 280 million years ago during the Hercynian mountain-building period. Movement between the Eurasian and North American plates at that time also raised up fold mountains, such as the Verkhoyansk Range to the east of the Lena river and the Chukot Range in the far northeast of the country.

A turbulent past

The Alpine mountain-building period, which began about 30 million years ago, affected only the southern fringes of the region. The southerly movement of the Eurasian plate against the Indian and Arabian plates folded the deep sediments that had accumulated between them to form mountain ranges that include the Caucasus Mountains and the Pamirs. Some of the older mountains formed in the Hercynian period, such as the Altai range, were lifted up again. Lake Baikal occupies a trench formed by these upheavals. The movements are still taking place, and in 1988 were responsible for the tragic earthquake in Armenia, south of the Caucasus Mountains, which killed 25,000 people. Rebuilding was still being done at the start of the 21st century.

Along the southeastern and eastern boundaries of the Eurasian plate the movements caused magma to rise to the surface, forming volcanoes. The Kamchatka Peninsula contains Siberia's highest mountain, the volcano Klyuchevskaya Sopka, 4,750 m (15,580 ft). The Kuril Islands are a continuation of the mountains of Kamchatka.

Plains and plateaus

The great plains have nearly always been low-lying, and the sea has advanced and retreated regularly over them. Only the northwest has remained permanently above sea level. With each marine invasion sedimentary rocks were deposited under the sea. The younger rocks occur to the south, with Tertiary rocks 65–2 million years old in the Crimea, the middle Volga plateau and elsewhere.

To the east of the Yenisei river, beyond the West Siberian Plain, the Central Siberian Plateau begins. The land becomes higher, lying mainly between 450 and 900 m (1,500–3,000 ft) above sea level. Here the rocks have not been much disturbed, but there are gentle undulations where they have sagged following small depressions in the platform below.

GREAT INLAND WATERS

The Caspian Sea and the Aral Sea are both saltwater remnants of a former ocean. Lake Superior and the other freshwater lakes of North America are a legacy of ice sheets that covered the land. The greatest freshwater lake by volume, Lake Baikal, contains some 22,000 cu km (5,500 cu mi) of water. It lies in a rift valley formed as a result of tectonic activity in the Earth's crust.

Lake	sq km	sq mi
Caspian Sea, Azerbaijan/Iran/ Kazakhstan/Russia/Turkmenistan	371,000	143,240
Lake Superior, Canada/United States	83,270	32,150
Lake Victoria, Kenya/Tanzania/Uganda	62,940	24,300
Lake Huron, Canada/United States	59,600	23,000
Lake Michigan, United States	58,000	22,400
Lake Tanganyika, Tanzania/D. R. Congo	32,900	12,700
Great Bear Lake, Canada	31,800	12,100
Lake Baikal, Russia	30,500	11,800
Lake Malawi, Malawi/Mozambique/ Tanzania	29,600	11,400
Aral Sea, Kazakhstan/Uzbekistan	28,687	11,076

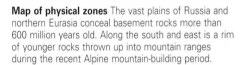

ARCTIC OCEAN

Franz Josef Land

Barents Sea

Novaya Zemlya

Severnaya Zemlya

Kara Sea

Wrangel Island

East Siberian Sea

New Siberian Islands

Chukot Range

Koryak Range

Bering Sea

Taymyr Peninsula

Laptev Sea

Byrranga Mts

Kola Pen

RUSSIA ESTONIA
LATVIA
LITHUANIA
BELARUS

L Ladoga

Northern European Plain

L Onega

N Dvina

Moscow

MOLDOVA

UKRAINE

Dnieper

Dniester

Volga

Don

Sea of Azov

Black Sea

Sochi
Elbrus 5642
GEORGIA

Caucasus Mts

ARMENIA

AZERBAIJAN

Caspian Depression

Ural

Kirghiz Steppe

Mangyshlak Peninsula -132

Caspian Sea
Cheleken

Aral Sea

KAZAKHSTAN

TURKMENISTAN UZBEKISTAN

Kara Kum

Kyzyl Kum

Amu Darya

Syr Darya

L Balkhash

L Zaisan

Pamir
Qullai Garmo 7495
TAJIKISTAN

KYRGYZSTAN
Pobedy Peak 7439

Ural Mountains

Ob

Tobol

Irtysh

West Siberian Plain

RUSSIA

Ob

Yenisei

Central Siberian Plateau

Verkhoyansk

Cherskogo Range

Pobeda 3147

Lena

Verkhoyansk Range

Kamchatka Peninsula

Klyuchevskaya 4750

Kolyma Range

Dzhugdzur Ra

Sea of Okhotsk

Sakhalin

Kuril Islands

Angara

Lena

L Baikal

Eastern Sayan Mts

Yenisei

Western Sayan Mts

Altai Range

Ulan Bator

MONGOLIA

Gobi

Stanovoy Range

Yablonovy Range

Amur

Amur

Ussuri

Sikhote-Alin Mts

Sea of Japan

Vladivostok

Physical zones
- tundra
- mountains/barren land
- forest
- grassland
- semidesert
- desert

▲ mountain peak (meters)
▼ depression (meters)
☀ climate station

Map of physical zones The vast plains of Russia and northern Eurasia conceal basement rocks more than 600 million years old. Along the south and east is a rim of younger rocks thrown up into mountain ranges during the recent Alpine mountain-building period.

The deepest lake in the world, with a maximum depth of 1,940 m (6,365 ft), Lake Baikal lies in a rift valley. It is fed by no fewer than 336 rivers, and contains about one-fifth of all the fresh water on the surface of the Earth.

A SUCCESSION OF CLIMATES

The great scale and low relief of the region means that large areas have similar landscapes, climates, vegetation and soils. With few natural boundaries formed by bold changes in topography, one zone merges almost imperceptibly into the next.

The continental interior
The huge interior expanses, which are cut off from the ameliorating effects of any warm ocean except in the extreme northwest, have a continental climate. This is characterized by large differences in temperature between winter and summer, very short spring and fall seasons, low rainfall and strong winds. The country lies farther north than many people imagine, and this makes the continental climate very severe. Moscow lies on the same latitude as Labrador in northeast Canada, and large stretches of the country are north of the Arctic Circle. Verkhoyansk

in eastern Siberia has been called the "cold pole" because winter temperatures there can fall as low as –50°C (–58°F). During its short summer, temperatures may reach 37°C (100°F).

Three areas have a more favorable climate. The east coast, particularly the basin of the Amur, has onshore winds in summer that bring rainfall of about 750 mm (30 in). South of the Caucasus Mountains the valleys are well sheltered from the cold north winds, and winters are mild. Summers are hot because of Transcaucasia's southerly latitude, and the climate may best be described as subtropical. The third area with mild climates is the south coast of the Crimean Peninsula in the Black Sea, which is also protected by mountains from cold north winds in winter. With wet, warm winters and hot, dry summers it has a Mediterranean climate.

The plains can be divided into four main zones, running roughly east to west, that reflect gradual climatic transitions from tundra to arid conditions. From north to south they are: tundra, where conditions are too cold for trees; forest; grassland (steppe); and desert, where there is too little moisture available for a rich plant cover. One vegetation zone slowly changes to another over several hundred kilometers in a transitional zone, so it is never possible to state exactly where one starts and the other finishes. The wooded steppe is an example.

The sluggish rivers of Siberia form large deltas. Water readily lies on the surface of the tundra, prevented from draining away by the frozen subsoil.

Dark coniferous forests or taiga, a quarter of all the world's forests, extend over nearly half the country, covering the infertile podzol soils of the northern plains.

The great forest

The dominant impression of the northern landscape is a vast plain, but in fact glaciation has created some relief. Shallow valleys that run east-west mark where meltwater flowed along the front of the ice sheets that advanced over the plains during the ice ages of the past 2 million years. In the northeast material deposited by ice sheets has blocked old valleys and created lakes such as Lakes Ladoga and Onega. Rivers have cut shallow valleys as the land has risen since the great weight of the ice was removed.

Forest is the natural vegetation over the greater part of the region. Coniferous forest (taiga) is the most common, covering over a third of the country. It spreads across the land from the Baltic Sea to the Pacific Ocean, and stretches through 2,000 km (1,240 m) of latitude in east Siberia. Forests present a monotonous landscape with only the density of the trees changing – tall, dark thickets on the higher, well-drained ground, thinner forest on the swampy lowlands. Few plants live on the forest floor, but on the trees there are various species of moss and lichen. In the west the main tree species are spruce, pine, fir and cedar, whereas in the east the Siberian and Dahurian larches prevail.

To the south the coniferous forest merges into mixed and then deciduous broadleaf forest. This change reflects the longer growing season and higher temperatures. This is good agricultural land; only isolated patches of the forest remain in a landscape dominated by farming. The largest area of deciduous forest is found in the southeast, where both rainfall and temperatures are higher in the basin drained by the Amur.

Steppe grasslands

Farther south steppe grasslands become more widespread. Flat plains dissected by gullies and ravines are the most typical scenery. The forest steppe is a broad transitional zone in which patches of

forest on the cooler north-facing slopes alternate with steppe on the warmer south-facing slopes.

The steppe is too dry for trees to grow except along the side of river valleys. There are few features to break the uniformity of the landscape apart from some small basins formed by erosion, and a few ancient burial mounds raised by human inhabitants. The steppe extends southeast in a broad sweep from the Sea of Azov through the lands between the Ural Mountains and the Caspian and Aral Seas, to the mountain fringe north of Lake Balkhash. The rich black chernozem soils, formerly an expanse of grasses and herbaceous plants adapted to a dry climate, were extensively plowed and cultivated under the Soviet regime, making them into substantial grainfields.

THE GREAT RIVERS

In such a huge landmass, where there are few indentations in the coastline and where the sources of the rivers are such a long way from their mouths, the main rivers are immense. The drainage basins of the Siberian rivers such as the Amur, Lena, Ob and Yenisei could each contain Texas at least three times and France four times over.

As well as their size, the rivers have many other features in common. Their gradients are very shallow because they flow over extensive low-lying areas. The steepest gradient is that of the Volga at 1 : 1,000, about six times less than the Seine in Paris. Still about 2,000 km (1,200 mi) from the Arctic Ocean, the Yenisei is already only 152 m (500 ft) above sea level. This low gradient is associated with relatively slow river flow, but because the volume of flow is so large the rivers and the valleys they occupy are wide: the estuary of the Yenisei, for example is almost 50 km (30 mi) wide.

The flow of the rivers is seasonal, and generally at their lowest level in February, when the catchment areas are frozen. The highest volumes are reached in early summer, when the snow melts and there are summer storms. At this time the rivers flowing into the Arctic overflow their banks, because their mouths are still blocked by ice long after the southern courses have melted. At the mouths of the rivers huge deltas have been deposited. The Volga enters the Caspian Sea through a fan of river channels 200 km (124 mi) wide.

THE ARID SOUTH

Mountains to the south and east, the Caspian Sea to the west and the Kirghiz Steppe to the north mark the boundaries of the regions main desert area in central Asia. It covers a huge plain with slopes generally so gentle that they are barely visible. Several types of desert, including clay, gravel and pebble deserts, have developed here but sandy deserts are the most common.

In the central Asian desert large areas of dry land have very little vegetation except in occasional small depressions that collect moisture. In the north there are rich loess soils that can be cultivated if irrigated, but elsewhere wind erosion has left rocks with very thin soils, and over large areas the sand is blown into lines of shifting dunes.

Three main areas within the desert can be identified. The Ustyurt plateau, on the northeastern border of the Caspian Sea, is a block of land about 200 m (650 ft) above seal level surrounded by lines of fractures. To the south lies the mainly sandy Kara Kum (kum means desert); between the Syr Darya and Amu Darya rivers is the Kyzyl Kum, which has a thick mantle of sand covering a broken relief, with flat-topped ridges up to about 910 m (3,000 ft).

Beyond the mountains of the Altai range in the southeast of the region lies another great desert area. The Gobi desert extends across half of Mongolia. An area of great extremes of temperature, the Gobi ranges from sandy in the east to stony in the west.

Inland seas

Although precipitation is normally less than 200 mm (8 in) a year in the deserts of central Asia, with the potential for evaporation in the intense summer heat more than 1,000 mm (40 in), the large desert basin of the former Soviet Union has two major lakes, the Aral Sea and Caspian Sea.

The Aral Sea is the smaller of the two and has an average depth of about 15 m (50 ft). It is fed by two major rivers, the Amu Darya and Syr Darya, which flow across the desert from the mountains in the southeast. The Caspian Sea, the world's largest inland expanse of water, is 1,945 m (6,384 ft) deep at its southern end. It is fed by the Volga (Europe's longest river), the Ural and the Emba, which flow in from the plains of the north.

Satellite view of the Gobi desert in southern Mongolia. Streambeds formed by flash floods thread the barren slopes of rocky material washed down from mountain ranges. A dry salt pan and a lake occupy the inland basin to the south.

The desert tableland of Ustyurt, near the Aral Sea, a striped landscape of horizontally bedded sandstone. At some time in the past the sandstone was eroded; new, coarser sediments were deposited on the old land surface. In the harsh desert climate these younger rocks are now weathering, and rock fragments are tumbling down the sandstone slopes.

The mountain fringe

Mountains occupy almost a third of the region. Many of them, including the Urals, the mountains south of Lake Baikal and the far eastern mountains, do not have very conspicuous relief. The most common landscape is of flattish, rounded hills, broken here and there by higher summits. They represent old mountain systems that have been worn down, pushed up again to form elevated plateaus and then eroded once again.

The principal mountain ranges form a ring around the south and east. The exception is the Ural Mountains, which rise in isolation to separate the European or Russian plains from the Siberian plains. Erosion has reduced their height, and the traveler arriving from the west is hardly aware that the Urals have been reached. For much of their 2,000 km (1,200 mi) length the peaks do not even reach 600 m (2,000 ft).

The highest and most spectacular mountains are found around the edge of the region, where the earth movements during the Tertiary period have had most effect. In the east the Kamchatka Peninsula, lying on the edge of the Pacific fault line, is marked by intense volcanic activity. The highest peaks are found in the Pamirs and other ranges to the south of the Siberian plain and Central Asia. Where the old plain has been pushed up and broken into blocks the mountains look like a giant staircase. Elsewhere earth movements have caused intense folding and faulting and deep rift valleys. High-level deserts have formed in the sheltered basins between the ranges.

The Caucasus Mountains extend for about 1,200 km (750 mi) between the Black and Caspian Seas. They were formed at the same time as the Alps in Europe. Although glaciers still exist, many of the landscape features associated with the ice ages of the past 2 million years, such as U-shaped valleys, hanging valleys and glacial lakes, have been removed by subsequent erosion and deposition. Within the mountains there are small basins separated from one another by high ridges and passes. Most of the mountain areas have been eroded to expose the ancient crystalline rocks lifted up by earth movements. In contrast, the hills in the south of the Crimea and in parts of the Caucasus are limestone, and contain the gorges, pavements and caves typical of karst scenery.

History in the landscape The military road to Georgia passes through the Caucasus Mountains, which began to rise some 30 million years ago and are still rising today. After each uplift the river, faced with an increased gradient, cuts deeply into its old bed, leaving the former valley floor to form a terrace. The many terraces in this valley are evidence of successive periods of uplift.

THE FERGANA VALLEY

Isolated basins surrounded by high mountains are a feature of many of the mountain areas. One of the largest is the Fergana Valley, a depression running east-west that covers 22,000 sq km (7,720 sq mi) between two mountain ranges north of the Pamirs. The eastern end of the valley is blocked by high mountains that form part of the Tien Shan range, which extends east into China; the western end opens up along the course of the Syr Darya into the Kyzyl Kum. This has made Fergana more accessible than most basins.

Unlike basins in lowland areas, which are formed when the great weight of sedimentary rocks warps the crust to form a geosyncline, the Fergana Valley was created as a result of faulting. The mountains around it rise very steeply from the valley floor, which is covered by a thick layer of sediment.

The area has a very low rainfall, of some 100–300 mm (4–12 in) a year. However, the fertile soils, irrigated by water from the Syr Darya, from oases and from underground sources, have been used to transform the desert into a major agricultural area that produces fruit and a quarter of the region's cotton crop. Only small patches of desert remain in the center of the area and along ridges on the periphery.

Permafrost and thermokarst

Traditional houses half sunken into the earth, and more modern buildings abandoned because of cracks and gaps in their walls, dot the city of Yakutsk on the Lena river in Siberia. These are not the effects of an earthquake, but evidence that heat from human habitations has melted what used to be permanently frozen ground beneath them. The ground is as firm as solid rock while it remains frozen, but once the water in it melts it can move as easily as mud.

The northerly position and climate of Russia are such that half the country is underlain by a layer of permanently frozen ground, or permafrost, between 3 and 1,400 m (10-4,600 ft) deep. The thickness of the permafrost reflects the relationship between the extreme cold of the climate on the surface and the heat from the interior of the Earth. Water occupying the spaces in the soil or rock becomes frozen, making it as impermeable as solid granite.

During the brief summer, higher temperatures cause thawing from the surface downward. The thawed layer is known as the active layer, the permanently frozen ground below it as the permafrost table. The depth of the active layer depends both on how high and for how long surface temperatures remain above freezing and on local characteristics. The layer is deeper in sands and gravels than in finer silts and clays. Vegetation at the surface acts as insulation, and can reduce the depth to which the summer warmth penetrates. Under lakes and in river valleys there may be no permafrost at all.

At the end of the summer, freezing begins from the surface downward, with the result that an unfrozen layer with water under pressure may be trapped between frozen layers. Under these conditions any slight change in temperature, such as that caused by heat from an uninsulated home, for example, can thaw the surface frozen layer.

A pingo can be up to 90 m (300 ft) high and 360 m (1,200 ft) across. At the end of summer the soil water freezes from the surface down, and a layer of water may be trapped against the permafrost. If it freezes, expanding to form ice, a pingo may develop over many years as the surface layers of soil are pushed up.

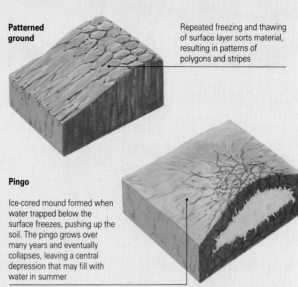

Patterned ground

Repeated freezing and thawing of surface layer sorts material, resulting in patterns of polygons and stripes

Pingo

Ice-cored mound formed when water trapped below the surface freezes, pushing up the soil. The pingo grows over many years and eventually collapses, leaving a central depression that may fill with water in summer

A distinctive landscape

Melted ice in the active layer cannot soak into the permanently frozen layer below, so water accumulates as the summer progresses. The active layer can become so moist and unstable that just a slight gradient or a small amount of pressure, such as that exerted by a building, is enough to make the whole layer move or start to flow, a process known as solifluction. This can produce ridges, terraces and small steps in the landscape, and can cause buildings to subside.

Another feature of the water-laden soils that undergo repeated freeze–thaw cycles is patterned ground. The name is given to patterns of stones, vegetation or topographical features with a natural regularity, ranging in scale from 1 sq m (11 sq ft) to several square kilometers. In permafrost areas ridges of stones are common that on flat ground form interlocking polygons, but on slopes become elongated until on the steepest slopes they become stone stripes. Mounds covered in vegetation follow a similar arrangment.

There is still much speculation about how such features are formed, but the development of convection cells in the meltwater within the ground seems to play a part. Water is at its most dense at 4°C (39°F). During the spring and summer the meltwater at the surface reaches this temperature sooner than the water lower down. The warmer, heavier water sinks and is replaced by cooler water from below, setting up a convection cell. Materials are moved in the process; the size and shape of the resulting feature will depend on the size and shape of the convection cell, which itself becomes elongated on sloping ground.

Thermokarst is the name given to the distinctive scenery in permafrost areas that is caused by changes in temperature. Its name comes from the karst scenery of limestone areas, which has similar landforms including collapsed features such as depressions. Thermokarst is characterized by subsidence-related features. The permafrost is supersaturated with water. If part of the permafrost layer melts, the excess water is lost by seepage, runoff or evaporation. This decreases the overall volume of the soil, and eventually causes the land surface to collapse.

A spectacular feature of permafrost areas is the pingo. Pingos are domes that rise up where water has collected under the ground and has frozen. As the water freezes it expands, forcing the surface upward into a dome. Pingos are often found in the center of depressions called alases, a feature of thermokarst scenery.

Permafrost areas are among the world's most sensitive environments, and are easily damaged by development projects, such as the construction of buildings, pipelines and roads, or simply the removal of the insulating layer of forest. The development projects themselves may be damaged, through flooding or subsidence, by the changes they cause to the permafrost layer. For both conservation and development to succeed, it is necessary to understand how changes to the environment can be minimized.

Spotted tundra, with its striking patterns of hummocks and furrows marked by distinct bands of vegetation, is widespread on peaty soils. It may be the result of thousands of years of alternate freezing and thawing of the upper layers of soil.

Predicting volcanic eruptions

Volcanic eruptions often take place unexpectedly, and as a result may cause great loss of life. Attempts to predict eruptions center on two techniques: the monitoring of the volcano's shape, and the detection of earth tremors associated with the volcano.

As the volcano's magma chamber fills with molten lava the mountain swells, especially where the overlying lava crust is weak. This swelling accelerates just before an eruption, as the intense pressure below forces molten lava toward the surface.

One of the sites where volcanoes are being studied closely is the Kamchatka Peninsula in the Far East of Russia. Lying on the Pacific "Ring of Fire", where two of the Earth's crustal plates are in constant slow collision, Kamchatka has many volcanoes.

A typical example of the use of earth tremors to predict eruptions came in 1955. Earth tremors began to take place frequently along the peninsula. The focus of these tremors was traced to the volcano Bezymianny, which was thought to be extinct. The number of tremors built up to over two hundred a day. Then suddenly Bezymianny erupted. Earthquakes continued for over a month as the volcano spewed out ash and smoke. When it went quiet, the earthquake subsided. Four months later a tremendous earthquake shook the peninsula. The volcano exploded so violently that the top 200 m (650 ft) were blown off.

Research into the patterns of earthquake and volcanic activity could help prevent a major disaster in the future, but very few volcanic areas are monitored regularly enough for accurate predictions to be made.

Trouble brews in a Russian volcano There are about 80 volcanoes on the Kamchatka Peninsula, some rising to 4,750m (15,675 ft) above sea level. About 33 of these are active.

HABITATS AND THEIR CONSERVATION

THE CHANGING LANDSCAPE · PRESERVING THE WILDERNESS · PROBLEMS ON A GRAND SCALE

The former Soviet Union and Mongolia contain some of the greatest stretches of untamed wilderness left on Earth. Extending from the Baltic Sea in the west to the fringes of the Pacific Ocean, from the frozen Arctic Ocean to the mountains of the Tien Shan and the Kara Kum desert in the south, this vast region encompasses an enormous range of habitats. They include broad, flat steppes, ice-packed Arctic coasts, desolate and remote tundra, seemingly endless forests, soaring mountains, hot springs and active volcanoes, scorching deserts, and numerous lakes and rivers. It is an area of superlatives. It has the world's largest forest, the taiga, which contains a third of the world's timber resources; the world's largest and deepest freshwater lake, Lake Baikal; and four of the longest rivers in Europe and Asia.

COUNTRIES IN THE REGION

Armenia, Azerbaijan, Belarus, Estonia, Georgia, Kazakhstan, Kyrgyzstan, Latvia, Lithuania, Moldova, Mongolia, Russia, Tajikistan, Turkmenistan, Ukraine, Uzbekistan

Major protected area	Hectares
Altai SR	863,861
Astrakhan SR BR	63,400
Baikal Region NP SR BR	1,564,019
Bolshoi Arkticheskiy NR	4,169,222
Central Black Earth SR BR	4,795
Chernomor SR BR	87,348
Great Gobi NP PA BR	5,311,700
Kavkaz SR BR	263,477
Kronot SR BR	1,099,000
Lake Baikal WH	8,800,000
Lapland SR BR	278,400
Matsalu R	48,634
Parapol Valley RS	1,890,000
Pechoro-Ilych SR BR	721,322
Repetek SR BR	34,600
Sayano-Shushen SR BR	389,570
Sikhote-Alin SR BR	340,200
Sokhondin SR BR	31,053
Taymyr SR	1,348,316
Virgin Komi forests WH	3,280,000
Volcanoes of Kamchatka WH	3,300,000

BR = Biosphere Reserve; NP = National park;
PA = Protected area; R = Reserve; RS = Ramsar site;
SR = State Reserve; WH = World Heritage site

THE CHANGING LANDSCAPE

Much of the area consists of vast featureless plains stretching, monotonous and unchanging, as far as the eye can see. From the Ural Mountains west to the Baltic Sea, south to the Black Sea, and east to central Siberia they represent some of the largest expanses of flat land in the world. Plant and animal life is restricted by the climate, which over much of the northern plains is harsh and cold. Winter lasts more than half the year and permafrost covers nearly half the country. In the north the barren tundra is hard and frozen in winter, a mudflow-covered swamp in summer.

The tundra herbs are mostly lowgrowing shrubby plants that shelter beneath an insulating layer of snow in winter. In the most exposed areas only lichens, mosses and algae survive, except in sheltered cracks and hollows where snow accumulates and a few flowering plants can gain a foothold.

Polar bears, seals, walruses and reindeer inhabit the ice-fringed shores, treeless cold deserts and tundra of the northern mainland and the Arctic islands. In summer the tundra teems with breeding birds – ducks, geese and waders that have migrated north to take advantage of the long summer days, the plentiful supplies of fish and the insects that swarm around the pools of melted snow.

Further south, the tundra gives way to a great zone of coniferous forest, the taiga. This dark forest harbors a wide variety of animals, including moose, lynx, brown bears, wolverines, sables, capercaillies and hazel grouse. Dominated by pine, spruce, fir and larch for much of its range, the taiga in the far east contains many species more typical of China and Japan; the Korean pine, Khingan fir, Yeddo spruce and Japanese stone pine.

In the drier south, the trees of the taiga thin out into the Eurasian steppe, a vast, usually treeless and flat expanse that is dominated by drought-resistant grasses and sedges. In the moister western parts of the Russian plain the taiga is replaced by broadleaf forests of oak and beech, while in the far southeast, along the border with China, lying in the path of moisture-bearing trade winds, there grow broadleaf forests of Mongolian oak, hornbeam, lime and maple draped with lichens and climbing plants.

Much of the steppe grassland is now under cultivation, for this was the granary of the Soviet Union and is still cultivated today. Beyond the steppe, the grasses give way to semidesert and desert in the south, or are interrupted by the great ranges of

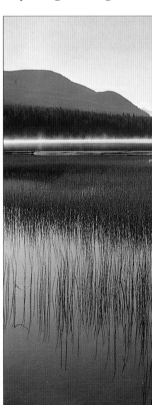

The taiga in winter Snow highlights the bare branches of larches, which shed their leaves in winter, unlike the other coniferous trees of the taiga zone. Larches are found mainly in eastern Siberia; dark, evergreen pines and spruce predominate elsewhere. The sloping shape of the trees prevents their branches breaking under the weight of snow.

A land of quietly flowing rivers In the lowlying plains of central Asia the northern forests give way to empty stretches of open, undulating steppeland interlaced by long, winding rivers and dotted with reed-fringed pools and marshes. These provide valuable breeding and feeding grounds for cranes, as well as waders and waterfowl.

ARCTIC OCEAN

Franz Josef Land

Wrangel Island

East Siberian Sea

Barents Sea

Novaya Zemlya

Severnaya Zemlya

Taymyr Peninsula

New Siberian Islands

Chukot Range

Koryak Ra

◆ Parapolsky Dol

Bering Sea

Kara Sea

Laptev Sea

○ ◆ Lapland
Kola Pen

ESTONIA
RUSSIA ◆ Matsalu
LATVIA
LITHUANIA

L Ladoga

◆ Central Forest

Northern European Plain

L Onega

N Dvina

Yamal Pen

Gydanskiy Pen

◆ Brekhovsky Islands

Byrranga Mts

◆ Taymyr

Cherskogo Range

Verkhoyansk Range

Kamchatka Peninsula

◆ Kronot

BELARUS

Dnieper

MOLDOVA UKRAINE

◆ Central Black Earth

○ Pechoro-Illych

◆ Oka River

Volga

Ob

West Siberian Plain

Yenisei

Central Siberian Plateau

◆ Central Siberian

Lena

Stanovoy Range

Sea of Okhotsk

◆ Chernomor

◆ Voronezh

Don

Black Sea

Sea of Azov

Ural Mountains

Ural

Tobol

RUSSIA

Angara

Dzhugdzhur Ra

Sakhalin

Caspian Depression

≈ Astrakhan/ Volga Delta

≈ Tobol-Ishim Forest-steppe

Irtysh

Ob

Yenisei

Eastern Sayan Mts

Lena

L Baikal

◆ Baikal Region

Yablonovy Range

Amur

Kuril Islands

GEORGIA

Caucasus Mts

◆ Kavkaz

Lake Sevan ◆
ARMENIA

◆ AZERBAIJAN

Kirghiz Steppe

KAZAKHSTAN

Aral Sea

Syr Darya

L Balkhash

○ Sayano-Shushen
◆ Altai

L Zaisan

≈ Mongol Daguur

◆ Sokhondin

Amur

◆ Kuril

Sea of Japan

◆ Sikhote-Alin

Ussuri

Caspian Sea

TURKMENISTAN

Kara Kum

UZBEKISTAN

Kyzyl Kum

Amu Darya

○ Repetek

◆ Chatkal Mts

Pamir

KYRGYZSTAN

TAJIKISTAN

Altai Range

≈ ◆ Har Us Nuur

Sayano-Shushen

MONGOLIA

Gobi

Biomes

- coniferous forest
- temperate broadleaf forest
- evergreen sclerophyll forest and scrubland
- cold winter desert and semidesert
- arctic desert and tundra
- temperate grassland

- mountain and highland system
- lake system

- ◆ major protected area
- ○ Biosphere Reserve
- ≈ Ramsar site

Map of biomes Nearly all the major zones are found within the region. Arctic tundra gives way to a wide band of coniferous forest, merging into broadleaf forest on its western and eastern edges, and then to temperate grassland. Farther south semidesert and desert are interrupted by the great mountain ranges of central Asia, and there are many large lakes in the region.

the Caucasus, Pamir, Tien Shan, Altai and Yablonovy mountains, with their mixed woodlands, alpine meadows and their high-altitude deserts. Beyond the peaks lie subtropical Georgia in the southwest and the barren lands of Mongolia and the Gobi desert in the east.

Centers of diversity

The area contains over 21,000 species of plants, of which 6 percent are found nowhere else in the world. During the last ice age, which ended about 10,000 years ago, ice covered much of the northern part of the country, and plant and animal species migrated south.

As the land warmed after the ice age, other species migrated into the region from Europe and Asia. In the mountains of the far southeast, and in the volcanic Kamchatka Peninsula and the Kuril Islands, these invading plants and animals found a wide range of habitats – mountains, river valleys, islands, monsoon-soaked coasts and volcanic hillsides. They diversified to form many new species.

PRESERVING THE WILDERNESS

In the late 1980s the Soviet Union had a network of 150 or so nature reserves. They were carefully distributed throughout the republics to preserve the best representative examples of the region's typical ecosystems. By the end of the 1990s there were over 700 reserves and 70 national parks on the UN list of protected areas.

The 1977 Soviet constitution outlined the duty of both state and citizens to protect nature, and reflected a long tradition of interest in conservation. Russia's earliest environmental laws were passed during the 17th century in the form of hunting, land-use and forestry regulations. The first conservation committees emerged in 1909, and the All-Russian Society for the Protection of Nature was created in 1924.

Today, conservation policies and legislation are diverging across the independent republics. Moldova and Ukraine have indicated that they wish to align their environmental legislation towards becoming members of the European Union. Elsewhere, the emphasis is on stricter implementation and enforcement of conservation legislation.

Degrees of protection

Nature reserves are the most extensive type of protected area throughout Russia and the republics. They are primarily used for scientific research and can have between 25 and 50 staff working in laboratories, museums and monitoring stations. Within the nature reserves, economic activity is forbidden, and tourists and non-specialist visitors are refused admission.

Many nature reserves across the region have been established to preserve threatened or endangered species, such as the bison in Oka River Valley Nature Reserve (which also has a breeding station for birds of prey and Siberian cranes). Other nature reserves extend protection to the Russian desman (a mammal related to the mole, that has been hunted close to extinction for its fur), the onager and goitered gazelle, the red-breasted goose and the Far East skink, a species of lizard. Yet other institutions specialize in research into such diverse topics as agricultural land use, recreational use and desert ecology. International cooperation between the new republics and the United States has led to the twinning of reserves so that comparative research may be carried out.

Steam rises from a hot spring in a waterfilled crater in the Kamchatka Peninsula. Many endemic species flourish in this volcanically active area, adding to the diversity of wildlife in Russia's far east.

A waterlogged landscape Surface water accumulates after the spring snowmelt and cannot drain away if permafrost lies beneath the surface. Only tussocky grass grows in the permanently waterlogged ground.

Nature sanctuaries are areas where protection is extended on a temporary basis at certain times of year, especially if the site contains breeding colonies of birds. There are more than 2,700 of these sanctuaries, covering more than 4 million sq km (1.5 million sq mi). Economic activity within their boundaries is permitted but subject to controls.

Of the region's 70 national parks at the end of the 1990s, 32 were in Russia. They are designed to combine conservation

MIXING THE SPECIES

The wildlife of the eastern edge of Russia is particularly diverse and has been given special protection by a network of state nature reserves. This narrow belt of land, 4,500 km (2,800 mi) long, stretches north from the Siberian tiger's stronghold in the Sikhote-Alin Mountains near China to the Koryak Mountains and the Kamchatka Peninsula bordering the Bering Sea. It encompasses a great variety of habitats, from taiga and tundra to meadows, warm temperate woodland and marshes, and from moist coastal plains to volcanic springs and high mountaintops. The area is the meeting point of Siberian, Chinese, Indo-Malayan, Mongolian and European species.

The taiga meets the subtropics in the area of the Ussuri river where a unique plant life is found. Ginseng, Amur lilac,

Amur maackia and a wealth of lianas all thrive in the forests of monumental black fir, Korean pine, Manchurian ash and walnut and Amur cork oak. The forests are inhabited by leopards, bears, the mysterious musk deer and over 340 species of birds.

In the shadow of volcanoes in the Krono State Nature Reserve on the eastern side of the Kamchatka Peninsula, 20 active geysers add to the diversity of habitats. Here endemic species such as the Kamchatka fir and the 3 m (9 ft) tall Kamchatka nettle are present.

More endemic species, such as the Far East skink and the Kunashir grass snake are protected in the recently created Kunashir Nature Reserve in the Kuril Islands, which extend south of the Kamchatka Peninsula between the Sea of Okhotsk and the Pacific Ocean.

objectives with recreational activities. There are also national hunting reserves and thousands of natural monuments. In addition to protected areas, green zones are being declared, which will raise the total area of reserved lands by a considerable degree. The largest reserve, declared in 1993, is the Bolshoi Arkticheskiy at 4,169,222 ha (10,302,147 acres). It is located to the east of Khabarovsk.

The administrative bureaucracy was streamlined and simplified in 1988, before the collapse of communism. A super-office for nature conservation was created – the State Committee for Nature Conservation (Goskompriroda) – which took over tasks

previously spread among more than 300 different organizations. Nongovernmental conservation organizations are springing up, with the creation of the Ecological Project Center, the Moscow Center of Ecological Youth Movement and the Association for the Support of Ecological Initiatives.

An international heritage

The region has many protected areas of international importance. At the end of the 1990s there were 29 Biosphere Reserves designed to preserve the genetic diversity of the plants and animals living there, and strictly controlled to facilitate scientific

Components of the ecosystem
1 Plant plankton
2 Animal plankton
3 Herbivorous protist
4 and 5 Freshwater shrimps
6 Osprey
7 Lake Baikal seal
8 Pike
9 Carp
10 Transparent bottom-dwelling fish

Energy flow
primary producer/primary consumer
primary/secondary consumer
secondary/tertiary consumer
dead material/consumer

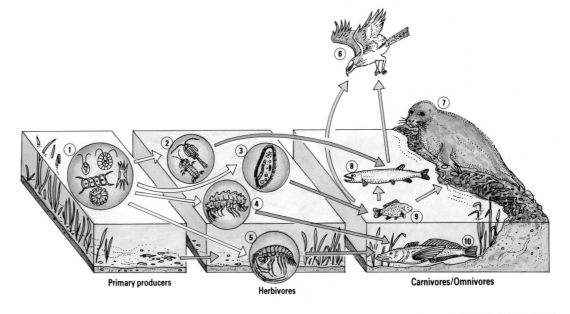

Primary producers

Herbivores

Carnivores/Omnivores

A freshwater lake ecosystem, such as that of the famous Lake Baikal, is based on algae and detritus from lakeside plants.

research programs. These Biosphere Reserves range from the Kavkaz Reserve, which protects the many species endemic to the area, to the Repetek Reserve in the sandy wastes of the Kara Kum, center of much research into desert ecology, and the Chatkal Mountain Reserve high in the lofty Tien Shan range on the border with China, another area that is rich in endemic species.

Under the international Ramsar Convention, 62 important wetland sites have been proclaimed as protected areas, over half of those in Russia and 32 of those which were established in 1994. These include the vast reed beds of the Matsalu Reserve in Estonia in the northwest and the Astrakhan Reserve situated on the Volga delta where it drains into the Caspian Sea. The latter is the summer molting retreat for many ducks and geese and an important spring and autumn stopover point for 5-7 million migrating waterfowl, as well as being the breeding ground for huge colonies of birds and a spawning ground for fish.

In addition, there are a number of successful captive-breeding programs, and considerable progress has been made in reintroducing captive-bred animals such as musk oxen into areas where the wild populations have been reduced and are close to extinction.

The Caucasus mountains are the most western of the great ranges that form a climatic barrier between the north and the south. Their highest slopes are a refuge for plants isolated after the last ice age, and lower down they are covered with forests, which include oak, chestnut and Caucasian fir.

PROBLEMS ON A GRAND SCALE

The 1986 nuclear accident at Chernobyl, near Kiev, brought home the danger of allowing a complacent attitude to the effect of industry and technology on the natural world. In less dramatic ways, humans have intruded into even the most remote parts of the region, such as Siberia. Today the untouched wilderness of popular imagination is only an illusion, and with the building of the Baikal-Amur Mainline (BAM) railroad even the most distant eastern expanse of Russia has been opened up for exploitation. Seas and lakes have been poisoned, forests covering entire mountain ranges burned, and the air in over a hundred major cities is polluted. Widespread soil erosion has caused desertification and the creation of massive dustbowls that affect an area equal in size to western Europe.

An indication that attitudes were beginning to change at the end of the Soviet era came with the creation of the State Committee for Nature Conservation at the highest level of Soviet bureaucracy. Its task was to ensure that environmental protection extended throughout the Soviet Union. The committee remains, but despite growing awareness, the nature reserve laws are still broken. Oil prospecting, domestic animal grazing, overfishing, trapping, hunting, tourism and illegal building encroach on several reserves, and at the start of the 21st century there are indications that the authorities, with economics firmly on their minds, are once again becoming less concerned for the conservation of nature.

The threat to the taiga
One problem that is likely to intensify is the economic exploitation of that greatest of wildernesses – Siberia. A highly visible sign of this is the aftermath of logging in the taiga forest. As much as one-fifth of the newly exposed soil may be washed away by rain after felling, and uncontrolled fires abound in the recently cleared areas. In the mid-1980s more forest was burned in Irkutsk province alone than was planted throughout the whole of the Soviet Union.

In recent years oil spillages have greatly increased pollution in Eurasia's largest freshwater basin, Lake Baikal, and the general opening up of the Siberian wilderness has led to increased air, soil and

water pollution. One result has been the southward retreat of the forest zone: loss of lichen and moss, plants that are highly vulnerable to airborne pollution, results in cooling of the soil, and a consequent fall in air temperature and increase in wind, conditions that are less favorable for the growth of trees.

These developments are connected with the building of the BAM railroad. The BAM has a development zone of 300–500 km (185–310 mi) on either side of its 4,670 km (2,900 mi) of track. The railroad will affect an area equivalent to the Amazon Basin. Exploitation zones for oil, gas, gold and minerals cover approximately 3.5 million sq km (1.35 million sq mi) – an area the size of Europe.

Waste disposal also poses difficulties. Siberia's cold climate slows down bacterial action so that the breakdown of waste takes longer. Siberian rivers need to flow some 1,500 km (930 mi) before they are cleansed, compared with 200–300 km (125–185 mi) for rivers elsewhere.

"Desert forest" in the Repetek Reserve. The roots of shrubby trees, predominantly black saxaul, retain the shifting sands of the Kara Kum desert. Many mammals and reptiles find shelter and food beneath their branches; in spring the desert becomes a sea of color as the shrubs burst into flower.

The silver trunks of birches are reflected in spring floodwater. They grow extensively on the margin between the tundra and taiga where conditions are too wet or altitude too great for conifers to flourish. They are often the first trees to colonize cleared woodland spaces.

REPETEK NATURE RESERVE

Quiet reigns in the empty corner of the Kara Kum desert in Turkmenistan where the Repetek Biosphere Reserve is situated. The main visitors are scientists, for the reserve – which includes more than 30,000 ha (75,000 acres) of unspoiled sand desert with 10 m (33 ft) high sand dunes – is the area's foremost center for research on desert ecology.

Repetek Nature Reserve was created in 1928 as a place to study quicksands. Investigations now cover the entire desert ecosystem, so that the work carried out here will benefit desert protection more generally: the strict habitat protection creates the ideal conditions for such research. Studies initially conducted as part of the international Biological Program, and later under the UNESCO Man and Biosphere Program, brought the center worldwide attention. In 1978, on the 50th anniversary of its foundation, Repetek was designated a Biosphere Reserve.

The reserve's expert staff run sessions for overseas scientists as part of the United Nations Environment Program (UNEP). Courses deal with the control of shifting sands and the ecology of desert pastures.

Repetek's desert habitats include creeping sand ridges hundreds of meters long that are entirely free of vegetation. Where there are valley depressions in the dunes, leafless, drought-resistant black saxauls grow, creating a unique "desert forest".

More than a third of the 211 plant species recorded in Repetek are found nowhere else in the world. These "forests" provide shade during the day for large, rare mammals such as the goitered gazelle, the caracal and the marbled polecat. Smaller jerboas, ground squirrels and shrews stay in the cool of their underground burrows during the day and emerge at night. The reserve boasts 23 reptile species including the desert monitor.

Re-routing the rivers
No less epic than the BAM undertaking was the plan to divert north-flowing Siberian rivers to flow south to irrigate the dry southern deserts of Central Asia – the unprecedented long-distance transfer of an estimated 120 cu km (29 cu mi) of water a year. Although the scheme was abandoned in 1987, the idea was resurrected by Kazakhstan in the late 1990s. The environmental consequences of such a gigantic project are unknown, but similar, smaller projects affecting the Aral, Caspian and Azov seas have had devastating environmental effects, causing drastic shrinkage of these lakes and widespread soil erosion and desertification.

A growing awareness
In the Soviet Union all land and resources were under the control of the state. Now that the union has fragmented into separate republics, privatization is taking place. There is greater environmental awareness at all levels, so the door is opening for the introduction of private and leased reserves. Pressure groups have proliferated and environmental issues are now fully discussed and examined in the media. Scientists and academics are freer to voice their concerns. There are Greenpeace movements, and environmental groups, lobbying against local centers of industrial pollution, were a powerful force in the development of nationalism in the Baltic states.

As in the West, natural history is popular with the general public. A quarter of the television audience might tune in to a natural history program.

Lake Baikal Region Biosphere Reserve

Lake Baikal lies in the heart of Siberia. Russians call it "a part of their souls"; its water is of exceptional purity and clarity. Formed over 25 million years ago, Lake Baikal is the world's deepest (1,620 m/ 5,314 ft) and largest inland body of fresh water with an area of 31,500 sq km (12,200 sq mi). Its 23,000 cu km (5,500 cu mi) of water are equivalent to a fifth of the world's fresh water and four-fifths of the area's surface fresh water. More than 330 rivers enter the lake's catchment area of 600,000 sq km (231,600 sq mi), but only one, the Angara, leaves it.

There are three state nature reserves on its shores, the Baikal and the Barguzin Reserves, both created in 1916, and the Baikalo-Len Reserve, designated in 1986. In the latter year the Pribaikal and Zabaikal National Parks were added. The

Lake Baikal Coastal Protection Zone was established in 1987 and in 1994 the Selenga Delta became a Ramsar site. Between them the reserves cover a large area of the shores around the lake and the surrounding mountains.

Numerous hot springs are refuges for plant species that remained after other species were forced to retreat south with the onset of the last glacial period some 60-70,000 years ago. Much of the area is covered in taiga, dominated by larch, pine and Siberian stone pine. These dense forests are inhabited by sables, Siberian red deer, musk deer, bears, lynx and wolves. Woodlands of poplar, willow and cherry grow bin the more sheltered valleys. Above the forests, elfin cedar woodland gives way to alpine meadows and wind-resistant plants.

The climate is severe. In the high parts temperatures remain below freezing for more than 200 days a year. For five months of the year the lake is covered in 2.5 m (8 ft) or more of ice, though many of the streams that supply it, warmed by the geothermal springs, remain free of ice.

Lake Baikal Biosphere Reserve contains around 1,000 species of animals and 400 species of plants that are not found anywhere else in the world. There are also some 50 species of fish, many of them endemic too. Its most famous inhabitant is the small Baikal seal, but the key to the ecology of Baikal is the epishura, a tiny crustacean unique to the lake. The epishura comprises up to 98 percent of all the minute animal life (zooplankton) in the water. It feeds on algae and is a major link in the food chain that supports

The "blue eye of Siberia" The sun sets over Lake Baikal, which is covered in thick ice during the winter. The largest body of fresh water in the world, it supports thousands of unique species of animals and plants.

Dense taiga forest comes right down to the unspoiled shore. The reserves surrounding the lake protect many rare mammals, especially the sable, a large relative of the weasel hunted for its fur.

The Baikal seal, an endemic species, is related to the Arctic ringed seal. It is thought to have arrived in Lake Baikal before it was cut off from the sea.

Baikal's unique forms of life. In addition, the epishura acts as a filter capable of extracting 250,000 tonnes of calcium each year: water as pure as that of Lake Baikal is almost unknown elsewhere on Earth. Forests of green freshwater sponges and no fewer than 258 species of shrimps also contribute to the filtration process.

The Barguzin Nature Reserve was created specifically to protect an endemic species of sable, much hunted for its highly valued fur, which earned it the name "soft gold". Today the population has risen to over 2,500 animals. However, the rapid growth in tourism has brought new dangers: the shores of the lake are littered with waste, while sheep have taken over in areas once grazed by moose and wolves. Fire and soil erosion, the inevitable accompaniment of human intrusion

in the taiga, are a constant hazard. Pollution of the lake is blamed for a decline in the numbers of birds that use it as a stopover point or breed along its reedfringed shores, and for an even sharper fall in birds of prey.

Apart from the research staff, there are no people living in the reserves, and no visitors. So remote is this wilderness that it took more than four years to lay the first tracks for the BAM railroad. But isolation is no protection against the pollution of industrial development.

The building of paper and pulp factories in Ulan-Ude and along the Selenga and Barguzin rivers southeast and east of the lake, together with thermal power plants, chemical and petrochemical installations and the BAM railroad, have destroyed life on some 2,000 ha (5,500

acres) of the lake bottom. The consequent reduction of the annual Baikal fish catch has undermined the traditional way of life carried on by the local people, which was based on fishing.

In the 1980s the Central Committee of the Communist Party put through a comprehensive protection plan for the lake. A number of officials were dismissed from their posts for grave environmental negligence. Production facilities began to be closed, lead and zinc waste was diverted, and the inflow of polluted water was completely stopped. A special zone 1.6 km (1 mi) wide was created on either side of the BAM to protect air, water, soil and vegetation from pollution. Much has been done to protect the area and there are plans to do more. The future for Lake Baikal looks brighter than in the past.

ANIMAL LIFE

LEGACY OF THE ICE AGE · ADAPTING TO EXTREMES · PUSHING NATURE TO THE LIMIT

Russia and the newly independent states around it contain within their vast boundaries animals as diverse as Polar bears, African wildcats, Snowy owls, flamingoes, walruses and cheetahs. Atlantic sturgeon inhabit its western waters, while the Japanese crane and Oriental cuckoo are found in the east of the region. Much of the diversity comes from areas on the margins, such as the high peaks of the south and the mixed forests that span the European frontier. The richest areas are those that were left relatively unscathed by the last period of glaciation: the forests around the Ussuri on the Pacific coast, and the zone between the Black and Caspian Seas. Animals that took refuge here from the advancing cold of the ice age later mingled with others that invaded from the warmer regions to the south as the ice receded.

COUNTRIES IN THE REGION

Armenia, Azerbaijan, Belarus, Estonia, Georgia, Kazakhstan, Kyrgyzstan, Latvia, Lithuania, Moldova, Mongolia, Russia, Tajikistan, Turkmenistan, Ukraine, Uzbekistan

ENDEMISM AND DIVERSITY

Diversity Low to medium
Endemism Low to medium to high (for example, Lake Baikal)

SPECIES

	Total	Threatened	†Extinct
Mammals	275	23	1
Birds	*730	38	2
Others	unknown	34	0

† *species extinct since 1600 – Steller's sea cow (Hydrodamalis gigas), Spectacled cormorant (Phalacrocorax perspicillatus), Great auk (Alca impennis)*
* *breeding and regular non-breeding species*

NOTABLE THREATENED ENDEMIC SPECIES

Mammals Manzbier's marmot (*Marmota menzbieri*), Russian desman (*Desmana moschata*)
Birds none
Others Amur sturgeon (*Acipenser schrencki*), Balkhash perch (*Perca schrenki*), Caucasian relict ant (*Aulacopone relicta*)

NOTABLE THREATENED NON-ENDEMIC SPECIES

Mammals tiger (*Panthera tigris*), Amur leopard (*Panthera pardus*), European bison (*Bison bonasus*), Asiatic wild ass (*Equus hemionus*), Przewalski's horse (*Equus przewalskii*)
Birds Crested shelduck (*Tadorna cristata*), Steller's sea eagle (*Haliaeetus pelagicus*), Siberian crane (*Grus leucogeranus*), Relict gull (*Larus relictus*), Great bustard (*Otis tarda*)
Others Caucasian viper (*Vipera kaznakovi*), Large copper butterfly (*Lycaena dispar*), Freshwater pearl mussel (*Margaritifera margaritifera*), Baltic sturgeon (*Acipenser sturio*)

DOMESTICATED ANIMALS (originating in region)

horse (*Equus 'caballus'*)

LEGACY OF THE ICE AGE

In the dark, silent boreal coniferous forest or taiga, which covers more than a third of Russia, the animals are not abundant, and are generally hidden from view; the number of species is low in most parts of the forest. North of the taiga, the tundra (treeless plains where the subsoil is permanently frozen) also has relatively few species. However, in summer the tundra bustles with activity, for the species that are there are represented in huge numbers. Many are migratory birds that come to exploit the abundant insect food of the Arctic summer and feed their chicks; they then fly south at the end of the brief breeding season to escape the Arctic winter.

Twenty thousand years ago tundra would have covered most of the area. Gradually, as the Earth became warmer and the tundra decreased in area, animals such as the reindeer, Arctic fox and Snowy owl returned to the most northerly areas. During the ice age so much water was locked up in the glaciers and ice caps that there was a worldwide fall in the sea level. In the far north this created a land bridge between Asia and America, across what is now the Bering Strait. Animals hardy enough to survive so far north were able to move freely between the two land masses; as a result, many of the species resident in the Arctic tundra of Russia are also found in the tundra of North America.

As the land grew warmer and the sea level rose, about 10,000 years ago, the animals of the two continents were separated. Despite their isolation, most are still technically single species: if brought together they can interbreed. In time they will undoubtedly become different species, but for now they remain linked by their shared past. Similarly some of the taiga animals have counterparts in the boreal forest of the New World: for example, the elk (moose), the Brown bear and the wolverine.

The legacy of the period of glaciation can also be seen in the southern mountains. Here, tundra and taiga animals, such as the Mountain hare, the Hawk owl and the Red crossbill, live in the same mountain ranges as invaders from the subtropical south, for example, babblers, Paradise flycatchers and Asian wild dogs. The cold-adapted species normally associ-

ated with the north would have been widespread in the surrounding lowlands during the ice age. As the climate gradually warmed up they moved up into the mountains to escape the unfamiliar heat of the plains, and settled as isolated populations surrounded by hot desert.

The warm, dry south

The animals of the region's deserts have a less complicated history than those of the mountains. Most of the species are the descendants of southern immigrants from the deserts of central Asia and the Middle East, which provided a link with the Sahara. This corridor of desert and semi-desert enabled animals such as the African wildcat, the cheetah and the ratel or Honey badger to migrate from Africa into Asia. The cheetah may now be locally

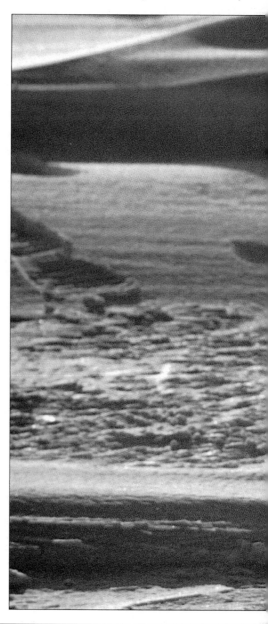

Hunter of the night (*above*) The Striated scops owl is the most widespread nocturnal predator of the steppes. Compared with most owls, it has very long wings, and is capable of gliding flight. It migrates in the fall to the warmer climates of the south.

Camouflaged for survival (*below*) An Arctic fox in its white winter coat merges with the snowy landscape. In summer its coat turns brownish-gray. Arctic foxes are often observed following Polar bears in order to scavenge from their kills.

extinct due to hunting, but there are plans to reintroduce it into a nature reserve. The deserts also support many reptiles, including tortoises, skinks, geckos and many species of snake.

Many desert animals also inhabit the steppe grasslands, especially in the drier areas, and some animals have moved in from the mixed woodlands to the northwest. These outsiders share their domain with true steppe mammals, such as hamsters, sousliks (ground squirrels) and Saiga antelopes, along with birds such as larks and bustards.

Specialists and exotics

Endemic species are relatively rare in the region, possibly because so few areas were unaffected by the last ice age in the Pleistocene. Clusters of endemics are found only in isolated and enduring habitats such as Lake Baikal in southeastern Siberia. The phenomenal depth of the lake prevented it from freezing solid during the ice age. Lake Baikal supports about 1,200 animal species, of which 60 to 80 percent are endemic. Among them is the Baikal seal, a distant relative of the Ringed seal whose ancestors must have swum inland about 10 million years ago.

The peaks of the southern mountains also support some endemic species: for example, each mountain range has its own species of snowcock – specialized mountain birds whose ancestors probably originated in the Himalayas. The Caucasus, the area of land between the Black and Caspian seas, is also rich in endemic species, having once been isolated from the rest of the region by water.

ADAPTING TO EXTREMES

Only two areas in the region have a consistently benign regime: the mild, damp coastal area between the Pacific coast and the Ussuri river in the far southeast of the region, and the subtropical lowlands between the Black Sea and the Caspian. Throughout much of the area climatic conditions are extreme, and many animals find survival difficult in summer and winter.

The Arctic ground squirrel has adapted to the difficult conditions by entering a state of suspended animation not just once but twice a year. It hibernates in winter to escape the severe weather; during the driest part of the summer, when the vegetation withers, it repeats the process to avoid starvation.

The effects of the cold mass of air that hangs immovably over the continent in winter are felt even in the southern deserts. Although hot and dry in summer, temperatures can fall to below freezing in winter. The jerboas – desert rodents commonly found throughout northern Africa and the Middle East – do not usually hibernate, but in these deserts they do so for as much as seven months of the year in order to avoid the cold weather.

Another group of desert rodents, the gerbils (or jirds) have evolved into a specialized genus, *Meriones*, within these inhospitable central Asian lands. They live communally, unlike other gerbils, and may store food for use in winter. Digging a deep communal burrow and huddling together helps them to conserve their body heat.

A scarcity of food
Cold is only one aspect of the problems that these animals face. Lack of food is also common, especially in the taiga. Conifers offer relatively little in the way of food, with their tough, waxy, indigestible leaves. Resins – which give conifers their aroma – are there to defend the wood and needles from attack, and they prove noxious to most animals. With the exception of a few insects, the most successful needle-feeders are the large, sturdy game birds known as capercaillies; these vegetarian birds specialize in feeding on pine needles and must have some mechanism for detoxifying and digesting their food.

Broadleaf trees, notably hardy birches, and undergrowth shrubs such as cran-

Imperial eagle
Aquila heliaca

Pallas's sandgrouse
Symhaptes paradoxus

Birds of plains and deserts The majestic Imperial eagle breeds throughout central Asia from Iran to China. The world population is only a few thousand pairs; the European population has been reduced to between 320 and 570 pairs. A bird of desert and steppe, Pallas's sandgrouse flies long distances every day in search of water. Its breast feathers are specially adapted to soak up water, which it carries back to its thirsty chicks.

berry provide an alternative food source for many herbivores. Where the canopy is closed, however, little undergrowth can spring up, so this potential source of food is also lost. More open areas and swampy ground – of which there are plenty – are the feeding grounds for many animals. The elk, for example, browses on succulent undergrowth and wades into the water to feed on aquatic plants.

The only form of rich and trouble-free food that conifers provide is their seeds, packaged inside woody cones. The cones have evolved to protect the seeds from predators, and they are far from easy to open. Mammals invariably gnaw them but this method is slow and uses up energy.

Animals that can tackle the cones, such as crossbills (members of the finch family) and squirrels, are an important link in the forest food chain, providing sustenance for birds of prey, martens and other predators. The unusual beaks of the crossbills are specialized cone-opening tools: the abnormal jaw joints allow the lower half of the beak to move side to side, not just up and down.

Unfortunately for the seed-eaters, conifers are inconsistent in the amount of seed they produce. A poor cone-bearing year, especially if it follows a good year, may result in an "irruption" of crossbills scattering from their Siberian homelands in search of other food; they often fly as far as Spain and Portugal.

Many animals store food as a means of ensuring that they have a regular supply throughout the long winter. For example, the Siberian chipmunk, a small ground-dwelling squirrel, has enormous cheek pouches in which it carries seeds to its burrow. A single animal may cache tip to 6 kg (13.5 lb) of food before winter sets in.

A unique meeting place
In the still-unspoiled wildernesses around the Ussuri, river valleys provide north-south migration corridors between the mountains, which otherwise tend to form barriers to migration. In this area, animals that are native to Siberia have mixed with others from China, Japan and southeast Asia. A wealth of different habitats favors

Saiga
Saiga tatarica

A NOSE FOR THE STEPPES

The saiga is an unusual animal; although often referred to as an antelope, it has in fact many anatomical features that are more like those of a goat. It is a true steppe animal, but in winter it migrates southward to the warmer lowlands around the Caspian Sea. In the 1920s overhunting in Central Asia brought the saiga close to extinction; since then strict protection has allowed its numbers to increase, and there are now more than a million.

The saiga's bulbous nose contains enlarged nasal passages that are lined with unusually luxuriant hairs and mucus-producing glands. The nose helps to warm the cold air that the animal inhales, and to filter out the dust that the hooves of the herd chum up as it runs. Why the nostrils should point downward is something of a mystery. During the mating season, the male's nose enlarges, which suggests that a large nose may be intimidating to other males or attractive to females. If this is so, then sexual selection may have played a part in the evolution of this unusual feature.

Sand cat
Felis manul

Mongolian jird
Meriones unguiculatus

Sable
Martes zibellina

the presence of abundant and diversified wildlife.

Among the many species that have arrived from the south are giant silk moths, numerous exotically colored butterflies and beetles, praying mantids, and the only softshelled turtle in the region. Mandarin ducks, whose center of distribution is in China, nest in tree holes close to forest streams, while the rare Blakiston's fish owl snatches fish from the surface of the larger rivers and lakes. Other exotic species include a type of roller (a large, colorful insect-eating bird), a paradise flycatcher, orioles and drongos – all birds that originated in subtropical forests. Leopards, Asian black bears and Sika deer may be found here too. Yet this mountainous area also boasts mountain hares on some of its peaks, and Siberian flying squirrels in its coniferous forests.

Mammals of steppe, desert and forest The saiga antelope of the central Asian steppes has evolved excellent vision and the ability to run very fast to escape predators. Pallas's cat is a rare predator of deserts, slopes and mountains, where it preys almost exclusively on rodents. The Mongolian jird is adapted to life in arid areas; it is well camouflaged, has long hind legs for jumping and running, and well-developed claws for burrowing to avoid summer heat and winter cold. It breeds rapidly to compensate for high predation. The sable is perhaps the most prized of all animals. Its thick pelt, which evolved to withstand the rigors of the Siberian winter, is highly valued in the international fur trade. As a result, it has been hunted almost to extinction, but is now protected in several reserves.

PUSHING NATURE TO THE LIMIT

It was once an article of faith in the former Soviet Union that nature was boundless and inexhaustible. Such a view was understandable, given the vastness of the land, but it is now changing. Many animals face a bleak future, and if the present range of wildlife is to survive, the scale of the human impact on the environment must be reduced.

Threats to steppe- and forest-dwellers
The animals that have suffered most from human activity are the steppe-dwellers, as their native habitats are particularly well suited to cereal growing. As in North America, this has resulted in the disappearance of millions of hectares of native grassland in favor of wheat fields. Some animals can adapt and thrive in the new environment, but many cannot, and the heavy use of chemical pesticides makes life yet more difficult. The Great bustard is now endangered by both changes to its habitat and overhunting; it has been part of a captive breeding program and the number has risen from between 3000 and 4000 in the late 1980s to around 12,000 today, about 11,000 in Russia.

A seal rarity (*above*) The freshwater Baikal seal is believed to be related to the northern Ringed seal. The females give birth in early spring in solitary snow lairs over breathing holes in the ice.

Northern tiger (*right*) The endangered Siberian tiger – the largest subspecies of tiger – has a thick coat to protect it from the Siberian winters. Only about 500 individuals survive today, for the tiger needs a very large area of wilderness to catch sufficient quantities of prey.

Surviving areas of steppe are protected as nature reserves. Their total area, however, is no more than 12,000 ha (30,000 acres), and most reserves are very small. The wildlife of these tiny islands of protection tends to become more and more impoverished as time goes by.

To the south, the rich subtropical forests of Transcaucasia have also given way to cultivation – mostly to extensive tea plantations. The varied wildlife of the area has suffered greatly as a result; for instance, the Anatolian leopard is now an endangered species.

The mixed forests of the Baltic republics and European Russia are intensively exploited for timber, with inevitable consequences for animals such as the beaver, Wild boar and Russian desman (a small aquatic mammal). The latter has declined greatly as a result of water pollution and competition from introduced coypus and

muskrats. Reserves in these forests may enable some of the animals to survive. A few of the reserves now support small herds of bison; hunted almost to extinction years ago, the bison has been reestablished by introducing animals from the United States. On the tundra plains of the Taimyr Peninsula, north of the Arctic Circle, Musk oxen from North America have also been successfully introduced.

Hunting and habitat loss
The capture of animals for fur is an ancient tradition in Siberia. European fur

The Soviet Union had considerable success in increasing the numbers of some of its rarest animals by captive breeding: for example, peregrines, lammergeiers (Bearded vultures), waterfowl and desert wildlife such as the Great bustard and Goitered gazelle. The aim was to provide captive populations from which animals can be reintroduced to their former habitats. Most programs have survived the breakup of the Soviet Union.

Operation Siberian Crane is a joint program between Russia and the International Crane Foundation based in Wisconsin in the United States. The female crane lays two eggs, but in the wild only one chick usually survives. In this program the second egg is removed and hand-reared, or placed with foster parents of other species of crane. The program is being extended to include the rare Oriental stork. A further measure has been the establishment of a new population at the Oka River Nature Reserve to the southeast of Moscow. The hope is that this population will settle and over-winter here, thus avoiding the threat from hunters while on migration.

Captive breeding of the rare Snow leopard has also been successful – though under zoo conditions the young have no opportunity to learn how to hunt from their mother. The leopards are released into reserves so that they can return to base to be fed until they gradually become independent.

At Askaniya Nova in southern Ukraine, animals such as Przewalski's horse and the Wild ass or kulan have been saved from extinction. A breeding group of Przewalski's horse was reintroduced in 1992 in Mongolia and is doing well. The African eland is being domesticated here, and ostriches, rheas and emus are bred to supply zoos, avoiding the need to capture more wild animals.

traders moved into the area at the beginning of the 15th century, and from then on huge numbers of furs were taken. The Russian desman was once a staple of the fur trade, with tens of thousands of skins being exported annually to meet the demands of western Europe. Stoats, too, have suffered, with as many as 12,000 animals being taken every year from the Kamchatka peninsula alone in the far northeast of the region. The species that have suffered most from the trade are big cats such as the Amur leopard and the Turanian tiger; both are now endangered.

The sable has required legal protection since the 17th century; one of the first forest nature reserves was set up by Peter the Great nearly three centuries ago to protect the sable's habitat. Today sable are being reintroduced, with some success. Hunting has also taken a toll on birds. It has been estimated that 100 million game birds are shot every year. Migrants such as the Siberian crane and Japanese crane are especially vulnerable.

Pollution and destruction of habitats are ultimately a far greater threat to wildlife than hunting. Many birds have been killed by poisoned grain scattered by aircraft to kill rodent pests in agricultural areas.

Large areas of wetlands around the Caspian Sea have been lost because of land reclamation and the use of water for irrigation. This has destroyed most of the wintering grounds once used by wildfowl. Farther east the water level of the Aral Sea is also falling and this, combined with widespread pollution from pesticides used in cotton growing, threatens many thousands of species, while exploration for oil and minerals threatens parts of the Arctic tundra.

Migrant birds of the tundra

In summer the vast treeless Arctic tundra is alive with birds. The myriad pools of snowmelt are the breeding grounds of millions of insects, providing a rich diet for warblers, wagtails and wheatears. The thin layer of thawed soil contains succulent grubs and other small creatures favored by waders, there are plenty of tender young shoots for the geese, and the Arctic seas abound with fish and crustaceans in summer.

Gains and losses

Many millions of migrant birds take full advantage of the abundant food and long summer days to raise their young in the tundra, so the temporary glut of food is put to good use. Warblers and wheatears, make astonishingly long journeys from southern Africa, Southeast Asia, Australia and New Zealand. One exceptional bird, the Pectoral sandpiper, makes the journey back via Alaska to spend the winter in South America.

Such long migration routes represent a vast expenditure of energy and food resources, and the birds face enormous risks on the way from exhaustion, bad weather and predators. The breeding success of these birds has to compensate for the loss to their numbers that occurs during migration. Many of the birds, especially the warblers and other small species, switch from a diet of seeds to one of insects to feed their young. Were they to remain in the south to breed, they would have to compete with the resident birds for a food supply that, in many parts of the tropics and subtropics, does not produce a seasonal glut.

Frontiers of exploration

The flight paths of these migratory birds tell us a great deal about the recent past of the region. Twenty thousand years ago, with the world in the grip of the last ice age, tundra covered most of the area: Siberia very largely escaped the glaciers that scoured North America, Scandinavia and Britain but, with the soil permanently frozen even close to the surface, conditions would have been arid, profoundly cold, and inhospitable to most forms of life. As the Earth gradually grew warmer migratory birds pushed back the frontiers of exploration a little more each year. The track of the wheatear shows that it has slowly progressed northward and then eastward and westward from its African wintering grounds. The Pectoral sand-

piper worked its way north into Alaska with successive summers, then edged westward to reach Siberia.

Most birds are remarkably conservative in their choice of migration routes, faithfully following the paths by which their first ancestors reinvaded the north. The wheatear still spends the northern winter in Africa, despite the fact that similar conditions may be found in South America and Southeast Asia. Greenland wheatears fly across the Atlantic to Britain before they head south, and birds from eastern Canada traverse Russia and central Asia.

By contrast, other species, such as the Lesser golden plover, have two distinct populations: one in North America, the other in Russia. Each has its own migration route – the American population flying to South America, the other migrating to Southeast Asia, the Pacific islands, Australia and New Zealand. Whether these routes have diverged with time, or whether they represent two distinct centers of recolonization of the north, is not known.

The northward migration of birds is not confined to the tundra. Little by little, many birds of the taiga and the temperate forests are also extending their range northward; the progress of the Collared dove across Europe during the present century is just one example. These birds are still extending their breeding grounds – a sure indication that gradual changes in the climate are taking place. The final acts of the great ice age drama are still being played out.

Living in perpetual summer (*above*) The Arctic tern migrates from the coasts of northern Europe, North America and Russia to the Antarctic and back each year, a round trip of some 40,000 km (25,000 mi), taking advantage of both polar summers for hunting.

The Little stint (*left*) is the smallest breeding wader of the tundra, with a body little bigger than a sparrow's. Despite its small size, it makes the long migration from the northern tundra to Africa, southeast Asia, Australia or Tasmania in the fall.

Invading the Arctic (*right*) Northern areas are part of a great belt of boreal forest, tundra and Arctic coast that extends to Greenland and North America. Since the ice retreated following the last glaciation, birds have been reinvading the region from the south. They still migrate south in winter.

Migration routes

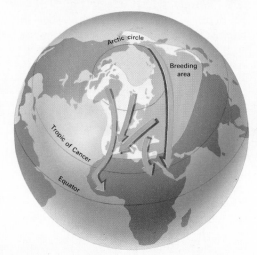

Wheatear The wheatear has recently expanded its range from Eurasia to Greenland and northern North America. Migrating birds still follow the routes by which they colonized the region in the first place, traveling great distances back to Africa and the Middle East.

Brent goose Many of the Brent geese that breed in the Arctic winter in the British Isles and northwest Europe, but one population heads for the United States' east coast, and another flies south from Alaska down the west coast.

American golden plover Birds following one migration route cross over the Atlantic Ocean to South America and return by a different route across Central and North America. Another route crosses the Pacific Ocean to New Zealand.

PLANT LIFE

TUNDRA, TREES AND GRASSLANDS · ADAPTING TO WATER STRESS · EDIBLE, HEALING AND DECORATIVE PLANTS

The plant life of the former Soviet Union and Mongolia has developed in every niche in these vast territories, with their enormous variations in climate and landscape. The Arctic poppy clings to life in the frozen wastelands of the north; twisted and stunted shrubs struggle to exist in the bleak, boggy tundra; and many strange succulents are unique to the burning deserts of the south and Mongolia. Across the land a belt of conifers and broadleaf trees grow together to form the taiga, the largest forest belt in the world. In the southeast subtropical trees support luxuriant vines and kiwi fruits, while in the south trees give way to great seas of grass, often bright with flowers in spring. The mountain ranges are home to many beautiful, much sought-after flowering shrubs, herbs and alpines.

COUNTRIES IN THE REGION

Armenia, Azerbaijan, Belarus, Estonia, Georgia, Kazakhstan, Kyrgyzstan, Latvia, Lithuania, Moldova, Mongolia, Russia, Tajikistan, Turkmenistan, Ukraine, Uzbekistan

DIVERSITY

Number of families	200
Number of genera	1,865
Number of species	21,000
Endemism	5.5%

PLANTS IN DANGER

Number of threatened species	c. 350
Number of endangered species	c. 167
Number of extinct species	c. 22

Examples *Astragalus tanaiticus; Elytrigia stipifolia; Eremurus korovinii; Fritillaria eduardii; Iris paradoxa; Lilium caucasicum; Potentilla volgarica; Rhododendron fauriei; Scrophularia cretacea; Tulipa kaufmanniana*

USEFUL AND DANGEROUS NATIVE PLANTS

Crop plants *Cichorium intybus* (chicory); *Ficus carica* (fig); *Ribes nigrum* (blackcurrant); *Rubus ulmifolius* (blackberry); *Secale cereale* (rye)
Garden plants *Bergenia cordifolia; Campanula carpatica; Elaeagnus angustifolia; Hemerocallis flava* (day lily); *Paeonia lactiflora; Tanacetum coccineum*
Poisonous plants *Daphne mezereum; Euphorbia peplus; Ligustrum* species (privet); *Taxus baccata* (yew)

MAJOR BOTANIC GARDENS

Kiev State University (10,000 taxa); Komarov Botanical Institute (8,500 taxa); Moscow (16,000 taxa); Siberian Central Novosibirsk (9,000 taxa); Irkutsk State University; Petrozavodsk State University

A bright flower braves the harsh, hostile environment of a rocky gorge in Central Asia. This southern area is largely dominated by desert and semidesert; in such an enormous area there are many favorable environments for plants as well as difficult ones.

TUNDRA, TREES AND GRASSLANDS

The vast span of the region, from both west to east and north to south, means that it can support an enormous range of vegetation zones, and encompasses the various extremes of climate that accompany great latitudinal extent.

In the Arctic islands and the northern part of the Taymyr Peninsula the freezing temperatures enable algae, mosses and lichens to survive, along with only about 40 to 50 species of flowering plants. These include dwarf willow (*Salix polaris*) and Arctic poppy (*Papaver polare*), which grow in isolated patches.

Farther south conditions in the treeless tundras are less harsh. Mosses and lichens predominate, and sphagnum bogs occur in areas with poor drainage. Dwarf shrubby birches (*Betula*), alders (*Alnus*) and willows (*Salix*) grow densely in places, along with perennial grasses. Scattered stunted trees, such as the ground-hugging Dahurian larch (*Larix gmelinii*) and the crooked birch (*Betula tortosa*), form forest tundra.

Forest belts and mountain plants

In a wide belt south of the tundra is the taiga forest, which covers more than 50 percent of Russia. To the west the taiga is dominated by spruces (*Picea abies* and *P. obovata*), Scots pine (*Pinus sylvestris*), Siberian cedar (*Pinus sibirica*) and Siberian larch (*Larix sibirica*). The northern twinflower (*Linnaea borealis*) and the saprophytic ghost orchid (*Epipogium aphyllum*), which lives on decomposing matter, inhabit the forest floor, together with many mosses and lichens. In contrast, the eastern Siberian forest consists mostly of deciduous trees, in particular Siberian and Dahurian larch. The trees of the far east are mainly evergreen and similar to those of the Eurosiberian taiga, but with different species of spruce and fir.

Birch forests and the rich field layer that grows beneath them characterize the

Floristic regions

Holarctic Kingdom

Circumboreal Region Cool northern temperate zone; here distinctive genera include cabbage-relatives, primula-relatives and the valerian *Pseudobetckea*.

Irano-Turanian Region Reflects in its plants the aridity of Central Asia; examples include the many genera of saltbush, cabbage-relatives and bellflowers.

Eastern Asiatic Region Northeastern extremity of large region with humid climate, here containing heathlike and roselike genera, cucumber-relatives and skimmias.

Pacific forest-meadow of the Kamchatka Peninsula; in the south, the mixed forest contains such rarities as Korean pine (*Pinus koraiensis*) and the Japanese yew (*Taxus cuspidata*). The understory has a number of endemic shrubs such as the Amur lilac (*Syringa amurensis*) and a mock orange (*Philadelphus schrenkii*). Attractive lianas abound; they include wild kiwi fruits (*Actinidia*) and the fragrant-flowered *Schisandra chinensis*.

The various mountain ranges have a distinct plant life of their own. The lower slopes of the Caucasus are covered with oak-beech forest, Caucasian hornbeam (*Carpinus caucasica*), maple (*Acer*), elm (*Ulmus*) and lime (*Tilia*), with an understory of *Rhododendron luteum*. The upper slopes are cloaked with conifers, mostly

Caucasian fir (*Abies nordmanniana*), occasionally mixed with oriental spruce (*Picea orientalis*). Birch groves and thickets of *Rhododendron caucasicum* and *Juniperus hemisphaerica* grow at the treeline. The subalpine and alpine meadows beyond the treeline are home to some beautiful endemic species of *Gentiana*, *Campanula* and *Primula*.

The high desert plateau of the eastern Pamir, in contrast, is dominated by scrubby *Artemisia pamirica* and *Ceratoides papposa*, with cushions of prickly thrift (*Acantholimon*) and thistly *Cousinia* also widely spread.

Steppe and desert

The steppes, which stretch from the river Danube in central Europe to the Ussuri in the far east, are dominated by drought-resistant grasses such as feather grass (*Stipa*). In the north, tall grasses and colorful flowers such as *Filipendula vulgaris*, *Salvia pratensis* and *Scorzonera purpurea* form the northern prairies and surround occasional islands of broadleaf

Map of floristic regions Much of the region is included in the Circumboreal region, the largest floristic region in the world. The desert areas in the south and the humid southeast each contain a quite different plant life.

trees. In the drier south, shorter grasses predominate, together with drought-resistant herbs such as sagebrushes (*Artemisia* and *Seriphidium*).

In the dry deserts of the south and Mongolia the plant life is sparse, though members of the goosefoot family (Chenopodiaceae) are widespread. Clay deserts support species of sagebrush or wormwood, whereas the sandy deserts of Central Asia are home to saxaul (*Arthrophytum*) and *Calligonum*. Here, plants such as the sedge *Carex physodes* and the grass *Stipagrostis pennata* bind the sand dunes, and giant fennels (*Ferula*) and a wild rhubarb (*Rheum turkestanicum*) colonize the lower slopes. These deserts contain some unique endemics, such as *Borszscowia aralocaspica* and *Alexandra lehmannii*, each so distinctive that it is the only species in its genus.

ADAPTING TO WATER STRESS

The two largest vegetation zones in the region are the taiga and the steppe. They have very different climates, but both are affected by a lack of water at certain times of year; in the taiga the water is frozen, while the steppe suffers from drought. The plants have adapted in different ways to survive this difficulty.

Living through low temperatures
The conifers are the dominant plants of the taiga because they have successfully adapted to very low winter temperatures and the consequent shortage of water. In contrast to that of many broadleaf species, the structure of their wood enables them to store water for use in times when groundwater is unavailable. This allows the trees quickly to replenish parts such as leaves that lose water through evaporation. The risk of water stress is greatest during early spring, when the sap begins to rise in response to the increased sunlight and warm air temperature, but the roots are still unable to take in water from the frozen soil.

The leaves of the evergreen conifers are also modified to reduce water loss by desiccation; they are small in size, have

Succulent glasswort of the salt steppe The branched stems and fleshy leaf "segments" are capable of absorbing moisture from the air, and even their inflorescence is fleshy to help cope with the permanent water stress.

sunken ventilating pores (stomata) and thick, protective, waxy cuticles.

Some trees, such as the Siberian larch, avoid damage from freezing by lowering the temperature of the water in their cells to at least −70°C (−95°F) without it freezing. They can do this by increasing the amount of unsaturated fats, sugars, sugar alcohols and membrane proteins in their stored water, which lowers the freezing point. These and other changes in the leaf and bud structure take place just before and during the winter; this enables trees such as the Dahurian larch to survive as far north as 72° 50′.

The Dahurian larch additionally has a superficial root system that is specially adapted to grow in permanently frozen ground (permafrost), which melts in summer to a depth of only 50–100 cm (20–40 in). This root system is supplemented by adventitious roots that form above the base of the trunk. Individual larches can survive in the growing peat bogs for 300 to 400 years, whereas pines, which do not have adventitious roots, are suffocated by the moss growth after 50 to 70 years.

Survival in the steppe
The desert steppes of the eastern Pamir, the Altai, central Tien Shan and Mongolia are covered with needlegrass (drought-resistant species of *Stipa*) and needlegrass growing with subshrubs. North of the Gobi, Mongolian needlegrass and onion species (*Allium*) are common. They have all developed adaptations that enable them to reduce or tolerate the effects of drought, and so are able to survive and reproduce successfully.

On the Kirgiz Steppe the plants avoid water stress by completing their cycle of growth and reproduction rapidly, while water is available. These plants are ephemeroids – perennials that spend the dry season underground as storage organs such as bulbs or tubers – and ephemerals, which are annuals that spend the dry season as dormant seeds. Most of them flourish in spring, such as tulip

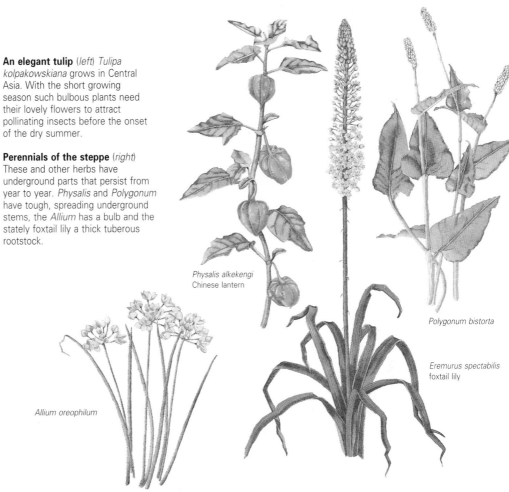

An elegant tulip (*left*) *Tulipa kolpakowskiana* grows in Central Asia. With the short growing season such bulbous plants need their lovely flowers to attract pollinating insects before the onset of the dry summer.

Perennials of the steppe (*right*) These and other herbs have underground parts that persist from year to year. *Physalis* and *Polygonum* have tough, spreading underground stems, the *Allium* has a bulb and the stately foxtail lily a thick tuberous rootstock.

Physalis alkekengi
Chinese lantern

Polygonum bistorta

Eremurus spectabilis
foxtail lily

Allium oreophilum

species (*Tulipa*), the grass *Poa bulbosa*, and *Valeriana tuberosa*; a few plants bloom in the fall, such as the autumn crocus (*Colchicum laetum*).

For those plants that live above ground during the dry season there are two main adaptations to overcome water stress. One involves taking in the maximum amount of water possible at times when it is available, the other the efficient use and conservation of the water that has been acquired. To take in water rapidly the plants need to have deep, penetrating root systems or abundant but shallow root systems, rapid root growth in the seedling and at the start of the growing season, and the ability to absorb what little water there is in fairly dry soils.

To conserve water some plants have a reduced leaf area, an increased ratio of green photosynthetic tissue to leaf area, or shed their leaves at the onset of drought. Plants that retain their leaves display other protective features such as sunken leaf pores (stomata), a thick, protective cuticle covering the leaf, a coating of wax on the leaf surface, hairs on both the leaf and the stem surface, inward-rolling leaves, and leaves that are positioned at an acute angle to the stem – all of which help to reduce water loss from the leaves through transpiration.

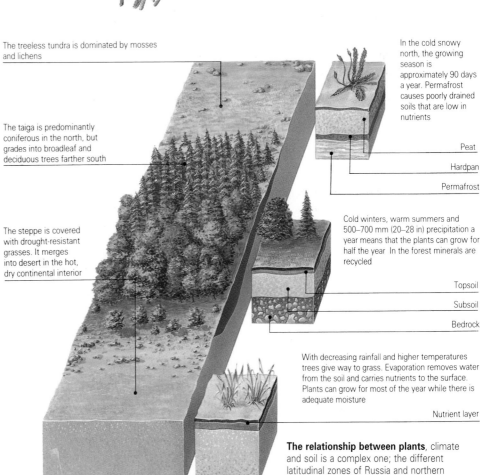

The treeless tundra is dominated by mosses and lichens

The taiga is predominantly coniferous in the north, but grades into broadleaf and deciduous trees farther south

The steppe is covered with drought-resistant grasses. It merges into desert in the hot, dry continental interior

In the cold snowy north, the growing season is approximately 90 days a year. Permafrost causes poorly drained soils that are low in nutrients

Peat

Hardpan

Permafrost

Cold winters, warm summers and 500–700 mm (20–28 in) precipitation a year means that the plants can grow for half the year In the forest minerals are recycled

Topsoil

Subsoil

Bedrock

With decreasing rainfall and higher temperatures trees give way to grass. Evaporation removes water from the soil and carries nutrients to the surface. Plants can grow for most of the year while there is adequate moisture

Nutrient layer

The relationship between plants, climate and soil is a complex one; the different latitudinal zones of Russia and northern Eurasia provide a number of examples.

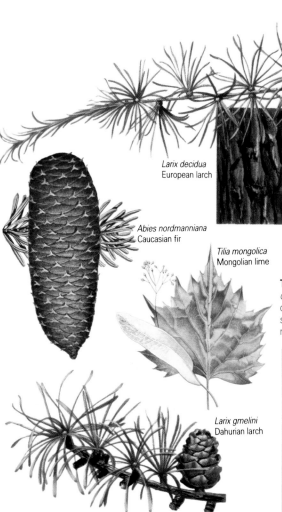

Larix decidua
European larch

Abies nordmanniana
Caucasian fir

Tilia mongolica
Mongolian lime

Larix gmelini
Dahurian larch

Juniperus chinensis
Chinese juniper

Zelkova carpinifolia

Trees of the taiga (*above*) The Caucasian fir, *Larix decidua* and *Zelkova* grow in western regions, the others are found to the east as their specific names suggest. Trees for timber and pulp are one of Russia's most important commodities.

Siberian iris (*below*) *Iris sibirica* is an elegant iris of streamsides and moist places; it is a variable species in the wild, and forms with white flowers instead of blue are sometimes to be found. It is cultivated in gardens and as a cut flower.

EDIBLE, HEALING AND DECORATIVE PLANTS

The very diverse plant communities of the region have always played a significant role in the life of the people. The steppes, meadows, deserts and tundra form a natural pasture and source of hay for livestock, and the forests are an extremely valuable source of timber. Wild plants also have innumerable uses, and are exploited both in medicine and as foods. In the Caucasus, for example, plants are the source of rodenticides and insecticides, vitamins, essential and industrial oils, soda and potash, gums and resins, rubber and gutta-percha (a latex obtained from trees), fibers and foaming agents; they have also been used in the manufacture of cheese, papermaking, wickerwork, tanning and metallurgy.

Culinary and medicinal plants

Many of the wild plants found in Russia and neighboring countries are of culinary importance. Wild fruits, nuts and certain fungi from the forests are eaten throughout the region. The seeds of the Siberian cedar, known as cedar nuts, can be eaten both raw and cooked; they also yield an

PLANNED CONSERVATION

The long and intensive use of the natural vegetation for grazing, settlement, fuel, agriculture and industry has inevitably and dramatically changed or destroyed much of the plant life of the region. Most of the Kirgiz Steppe, for example, is now under the plow for cereal cultivation. For these reasons active conservation measures to protect the plants, the resources they represent and the environmental stability they engender, are an urgent priority.

Successful environmental conservation requires legal and political backing to restrict activities that degrade or pollute the environment. In the old Soviet Union there was mixed success. While protected areas were established and some run very effectively, others were

often damaged by development project. Many development decisions were taken that ignored the potential environmental impacts with disastrous ecological consequences. The shrinking of the Aral Sea as a result of irrigation schemes and pollution in Lake Baikal from paper and pulp factories are two examples. However, there is a network of protected areas across the region that has survived the collapse of communism and expanded in most of the new republics. For examples, the United Nations list of Protected Areas 1997 lists 709 nature reserves, 70 national parks and 62 Ramsar sites. There are several reserves over 1 million hectares (2.4 million acres). The largest reserve in Russia's Far East covers 4,169,222 ha (10,302,147 acres).

edible oil. Important food plants of the southern mountains ranges include the walnut (*Juglans regia*) and the pistachio (*Pistacia vera*), which is also a source of resin. In Mongolia, wild plants that are used include *Agriophyllum pungens*, which provides a cereal grain; wild rhubarb (*Rheum compactum*) is used as a vegetable, starch is extracted from the stems of the fleshy parasite *Cynomorium soongaricum*, and berries are collected from *Vaccinium*, *Rubus* and *Ribes* species.

The most important medicinal plants found in the regioin are species of the liquorice genus *Glycirrhiza*, especially *G. glabra* and *G. uralensis*. They are used in various forms as an expectorant (to relieve catarrh), and as an antiirritant and relaxant in the treatment of gastritis and stomach ulcers. Mixed with other substances they are administered as a diuretic and laxative, and in powder form they are added to other medicines to improve their taste and smell.

A few more of the many hundreds of species with medicinal uses include *Ephedra equisetina*, a shrub from montane steppe that contains alkaloids such as ephedrine, which are used in the treatment of bronchial asthma, hayfever and low blood pressure. The daisy-flowered *Leuzea carthamoides*, a perennial herb

endemic to the mountains of southern Siberia, is used as a stimulant in the treatment of nervous disorders and physical and mental exhaustion. *Ahnfeltia plicata*, a red seaweed harvested from the White Sea coasts, is a source of agar, which is used to treat chronic constipation, and also as a base for slowly dissolving tablets. *Sphaerophysa salsula*, a perennial herb of deserts and semideserts, has a long rhizome that yields alkaloids given to stimulate contractions of the uterus during childbirth.

Gifts to gardens

Many wild plants in the region are popular with gardeners. Some of the most decorative of all come from the Caucasus Mountains in the west. Here are found a great number of ornamental plants such as the Caucasian fir; *Zelkova carpinifolia*, a hardy deciduous tree of the elm family; *Daphne pontica*, a hardy evergreen shrub with fragrant yellow flowers; and *Elaeagnus angustifolius*, a decorative shrub with ornamental silvery white and yellow foliage. Ornamental grasses also grow in the mountains, such as *Erianthus purpurascens*, with plumes similar to those of pampas grass, and the feathergrass *Stipa pulcherrima*, whose flowerheads are dried for winter decoration.

The giant hogweed (*Heracleum mantegazzianum*) The inflorescence is composed of many tiny flowers arranged in an umbel, typical of the carrot family (Umbelliferae). Its sap makes skin vulnerable to ultraviolet light, which causes painful burns.

The herbaceous perennials of the Caucasus Mountains include the gentian *Gentiana septemfida*, the shell-flower *Molucella laevis*, with its unusual green bracts, cornflowers (*Centaurea*) of many colors, large-flowered yellow *Paeonia* species and the giant hogweed *Heracleum mantegazzianum*, whose sap can cause a painful skin rash that is slow to heal. Other common perennials include red pyrethrum *Tanacetum coccineum*, which is now represented in gardens by numerous cultivars, and the bold daisy-flowered *Inula magnifica*, *Telekia speciosa* and *Doronicum macrophyllum*.

The bulbous plants of the Caucasus are very colorful; they include the lovely *Onocyclus* irises (of which *Iris reticulata* is perhaps the best known), tulip species such as the scarlet and blue-black *Tulipa eichleri*, and the autumn crocuses *Merendera trigyna* and *Colchicum speciosum*. From high altitudes come many rock garden and alpine plants: stonecrops such as *Sedum*, *Sempervivum* and *Rosularia*; and *Draba*, *Saxifraga*, *Androsace*, *Campanula* and the prickly thrift (*Acantholimon*).

Desert plants of the Gobi

The Gobi ("desert" in Mongolian) extends across the south of Mongolia. It is an extreme environment, combining arid, salty soils with temperatures that rise and fall dramatically from day to night and throughout the year. In the cold, dry, cloudless winters, conditions reach almost the lowest limits at which plants can survive. Much of the Gobi is stony desert, in places devoid of plants or with sparse vegetation cover. The number of plant species is small – there are only about 600 species of higher plants, of which few are dominant, and most have had to adapt to resist drought.

Drought-tolerant plants of the Gobi

The drought-tolerant plants (xerophytes) of the Gobi differ from those of hot deserts; in some respects, they combine the adaptations of mountain and cold zone plants with those of mountain and arid zones. Their productivity is comparatively lower than that of hot desert plants, and they are dormant for longer. The plants of the southwestern (Transaltai) Gobi are typical examples.

The southwestern Gobi is a sandy desert in which the plants are either sclerophytes or succulents. The sclerophytes are woody plants with small, thick leaves (or grasses with narrow, often inrolled leaves). These have a thick outer covering (cuticle), and a high proportion of cell wall in which water can be stored. Species include a wild rhubarb, *Rheum nanum*, the ornamental shrub *Caryopteris mongolica*, many species of milkweeds such as *Astragalus pavlovii*, and daisy-flowered plants such as *Ajania fruticulosa* and *Artemisia scoparia*. There are also grasses such as *Stipa gobica* and *Cleistogenes songorica*.

Unlike plants of average moist conditions, sclerophytes have compact photosynthetic tissue (mesophyll) with less space between the cells, but like them (except for some of the grasses), they photosynthesize in the usual way.

There are two types of succulents. Some have a low surface area, and a high proportion of water-storing tissue to reduce water loss through transpiration. They have evolved a specialized method of photosynthesizing (the photosynthetic tissues are differentiated into two types of cell), and they manufacture food by a process called the Crassulacean Acid Metabolism (CAM). The pores open at night (instead of during the day as those

In a dry and salty desert (*above*) *Anabasis brevifolium* belongs to the goosefoot family (Chenopodiaceae). Chenopods are predominantly herbaceous, and are adapted to live in saline soils. Many species, this plant included, exhibit xerophytic adaptations.

Tamarisk in the Gobi (*right*) *Tamarix ramosissima*, like its relatives in northern Africa and Europe, is salt tolerant and survives in dry and stony places. It is frequently cultivated in Californian gardens in the United States, where it forms an attractive small tree.

of other plants do). Through the pores the plant takes in and stores carbon dioxide, which is then released into the cells during the day when the plant is photosynthesizing. These plants include *Nitraria sphaerocarpa*, *Sympegma regelii* and *Reamuria soongorica*.

The second type of succulent is even more highly adapted to drought conditions. These are known as Kranz-syndrome succulents (their compact photosynthetic tissue is differentiated into three types of cell), and they have a special photosynthetic metabolism (C_4), which is more efficient in high temperatures and intense sunlight. Typical

species include *Iljinia regelii*, *Haloxylon ammodendron*, *Anabasis brevifolia* and *Salsola arbuscula*. Some non-succulent plants, such as the grasses *Cleistogenes songorica* and *Enneapogon borealis*, also have C_4 photosynthesis.

Some plants survive the drought by having no leaves, such as the sclerophyte *Ephedra*, succulents with normal photosynthesis such as *Salicornia*, and Kranz-syndrome succulents such as *Haloxylon*, *Calligonum* and *Anabasis*.

These examples all demonstrate the extraordinary ingenuity of plants in finding ways to survive in the most inhospitable of environments.

AGRICULTURE

THE CHALLENGES TO AGRICULTURE · FEEDING THE PEOPLE · IMPROVING THE SYSTEM TO MEET DEMAND

The territory of the former Soviet Union is vast, but only about 10 percent of the land is suitable for arable farming; the remainder is too dry, too hot or too cold. Just under half the land area is covered by coniferous forest, and in the northern tundra zone (about 20 percent of the land area) the subsoil is permanently frozen, making it too cold for crop cultivation. Useful agricultural land is squeezed into a central band (the black earth belt), which is wider to the west, narrower and more broken to the east. These physical limitations are compounded by the legacy of inefficient state-controlled agriculture, exemplified by the fact that there are 24 million farmers, more than in the whole of the West and Japan together, but they produce only about a quarter as much.

COUNTRIES IN THE REGION

Armenia, Azerbaijan, Belarus, Estonia, Georgia, Kazakhstan, Kyrgyzstan, Latvia, Lithuania, Moldova, Mongolia, Russia, Tajikistan, Turkmenistan, Ukraine, Uzbekistan

LAND: Total area 23,967,200 sq km (9,251,339 sq mi)

cropland	pasture	forest/woodland
11%	22%	35%
(2,629,661 sq km)	(4,298,334 sq km)	(8,461,043 sq km)

FARMERS	Highest	Middle	Lowest
Agriculture as % of GDP	45% (Kyrgyzstan)	22% (Azerbaijan)	7% (Lat., Eston.)
% of workforce	over 90% (Mongolia)	55% (Ar.,Kyr.)	11% (Estonia)

MAJOR CROPS: Agricultural products fruit and vegetables; wheat, barley, flax;.cotton; sugar beet; sunflower seeds; grapes; tea; beef; sheep and goats; dairy products; fish; tobacco; wool

Total cropland (000 ha)	127,962 (Russia)	30,135 (Kazakhstan).	559 (Armenia)
Cropland (ha) per 1000 people	1,840 (Kazakhstan)	520 (Mongolia)	150 (Tajikistan)
Irrigated land as % of cropland	88% (Uzbekistan)	41% (Georgia)	2% (Lithuania)
Number of tractors	886,490 (Russia)	108,121 (Kazakhstan)	7,000 (Mongolia)
Average cereal crop yields (kg/ha)	2,860 (Moldova)	1,772 (Armenia)	670 (Kazakhkstan)
Cereal production (000 tonnes)	67,064 (Russia)	9,985 (Kazakhstan)	218 (Mongolia)
Change since 1986/88	Data not available		-72%

LIVESTOCK & FISHERIES

Meat production (000 tonnes)	4,943 (Russia)	642 (Belarus)	36 (Tajikistan)
Marine fish catch (000 tonnes)	4,164 (Russia)	349.6 (Ukraine)	3.7 (Georgia)

FOOD SECURITY

Food aid as % of total imports	10% (Mongolia)	Data not available	
Daily kcal/person	3,085 (Kazakhstan)	2,617 (Georgia)	1,917 (Mongolia)

THE CHALLENGES TO AGRICULTURE

Serfdom was well established in Russia by the mid-16th century. This system made the peasants who worked the land the property of the landowning classes, who could buy and sell them as they pleased. It was formally ended in 1861, when the land was divided between the original landowning class and the freed peasantry, organized into communes.

In the communes land was divided into small strips often less than a meter wide and several hundred meters long. A peasant family might use its strips for a year or two only, before they were re-allocated to others. This system, which provided no incentive to improve the land, was a major contributing factor to the backwardness of Russian agriculture at the beginning of the 20th century.

Reform and collectivization

In the years before World War I reforms were introduced with the aim of creating a class of landowning farmer peasants (kulaks). By 1915 about half of the rural households owned strips, and over a million had been able to consolidate their landholdings. Migration eastward was encouraged, helped by the opening of the Trans-Siberian Railway at the end of the 19th century: 3 million peasant farmers settled in Siberia between 1907 and 1909. After the communist revolution in 1917 these peasant farmers were absorbed into large state-owned farming enterprises, and agricultural settlement continued to extend eastward until the 1950s.

In the early years after the revolution force was often used to extract sufficient food for the urban and industrial populations from the peasant communes and farmers. It is hardly surprising that the majority produced just enough for themselves; there was little point in producing a surplus for confiscation. The food shortages in the cities became acute, and in October 1929 Stalin (1879–1953) started a violent campaign to compel the kulaks to amalgamate their holdings into collective farms, which meant that production was brought under direct state control.

Checking the work tally Workers on a collective cotton farm in Kazakhstan line up to have their sacks of picked cotton weighed. Under the Soviet system, all aspects of farming were regulated and controlled by the state, but that has changed since the 1990s.

Today vast tracts in the region remain virtually empty of agriculture. In the northern tundra the only agriculture that takes place is based on hunting, fishing and reindeer herding. In the broad belt of coniferous forest (known as taiga) agriculture is confined to clearings where potatoes and small amounts of rye, oats and barley are grown.

The mixed deciduous and coniferous forests to the south of the taiga were the first to be cleared for permanent cultivation: their fertile soils (the black earths or chernozems) make them very suitable for agriculture. By the beginning of the 19th century wheat was being grown here for export to Western Europe. Large areas of this productive land in Ukraine were contaminated by the nuclear accident at Chernobyl in 1986.

Still farther to the south are the natural grasslands of the great Russian steppe. The traditional pastoral economy that was practiced here for hundreds of years has given way this century to cultivation. At their dry southern margins, however, where the grasslands merge into semi-desert and desert, migratory agriculture based on herds of sheep still survives. Most of the herdsmen, though, are now permanently housed in settlements, and only the herds move.

ARCTIC OCEAN

Franz Josef Land

Barents Sea

Baltic Sea

Kola Pen

Novaya Zemlya

Kara Sea

Severnaya Zemlya

Taymyr Peninsula

Laptev Sea

New Siberian Islands

East Siberian Sea

Wrangel Island

Chukot Range

Koryak Range

Bering Sea

RUSSIA
ESTONIA
LATVIA
LITHUANIA
BELARUS

L Ladoga

L Onega

N Dvina

Northern European Plain

Byrranga Mts

Pobeda 3147

Cherskogo Range

Kolyma Range

Klyuchevskaya 4750

Kamchatka Peninsula

MOLDOVA

UKRAINE

Dnieper

Volga

Don

Sea of Azov

Black Sea

Ural Mountains

Ob

Yamal Pen

Gydanskiy Pen

Yenisei

West Siberian Plain

Central Siberian Plateau

Lena

Verkhoyansk Range

Dzhugdzhur Ra

Sea of Okhotsk

Sakhalin

Kuril Islands

Elbrus 5642

Caucasus Mts

GEORGIA

ARMENIA

AZERBAIJAN

Caspian Depression

Ural

Tobol

RUSSIA

Ob

Angara

Lena

Stanovoy Range

Amur

Yablonovy Range

Amur

Sikhote-Alin Mts

Sea of Japan

Mangyshlak Peninsula -132

Kirghiz Steppe

L Baikal

Caspian Sea

Krasnovodsk

Aral Sea

Syr Darya

L Balkhash

KAZAKHSTAN

L Zaisan

Eastern Sayan Mts

Yenisei

Western Sayan Mts

TURKMENISTAN

UZBEKISTAN

Kara Kum

Kyzyl Kum

Amu Darya

Pamir

Qullai Garmo 7495

TAJIKISTAN

KYRGYZSTAN

Pobedy Peak 7439

Altai Range

MONGOLIA

Gobi

Agricultural zones

- arable and pasture
- pasture with some arable
- rough grazing
- woods and forest
- nonagricultural land

▲ mountain peak (meters)
▼ depression (meters)

Map of agricultural zones Most productive arable land is found in the "black earth belt" in the west of the region. North and south of the vast taiga forest conditions for cultivation become too cold or too arid.

Cotton and rice are grown in the valleys of the rivers that flow into the Aral Sea. So much water is extracted for irrigation that the Aral Sea has shrunk to nearly half its former size. In the 1960s the lake's area was 66,820 sq km (25,800 sq mi). It is now about 40,000 sq km (15,500 sq mi), and in places the old sea bed forms a salt desert. The lake once supported many fishing communities, now abandoned.

In the northwest, a large area is characterized by heavy, acidic, poorly drained soils called podsols. Here cultivation is difficult, and the application of lime and extensive soil drainage is generally necessary. Potatoes remain the staple food crop, though recent heavy investment in agricultural improvement has allowed a sharp increase in cereal yields, especially near the large cities.

FEEDING THE PEOPLE

Agriculture in the former Soviet Union failed to feed the people. About one fifth of the food required was imported – mainly grain from the USA. Agricultural reform has been slow throughout the region partly because privatization has become very politicized. In many areas the future for farming was still uncertain at the start of the 21st century and food security continued to be an issue. The root of the problems for farming lies in its organization during the Soviet period. Despite changes to the ownership of farms, the basic organizational structures and farming practices still follow patterns laid down in the Soviet period.

The organization of farming

The old Soviet state managed all aspects of agriculture – what was grown, how it was grown, when it was harvested – and most of it was distributed through state marketing organizations. The government did this by setting the production plans and by controlling the farming units at local level. The two kinds of farming units still remain. The collectives, or *kolhozy*, were the instruments of Stalin's coercive policies against the kulaks. The state appointed the farm managers who implemented the production plans, which were set centrally within the context of a state agricultural program. The state farms, or *sovhkozy*, in which workers were employed directly by the state, were set up after 1918 to parallel state-owned industrial ventures. Expansion of state agriculture into areas east of the river Volga, where there were few peasants to collectivize, contributed to the growth of state farms.

The collectives and state farms both were, and still are, very large units. The former has, on average, 2,385 ha (8,610 acres) of cultivated land; the latter are even larger, with 4,767 ha (11,780 acres). Farm workers live in small villages and towns, and commute to work on the farms. Some of the state farm enterprises are highly specialized – producing, for example, only irrigated cotton, sugar beet or tobacco for export, or tomatoes and cucumbers under glass for the Moscow market. A "farm" of this sort may have 250 ha (620 acres) under glass and a small power station to provide the required heat early in the growing season.

There was little incentive for raising productivity in state farms and collectives. Prices charged to consumers were set without serious consideration of production costs, and the production of different crops was controlled by imposing quotas.

The principal crop of both the collectives and the state farms is wheat. The amount of land planted to both wheat and potatoes has been falling since 1960, while production of fodder for livestock has been increasing, especially barley, oats and maize.

Change in diet

As the standard of living of Soviet people rose between 1960 and 1990 there was a trend away from staple foods such as bread and potatoes toward more meat. In the past, following poor harvest years (1963, 1966) livestock, particularly cattle, were slaughtered to match herd sizes to the available fodder. Meat, milk and eggs were often unobtainable. After 1970, however, growth in livestock numbers became more or less continuous, even when there were poor harvests. This was made possible not only by the increased national production of fodder grains, but also by large imports of grain from countries outside the Soviet Union.

Since the political and economic upheavals of 1991, the diets of most people have suffered drastically. Disposable incomes for most people in Russia and the former Soviet republics declined and with that the demand for foods, especially the more expensive foods such as meat and dairy products. Subsidies for farming, which at first actually increased to keep farming going, have decreased – in Russia by 80 percent in real terms between 1997 and 1998. The amount of land under cultivation and agricultural production has declined. Stock, the least profitable type of farming, dropped by 50 percent between 1990 and 1996.

Falling incomes, stock raising and farm production has meant that once again there is a greater emphasis on grains and vegetables in the diet, the vegetables coming largely from a growing number of private farms. In 1998 Russia had to import $394.3 million worth of grain and ask for food aid from international organizations.

The Soviet grain harvest Despite mechanization, production levels never rose as high as targeted. Even when harvests were good, and after reform, the lack of bulk road and tall containers means that grain may go moldy before it can be moved from the farms.

A **milking shed** on a collective farm in Ulyanovsk, Lenin's birthplace, on the river Volga. Cattle are kept indoors during the long winters; however, milk supplies can be still very variable, as they are dependent on the availability of fodder.

THE PATTERN OF GRAIN HARVESTS

The expansion of agriculture east of the Ural Mountains that took place during the 20th century means that grain is now grown in areas that are prone to high temperatures in summer, and in soils that do not retain moisture well. In the traditional grain-producing areas to the west, conditions are generally much wetter. It is only in exceptional years that adverse weather occurs throughout the entire grain belt. This happened, for instance, in 1975, when hot dry conditions prevailed throughout the whole country, resulting in a disastrous harvest. More often, however, unfavorable weather conditions in one area, producing a poor harvest, is likely to be balanced by better weather, and healthier harvests, elsewhere.

Consequently, climatic patterns are a vitally important factor in helping to prevent great fluctuations in grain availability from one year to the next. But a major problem is that yields per hectare are increasing much faster in the western half of the grain belt than in the climatically more volatile east. If this trend continues, the west will once more come to dominate the total production. Overall harvest sizes will be dependent on whether there is a good or bad year in the west, giving rise to much greater variability in supply. Moreover, the tonnage of grain that needs to be imported annually to make up any shortfall will become far less easy to predict. It is not only climatic patterns that threaten grain production. Yields in 1999 were relatively low because of severe locust infestations in parts of the region.

"Agricultural technology of the future" (*left*) So reads the legend on this sign outside a state farm. Soviet investment in farm machinery such as combine harvesters and tractors was considerable. But failures in planning – which the reforms initiated under the *perestroika* movement have not effectively been able to overcome – meant that there was a very low level of return. Machines often broke down, and could not be easily repaired.

Branching out (*right*) Towards the end of the Soviet era reforms were taking place, and farmers were being given greater control over their operations. This flower nursery on a collective farm was privately owned. Some such businesses diversified from basic food production into a purely commercial enterprise as the opportunity arose to make a profit. Productivity promptly increased.

IMPROVING THE SYSTEM TO MEET DEMAND

As personal incomes in the Soviet Union began to rise in the 1960s there came an increase in the demand for consumer goods, and in particular for higher quality foodstuffs. The continued absence of such goods still inhibits the country's economic development and labor productivity. Why should people work harder if there is nothing for them to spend their wages on?

The fertile conditions of the region's "black earth" grain-producing belt had allowed surplus wheat to be exported since the ending of serfdom in the mid-nineteenth century. Except for a brief period in the mid 1960s, the Soviet Union continued to export grain even during times of shortage at home. The decision of the Soviet government in 1972 to import grain in order to meet the domestic demand for higher quality foodstuffs therefore came as a great shock to the international grain market. It had profound effects on the price and availability of food for much of the rest of the world.

Great secrecy surrounded the Soviet Union's dealings on the international grain market. Most of its purchases were made from grain companies based in the United States, even while relations between the two countries remained tense following the Cold War. In 1971–72 the Soviet Union imported 7.8 million tonnes of grain; this shot up to 22.8 million tonnes in 1972–73, and of this 13.7 million tonnes came from the United States. The world price of wheat increased almost fourfold between July 1972 and February 1974. Although other factors, including a rapid rise in the price of oil and fertilizers, were involved, much of this price rise was attributable to the Soviet Union's unexpected decision to start buying grain.

Soviet grain imports remained high as domestic grain harvests continued to be disappointing and the demand for meat remained largely unmet. Annual grain imports rose as high as 55 million tonnes, close to the maximum that could be handled by the existing port facilities in the Soviet Union. This had implications for the entire world, especially those countries that depend on food imports and food aid. World grain shortages following droughts and failed harvests have left other food-importing short, particularly those that do not have foreign exchange resources.

Since 1991 agricultural production has decreased by as much as one third. Investment in agriculture has fallen and farm incomes have decreased, as have incomes throughout most of the former Soviet countries. This has led to a decrease in food imports and an increase in local food processing industries. However, grain imports are still needed, some in the form of food aid which comes from USA and the European Union. The imported grain is mainly for animal feed.

High investment, low returns

The problems of low productivity that beset Soviet agriculture were not a result of a lack of investment in land improvement and farm technology. On the contrary, the scale of government investment was even higher than in the United States. Good intentions, however, tended to be frustrated by the ongoing practical difficulties of centralized planning and supply over such a vast country. Between 1965 and 1980 agricultural investment increased by 190 percent, but output rose only by a paltry 17 percent.

Part of the reason was that the money was not well spent. Heavy seasonal demand for fertilizers created bottlenecks in their manufacture, storage and transportation. Deliveries to farms often arrived too late in a crop's growing cycle,

Agricultural efficiency, never very high in Russia, declined after 1990 and was only expected to start recovering in the new millennium if there was a strongly pro-reform government. Between 1990 and 1996, agricultural production dropped by 37 percent and imports and food aid were necessary.

The causes of the agricultural crisis are many. The economic crisis meant there was less money available to support or invest in agriculture. Investment declined by 18 times from 1990 to 1996. Political instability and disagreement on agricultural policies gave farmers an uncertain future. Farmers were ill prepared for operating in an increasingly market economy. Controls were relaxed but cooperative systems and distribution systems became disrupted or collapsed in the aftermath. State budgets for agriculture were reduced and state purchase guarantees broken. Lower real incomes also led to a decline in the demand for food products. By the end of 1997, 80 percent of Russian farms were operating in deficit.

As delays in reform continued there was a marked increase in non-authorized privatization. The consequences of this failure to plan agricultural reform effectively are evident in the rural areas: higher death rates than birth rates, growing unemployment, greater social divisions and increased isolation of villages. Agriculture remains a problem in the 21st century as it was for most of the 20th.

and were simply left to lie by the roadside. At one time tractors and other machinery were held in centralized "tractor stations" from where they were supposed to be delivered to farms as required, but they rarely were. Machinery is now supplied direct to each collective and state farm, but even now, equipment is often unreliable and not always available when needed. Throughout the 1980s, labor productivity remained only a tenth of that of agriculture in the United States.

Moreover – as China discovered when it allowed cultivation of private plots alongside state farms – productivity was significantly higher on the private plots than on the state-controlled farms.

Prescribing solutions
President Mikhail Gorbachev launched a package of economic reforms (known as *perestroika*, or "reconstruction") in 1986. Farmers were given more control over what they grew and how they marketed it. On state farms the labor force was divided into teams and paid according to its production success. Productivity rose to more than ten times the national average in some cases. Today, agriculture in the region is making the transition to a market economy with great difficulty.

A prerequisite of further progress is land reform. This requires decisions from the relevant national officials, but decision-making on land reform in Russia and many of the newly independent republics has become embroiled in politicking and even corruption. At the end of the millennium, farmers in some countries such as Ukraine were still waiting to find out how

the issue of land tenure was likely to be resolved. There was little incentive for them to invest in land that they might soon lose. In other countries such as Estonia, privatization proceeded quickly and private farms have already become the foundation of a significant food processing industry. Even where state owned farms have become private companies with the farmers as the shareholders, farming practices have changed little and productivity remains low.

The private plots remain, and although limited in size to 0.353 ha (0.87 acres) they continue to make an important contribution to the food supply throughout the region. In Russia, 90 percent of potatoes, 76 percent of vegetables and 51 percent of meat production comes from these tiny parcels of land.

Farming the private plots

Even under the Soviet regime many people were permitted to control the use of a small private plot of land, to grow food for their own consumption.

Private plots were originally granted as compensation for those peasants whose lands were amalgamated into the collective farms. Of the 35 million private plots 13 million were still worked by the collective farmers, or *kolkhozniks*, and a further 10 million were worked by the employees of the state farms, the *sovkhozniks*. The remaining 10 million plots were divided among the employees of various other state organizations. The plots that belong to the kolkhozniks were the largest in size (an average of 0.31 ha/0.76 acres).

Having a plot involved control of its use, but not ownership. Control could be passed on within a family, but if the family moved or did not use the land, it reverted to the state. Today the ownership of private plots is being discussed within the land reform debate. Great care is lavished on the private plots, especially by grandparents and children, the incentive being the high prices that are available in the markets, and the pleasure of growing quality produce for the family.

Productivity is very high compared with other farming, but because the plots are so small the type of produce is limited. A cow, a pig or two and a few chickens are usually combined with a number of different vegetables, the choice depending on the season and climatic zone. Some 45 percent of the region's vegetable and potato production, 31 percent of dairy cows, but less than 1 percent of the cereal production comes from private plots.

Supplying the private markets

Because so much produce from farms is of poor quality and is subject to irregular supply, fresh food sold through private markets, which are found in every town and city, can be a very valuable source of income. Domestic transportation is cheap, so producers may travel long distances to sell relatively small quantities of produce from their private plots. A producer living in one of the southern republics may undertake a round trip of 1,000 km (over 600 mi) or more to sell fresh vegetables and fruit in the much larger, more demanding and more profitable markets of Moscow. Sales are made directly by the producing family without employing mid-

dlemen or traders of any sort, so there markets are noisy and colorful, with very large numbers of sellers from many parts of the country, each trying to dispose of relatively small quantities of produce.

As in the People's Republic of China, the success and importance of this parallel system of private agriculture remains something of an indictment of the failures of the state sector. All the same, cooperation between the private and the state sector is now encouraged by allowing the release of fodder from state and collective farms for consumption by privately-owned livestock. Moves have also been made to put private plot production under contract, using the seed, fodder and young livestock as well as the marketing channels of the state sector, harnessed to the superior productivity of the private sector. State and collective farms are allowed to sell produce in private markets, as the incentives for private production slowly spread into the state sector.

Marketing the produce A woman in a mountain village in the Caucasus displays the tomatoes, apples, pears and grapes grown on her private plot for sale. Markets like this are found in every town and village across the region.

The fruits of their own labor A couple at work on their private plot. The onion-domed church behind them is under repair – a sign of the changing political climate, which is more tolerant of private farming.

The private sector's share The small size of most private plots means that they are limited in what they can produce, but in some items, notably potatoes, milk and vegetables, their percentage contribution to overall production is considerable.

Percentage per year / Product	1940	1960	1970	1975	1980	1985
Meat	72	41	35	31	31	28
Milk	77	47	36	31	30	29
Eggs	94	80	53	39	32	28
Wool	39	22	20	20	22	26
Grain	12	2	1	6	1	1
Cotton	0	0	0	0	0	0
Sugar beet	0	0	0	0	0	0
Sunflower seeds	11	4	2	3	2	2
Potatoes	65	63	65	59	64	60
Vegetables	48	44	38	34	33	29

INDUSTRY

RESOURCES TO FEED RAPID GROWTH · ACHIEVING INDUSTRIAL SELF-SUFFICIENCY · PEOPLE AS INDUSTRIAL FODDER

Northern Eurasia's diverse natural resources are among the richest and most plentiful in the world. The region, comprising the former Soviet Union and Mongolia, is a world leader in the production of natural gas, iron ore, coal, manganese, mercury and potash; and ranks second or third in the production of oil, copper, lead, zinc, diamonds and nickel. Yet the very diversity of terrain and climatic conditions that helped to produce such a wealth of resources also creates major difficulties in extracting them. In many cases resources are so remote that transportation problems make it uneconomic to exploit them. Communist domination of the region from 1917 until 1991 shaped industrial development, encouraging production of engineering and the defense industries at the expense of consumer products.

In the pipeline (above) The source of Siberian oil is very distant from its users, so vast networks of pipes have been built to transport it. Sub-zero arctic conditions and the remoteness of the pipelines make routine maintenance extremely difficult.

COUNTRIES IN THE REGION

Armenia, Azerbaijan, Belarus, Estonia, Georgia, Kazakhstan, Kyrgyzstan, Latvia, Lithuania, Moldova, Mongolia, Russia, Tajikistan, Turkmenistan, Ukraine, Uzbekistan

TOTAL INDUSTRIAL OUTPUT (1997)

Russia US $155 billion   **Ukraine** US $17 billion

INDUSTRIAL PRODUCTION GROWTH RATE

Russia	8.1% (1999 est.)

INDUSTRIAL WORKERS (millions) for Russia
(figures in brackets are percentages of total labor force)

Total	Mining and Manufacturing	Construction
23.7	17.2 (23.5%)	6.5 (8.9%)

MAJOR PRODUCTS

Energy and minerals	1970	Output 1995	% of world production
Petroleum products (mill tonnes)	n/a	160	5.40%
Crude oil (mill tonnes, 1980)	582	301	9%
Natural gas (thou terajoules)	n/a	21,147	25.1%
Tin (thou tonnes)	n/a	5	2.4
Copper (thou tonnes)	n/a	550	3%
Zinc (thou tonnes)	n/a	150	–
Aluminum (thou tonnes)	n/a	2,700	10.2%
Steel (thou tonnes)	n/a	48,816	6.5%
Phosphates (thou tonnes)	n/a	7,922	6.2%
Iron ore (mill tonnes)	n/a	44	4.3%
Vanadium (tonnes)	n/a	10,000	29.4%
Nickel (thou tonnes)	n/a	203	22.1%
Nickel ore (thou tonnes)	n/a	240	24.8%
Cement (thou tonnes)	n/a	36,432	2.7%

Manufactures			
Beer (mill hectoliters)	n/a	25	2.1%
Fish (thou tonnes)	n/a	4,374	3.9%

RESOURCES TO FEED RAPID GROWTH

For most of the 20th century, through a series of five-year plans the Communist Party of the Soviet Union channeled labor, finance and resources into building up state-controlled heavy industry, especially the sector manufacturing machinery to equip new industrial plants, farming and construction. Huge oil and gas discoveries meant that between the 1920s and the 1980s the region's energy output soared eighty-fold. In the 1990s the dissolution of the former USSR opened the way for the considerable oil resources of the region – estimated to be between 15 and 40 billion barrels – to be commercially exploited. Hydroelectric and nuclear power also added to the region's ample energy resources.

Almost one-quarter of the world's reserves of coal are found in Northern Eurasia. The largest coal-producing area has always been the Donets basin (Donbas) in the Ukraine, which produces 190 million tonnes per year. The second most important area of coal production is the Kuznetsk basin (Kuzbas), which is in Siberia, Russia's inhospitable central zone that runs from the Ural mountains toward the Pacific Ocean. Fields at Karaganda in Kazakhstan and Pechora in the far north of Russia also contribute significantly to

the total output. In addition, there are two fields in the Tungusksa and Lena basins in Siberia that remain largely unexploited because of the brutally cold climate.

The region is one of the world's largest oil producers after the Middle East, producing around 355 million tonnes of crude oil annually. Before the 1930s, practically all of it came from the Baku fields in Azerbaijan. Since then reserves have been exploited in the Ural-Volga area of Russia and in western Siberia, making Russia second only to Saudi Arabia in oil production. Kazakhstan has further unexploited reserves off the Caspian shelf, assuring the country's supply in the 21st century. Huge reserves of natural gas are attracting foreign investment.

Hydroelectric power was first developed in 1928 on the Don and Volga rivers in the western part of the country. The Dnieper dam project began production in 1932, and since 1955 gigantic stations have been constructed in south-central and eastern Siberia, at Krasnoyarsk on the Yenisey river and at Bratsk and Ust-Ilimsk on the Angara river.

Nuclear power produces about 10 percent of the region's electricity, although almost all the reactors are the standard slow type, now overtaken by new technology. Most of the stations are in the energy-deficient west from the Kola Peninsula in northwestern Russia to Armenia in the south, and are run on uranium supplies from Krivoi Rog in the Ukraine and Narva in Estonia. Uranium is also found in Kazakhstan, eastern Siberia and the Tien Shan mountains near the Chinese border.

A treasure trove of minerals

At Norilsk in the Arctic Circle, there are huge reserves of platinum, nickel, gold, copper, cobalt and silver. Lead and zinc reserves are also vast in Kazakhstan at Leninogorsk and Ordzhonikidze in the northern Caucasus Mountains. The world's largest deposit of iron ore is in Russia at Kursk Oblast in the central plateau, and this together with six other large reserves, including those at Krivoi Rog and Karelia-Kola, yield over 236 million tonnes a year.

Nonmetallic minerals include apatite concentrate (used in fertilizers) mined from reserves in the Kola peninsula bordering Finland. Asbestos and potash are mined in large quantities in the central Urals and eastern Siberia. Eastern Siberia is also the world's second most important producer of diamonds, after the Democratic Republic of Congo.

Map of principal resources and industrial zones
(*above*) Northern Eurasia has plentiful resources, but geography and climate make them difficult to exploit.

Energy production and consumption (*far right*) Russia is the world's second largest producer of energy and the third largest consumer. It is, though, one of the least energy efficient in terms of GDP per kg of energy and needs to invest heavily in updating its power stations.

Resources and industry

- ◆ industrial center
- ○ port
- ● other town
- — major road
- — major railroad

mineral resources and fossil fuels
- • iron and other ferroalloy metal ores
- ● other metal ores
- ■ nonmetallic minerals

coal	natural gas
iron ore	oil
lignite (brown coal)	potash

Energy balance
(mill. tonnes coal equivalent)

Sources of energy output
- coal
- gas
- oil
- other

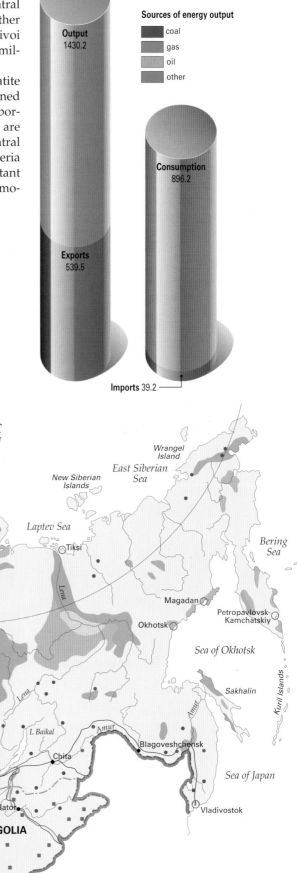

Output 1430.2

Exports 539.5

Consumption 896.2

Imports 39.2

ACHIEVING INDUSTRIAL SELF-SUFFICIENCY

It took the communist revolution of 1917 to quicken the pace of industrial growth in the region, which prior to this had a predominantly rural society. Once the controlling CPSU had decided that the state must be self-sufficient in manufactured goods, all natural resources were declared to be state-owned and then systematically exploited to meet the aims of the new political creed.

The overriding economic aim of early communist leaders under Vladimir Ilich Lenin (1870–1924) was to achieve industrial self-sufficiency. Without it they perceived that they would never maintain independence from the capitalist West. Under Joseph Stalin (1879–1953), large-scale heavy industries such as steel, metal processing and machinery manufacture took priority over the production of consumer goods such as clothing or household appliances. In fact, in the period from 1920 to 1980, engineering, industrial construction and heavy industry grew nine times faster than the consumer industries. By any standards the transformation of the country was extraordinary: during the same 60-year period over 40,000 new mines, power stations and manufacturing plants were opened.

Spreading the message

Another influential political aim was to spread the benefits of communism across the whole region, by giving each of the many distinctive areas its own industrial heartland and urban center. It was a herculean task and was achieved largely through military force and strong political conviction. Industrial processing plants were deliberately situated near raw materials, no matter how inhospitable the climate. Railroads and roads were built to open access to resource-rich areas such as Siberia, and to make it feasible to develop manufacturing complexes close to where resources were mined and processed, and distribute the goods from there. The country's largest tractor factory, for example, was constructed at Chelyabinsk in the Urals, and flourished as an industrial center because of its proximity to the Trans-Siberian Railroad.

After World War II the Soviet Union embarked on a period of building up its defense industries: weapons, tanks and

Developing the outlying regions Sumgait in Azerbaijan, north of Baku, had no tradition of steelmaking until Soviet economists decided to locate the industry there. Creating industrial centers from scratch was a hallmark of central industrial planning.

aircraft. At the same it developed a policy extending its political influence and the Soviet model of industrialization became widespread. Latvia, Lithuania, Estonia and Moldova were annexed in 1945, while Mongolia, eastern Europe and parts of east Asia and Central America began to develop centrally controlled heavy industry under Soviet guidance. China was also heavily influenced until the mid 1950s. During its expansionist period the Soviet Union initiated a program of space research. All these ventures required even greater exploitation of the region's natural resources and energy.

The central importance of Siberia

Before 1913 industry was concentrated in four main areas, three of them – Moscow, St. Petersburg and the fertile triangle of the Russian Republic – were in the west of the country. The other main industrial area was around the Baku oilfields of Azerbaijan. The rapid industrialization that began with the implementation of the first Five-year Plan (1928–32) changed this pattern in two significant ways. First, Siberia was developed enormously because of its substantial natural resources, better communications, transportation networks, and an increased labor force. In addition, new industrial clusters or "nodes" developed in far-flung regions where energy, forest resources and metals

THE SPACE PROGRAM

Until the mid 1980s the Soviet space program was the flagship of technological and scientific prowess in the region. This meant that the program benefited from the best scientists and resources that the state could provide, until economic accountability became an issue in this and other Soviet research programs. Although initial research started in the 1920s, real progress began after World War II when the Soviet Union acquired German expertise in rocket propulsion. However, it was the work of the brilliant rocket engineer, Sergey Korolyov, that gave the space program the technological capability to lead the world.

In October 1957 the launch of Sputnik 1 was a pioneering achievement, as was the first manned flight with Yury Gagarin in April 1961. The Soviet moon program culminated with Luna 17, which put a space vehicle, Lunakhod, on to the moon's surface in November 1970. Venera probes were sent to Mars and Venus in the 1980s, but thereafter scientists decided to concentrate on launching large Salyut space stations into orbit. Serviced by Soyuz spacecraft, these manned stations enable scientists to carry out research over longer periods, monitor the weather, supply communications facilities, and collect data for geological prospecting.

Salyut was superseded by Mir space stations in the late 1980s. In 1995 the US space shuttle Atlantis docked with Mir and exchanged crew members, a startling indicator of changed relationships between the former Cold War protagonists.

Generating business Hydroelectricity projects boost the construction industry as well as providing energy for additional growth. The Ust-Ilimsk dam, shown here under construction, is one of four large dams on the river Angara in southeastern Siberia.

attracted massive political and financial commitment until the twelfth Five-year Plan (1986-90), which put many of the projects that were designed for these regions into abeyance.

Trends in manufacturing have changed noticeably. A good example of this can be seen in the industrial area around Moscow, which before 1940 had a concentration of metal processing, machine manufacturing and vehicle industries. Since 1950, however, the area has specialized in skill-related industries such as research-intensive electronics, aerospace and nuclear technology, though in several

cases these have been situated in new satellite towns at a distance from Moscow.

During the 1970s the Soviet Union accepted some technical help from the West and by 1987, under the leadership of Mikhail Gorbachev, joint ventures with Western firms were officially sanctioned. Between 1987 and the dissolution of the Soviet Union in 1991 over a thousand such enterprises were officially registered and some three hundred began operating.

Other longterm projects initiated by the Soviet Union had a considerable effect on the distribution of industry in the region. A case in point was the Baikal-Amur Magistral (BAM) railroad project, which was opened in 1985 after 20 years of construction work. Running to the north of the existing Trans-Siberian railroad, it is a principal route for exporting freight from

eastern ports. This project consolidated the importance of Komsomolskna-Amure, which became one of the major areas in the Far East for the production of steel, oil-refining and pulp and paper mills. After the collapse of the Soviet Union in 1991, the government of the Russian Federation introduced radical reforms intended to establish privately owned industrial and commercial ventures, to privatize state-owned industries and to encourage foreign investment.

The transformation was slow, accompanied by a massive decline in production and an increase in unemployment that caused great hardship to many Russian citizens. In the late 1990s a financial crisis added to the problems faced by Russian industry and recovery to pre-1991 production levels looked a distant prospect.

PEOPLE AS INDUSTRIAL FODDER

The states of the former Soviet Union together with Mongolia house a huge range of nationalities, and after 70 years of communism newly emergent peoples are struggling for the right to express their regional identities. Under the leadership of Lenin and Stalin, people were often moved against their will from a local agricultural way of life to another area where they formed part of the work-force establishing an industrial base for the new communist state. By forcing industrial progress on the people Stalin increased production dramatically, open-ing 6,000 new enterprises during the first 10 years of his regime; but the human cost is not recorded. During the 1930s, for example, development of a large iron and steel complex transformed a Russian steppe village into the city of a Magnito-gorsk, making it a major producer of military equipment. The local population, along with imported labor, was drafted to work in the booming city.

Working for the state
In order to meet industrial goals, the government employed forced labor dur-ing the 1930s and afterward, especially for geographically remote projects such as the White Sea Canal, which cuts through Onega near the Arctic Circle. It is estimated that between four and five million people were forcibly put into labor camps and made to build railroads, canals and mines in the years up to 1939. During World War II when most men were conscripted, women were put to work in industry.

More than 10 million people were evacuated eastward to keep Soviet indus-try running, but destruction of industrial units by the Germans was massive. More than 82,000 enterprises were destroyed, 55 percent of steelmaking capacity and 60 percent of coal output were lost. After the war people were exhorted to work even harder, but cumbersome centrally planned policies were failing to achieve results. In the 1960s Siberia was singled out as a priority area because of its abundant energy resources, and there were govern-ment incentives for people to live and work there.

The continued dominance of manufac-turing in the machinery and arms sectors

led to chronic shortages of consumer goods, and discontent among the people flared up in demonstrations that were repeatedly quashed by the Red Army. Although Nikita Khrushchev (1894–1971), leader of the Soviet Union 1955–64, ex-panded production of consumer goods to some extent, his priorities were to de-velop the oil and gas-based industries, plastics and fertilizer manufacture. His attempts to integrate industry and agri-culture had only limited success, leaving many rural area with plentiful labor but few industries. Although government-run scientific studies called for full use of surplus labor resources in the 1960s and 1970s, local Party bosses lost sight of this aim in an effort to compete with each other in diverting industry to their areas. This led to "tugs of war" between those people who supported regional special-ization and those who were in favor of regional self-sufficiency.

TRADITIONAL CARPETMAKING

Northern Eurasia is one of the leading producers of handwoven rugs and carpets. There is a great tradition of craftsmanship that dates back to at least the 3rd or 4th century BC, a fact attested to by the discovery of what is thought to be the world's oldest known woolen carpet unearthed in a frozen Scythian tomb in southern Siberia.

The best known and most important regional carpets are the oriental style rugs woven in the eastern Caucasus Mountains and central Asiatic districts. Historically these rugs have always possessed a distinctive character – never as fine or densely knotted as Persian or Turkish carpets – but rather more coarsely woven with strong colors and innovative designs. Even now, many of the carpets produced in the region are woven on hand-held looms, usually by women and children who work either from home or in cooperative workshops and studios.

No one area has an absolutely pure regional pattern; the finished product is usually the result of a composite influence of different regional designs and colors. For instance, carpets woven in Armenia and Azerbaijan often display Persian, Anatolian or even Chinese influences, while the well-known Dagestan rugs display designs from Baku, Chichi and Kuba.

In central Asian districts carpets renowned for their durability and unique patterns are woven by various

The new silk road Tajikistan and Uzbekistan are two of the world's largest producers of cotton and silk. After 1990, a traditional Islamic weaving culture producing high-quality carpets and rugs reemerged in these independent states.

nomadic tribes, such as the Ersari, Salor, Tekke and Yomut. These rugs, sold in centers such as Ashkabad in Turkmenistan, Samarkand in Uzbekistan and Khodzhent in Tajikistan, owe much to the Islamic culture of the old Silk Road, which in medieval times was a trade route for silk from China.

Traditional carpetmaking was preserved as a craft by the communist state to earn hard currency from exports and to provide jobs and cultural continuity among ethnic minorities. The combination of Islamic revival and political independence in the southern republics is likely to stimulate even further development of the industry.

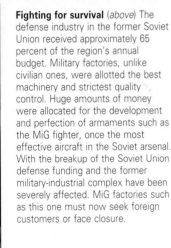

Fighting for survival (*above*) The defense industry in the former Soviet Union received approximately 65 percent of the region's annual budget. Military factories, unlike civilian ones, were allotted the best machinery and strictest quality control. Huge amounts of money were allocated for the development and perfection of armaments such as the MiG fighter, once the most effective aircraft in the Soviet arsenal. With the breakup of the Soviet Union defense funding and the former military-industrial complex have been severely affected. MiG factories such as this one must now seek foreign customers or face closure.

Trucks made by women (*left*) Gender barriers in most occupations were eliminated in the region, due more to labor shortages than ideology. Under Soviet rule, state-subsidized childcare provided by employers made it the norm for mothers of small children to continue working.

The more liberal policies of Mikhail Gorbachev, who took up leadership of the Soviet Union in 1985, sowed the seeds of reform and change. He tried to move labor from heavy industry and defense manufacturing to the construction of better social services and improved training and education. However, nationalist uprisings led to unresolved strife over the control and use of natural resources, and combined with longstanding discontent to cause political upheaval. With the breakup of the Soviet Union, the question of which national groups have the right to exploit the vast mineral, manufacturing and labor resources of the region is even more crucial and potentially dangerous.

Women in the workforce

Under the Soviet regime women formed an essential part of the labor force, even in heavy manual trades such as building and construction work. The rapid entry of

women into the urban industrial sector was accompanied by welfare programs superior to those in the West. Workplace crèches were provided, and even at the end of the 1980s were still more plentiful than in most Western countries. Maternity leave with the option of returning to a secure job was introduced as early as 1918, and in the factories women were allowed to take half-hour breaks every three hours to feed their babies.

Such measures were aimed at maintaining maximum productivity from a large sector of the potential workforce. In the late 20th century, women were predominantly employed in light industry and education. There were also more women economists, engineers and doctors than in the West. In the 1990s, reductions in welfare spending combined with the privatization of many industries were having a detrimental effect on welfare provisions for women.

The industrial Volga valley

The Volga river in Russia is arguably the most important waterway in the region, and has become the focal point of a giant industrial development. In total, the Volga measures 3,500 km (2,200 mi) and flows through an area containing some 40 million people. The industries along its banks produce 18 percent of the region's total industrial output – as much as the entire Ukraine. Two major advantages have contributed to this prominence: the river is a cheap and convenient way to transport heavy goods between the north and south, connecting most of the industrial centers in the area, and the force of the river can be harnessed to generate hydroelectric power.

When Soviet-planned industrialization began in 1928 experts considered the Volga valley to be lacking in sufficient energy resources. At first it looked as if this prediction was accurate. Nonrenewable reserves of oil and gas were rapidly depleted between 1937 and 1975, but hydroelectric power has increased the energy potential of the area far beyond any early expectations. The river has been transformed into a string of lakes with eight HEP stations providing 10,000 megawatts of generating capacity.

High-energy manufacturing

Despite these initial doubts, rapid manufacturing growth began in the Volga in 1933 and has been sustained ever since. The area has acted like a magnet, drawing investment and labor toward central Russia. During World War II as the Nazis overran the Ukraine, most of the major machinery, vehicle, armaments, aircraft and chemical factories were moved from the Ukraine to the Volga region for strategic reasons. As the industries expanded, new satellite towns were built around Nizhniy Novgorod, Samara, Yaroslavl and Volgograd (formerly Stalingrad). After 1945 oil refineries were set up to process local oil, and petrochemical plants were established nearby, making artificial fibers, tires, fertilizers and plastics.

Intensive riverside development The Volga valley is the industrial engine of Northern Eurasia. Major manufacturing centers are linked by the deep and navigable Volga river, but transportation to the east and west is relatively undeveloped.

Major industrial centers
- engineering
- iron and steel
- oil refining
- textiles
- hydroelectric power station

With the development of hydroelectric power came energy-intensive industries including smelting and electroplating. The largescale migration of families from the countryside created a growing male workforce for local heavy industry, and additional pools of female labor for work in food processing, textiles, clothing and shoe manufacture, the fur trade and a range of other light industries.

In addition, the Volga's geographic location between Europe and the western republics on one side (the potential market), and central Asia, the Urals and Siberia on the other (rich in energy and

River of steel This iron and steel mill is typical of the linked concentration of heavy industry in the region. Supplies and raw materials arrive by water from plants nearby and steel bars are shipped along the river for further processing.

resources) has encouraged the development of engineering assembly plants, especially of transportation equipment and, since 1965, motor vehicles.

East-west transportation problems
Although the Volga region has much in its favor as a flourishing industrial area, it is hampered by an inadequate transportation system with which to distribute its products to markets. The Soviet developers had overlooked this, regarding transportation, like all service industries, as nonproductive and low priority. As a result of neglecting distribution services, a good deal of labor, food, materials and energy have been squandered because rolling stock or haulage systems are inadequate, slow, unreliable and out of date. The situation is not helped by the huge distances between major cities in the region, or by the hostile physical environment of mountains, permafrost, marshes and deserts.

Although the mighty Volga river carries two-thirds of inland waterway traffic and is a significant link for boats from the connector canals between the Black and Caspian Seas in the south and the Baltic, White and Barents Seas in the north, it has always been a barrier to the east-west flow of commodities. The river is crossed by seven railroads and many pipelines, but few serve the river traffic and vice versa. Most Volga industry uses rail, pipeline or powerline transportation and though there is some major growth in the production of motor vehicles in the area, the condition of surrounding roads is poor and their network thin.

ECONOMY

FORCED PROGRESS · THE EMPIRE STRIKES BACK · THE NORTH-SOUTH DIVIDE

The economies of the republics of Northern Eurasia have long been closely knit together. As Russia came to dominate the region after 1700, a distinctive economic style became evident among them, with the state playing a vital role, trying to bring about rapid modernization. After the Bolshevik revolution of 1917 the new Soviet economy became increasingly centralized. Policies were isolationist, with little foreign trade except with satellite allies. Rapid growth was achieved at first and the Soviet Union became an economic superpower. However, this achievement was not sustainable and by 1991 socialist planning collapsed, as did the Soviet Union itself. In the 15 newly independent republics there is an emphasis on free market policies and trade with new foreign partners. An innovative and unpredictable era has begun.

FORCED PROGRESS

As it began to edge on to the international scene at the beginning of the modern era, Russia – though rich in natural resources and an important exporter of flax, hemp, fur and timber – was economically underdeveloped compared with its western European neighbors. Its lack of entrepreneurial energy and innovation threatened the empire's military effectiveness in its many wars. Peter the Great (1682–1725) was the first ruler to try to force development by pursuing policies of rapid modernization from above. British and Dutch experts were brought to Russia and the tzarist government established new manufacturing plants, notably ironworks, turning the region into one of the world's leading iron producers within a single generation.

Such rapid growth could not be sustained for long. By the mid 19th century the Russian empire, which had expanded southward and eastward into central Asia was still economically underdeveloped. Only 7 percent of the population were employed in the urban-industrial sector, compared with 50 percent in England during the same period. Again the government took the lead in investment and development, creating a huge rail network that culminated in the Trans-Siberian railroad (constructed from 1891

Home-grown designer capitalism (*below*) comes to Moscow with a fashion show that draws on Russia's Cossack and Communist heritage. A sign of the changing times, such a show cuts across the former emphasis on drab, inexpensive, utilitarian clothes.

COUNTRIES IN THE REGION

Armenia, Azerbaijan, Belarus, Estonia, Georgia, Kazakhstan, Kyrgyzstan, Latvia, Lithuania, Moldova, Mongolia, Russia, Tajikistan, Turkmenistan, Ukraine, Uzbekistan

ECONOMIC INDICATORS: 1996–97

	*LMIE Latvia	*LMIE Russia	*LIE Uzbekistan
GDP (US$ billions, 1997)	5.4	449.8	23.8
Aid as % of GNP (1996)	1.6	0.3	0.4
Central govt. expend. as % of GDP (1995)	32.2%	24.0%	n/a
GDP per capita (US$)	2,007	2,974	332
Manufacturing as % of GDP	n/a	62%	n/a
Labor force employed in agriculture (%)	16%	15%	44%
Labour force employed in industry (%)	41%	34%	20%
Merchandise exports (US$ million)	1.4	81.4	2.6
Merchandise imports (US$ million)	2.3	43.3	4.7

WELFARE INDICATORS

Infant mortality rate (per 1,000 live births)			
1965	17.9	23.0	31.0
1995–2000	18	18	44
Population per physician (1995)	293	235	284
Student life expectancy	12.1	n/a	n/a
Adult literacy (m/f)	99.8%	99.7/99.4%	93.5/85%

* LMIE (Lower Middle Income Economy) between $761 and $3,030 in 1997. LIE (Low Income Ecnomy) less than $760.

ARCTIC OCEAN

GDP per capita (US$)
- 2 000–4 999
- 500–1 999
- below 500

Profile of inflation (*above*) The Soviet Union's central planners kept inflation low and often manipulated figures to bolster the region's image. After the collapse of the regime, Russia's inflation peaked at more than 2000 percent, averaging 207 percent from 1991–98.

to 1915) connecting the industrial heartland west of the Urals with the largely untapped resources of Siberia in the east. Improved transportation and communications gave a fresh boost to the economy. Although the new infrastructure struggled with bad weather and the sheer distances involved, by the outbreak of World War I the Russian empire was an emerging industrial power.

The Communist state
The pressures of rapid economic change played an important part in provoking the Bolshevik revolution of 1917. The

leaders of the revolution aimed to create a classless and socially just society, and the role of the state in economic development became greater than ever before. Under the leadership of the first head of the Soviet Union, Vladimir Ilich Lenin (1870–1924), all banks and property were nationalized, though private enterprise was allowed to remain in the countryside, where peasants sold their own produce at market prices. Under Joseph Stalin (1879–1953) this practice was abandoned and the state established collective farms.

From 1928 the economy was directed through a series of Five Year Plans. State terror was widely used to force the cooperation of the workforce, with millions uprooted from the countryside and moved into large industrial complexes. State ownership was extended throughout the region, even to Outer Mongolia, which had become part of the Soviet orbit. Driven by the need to increase the country's military strength, the emphasis was on heavy industry – particularly manufacturing arms and weapons. Housing, agriculture and public services suffered neglect. Yet these policies transformed the country, enabling it to play a vital role in the defeat of Nazi Germany.

Map of GDP (*above*) The standard measure of Gross Domestic Product has now replaced the so-called "Net Material Product" (NMP), which was used to gauge economic performance in the former Soviet Union. NMP was defined as the total annual value of goods and productive services generated (excluding administration, defense and personal services). Isolated from the world economy from 1917 to 1991, the region has none of the world's top 500 banks or companies.

The post-Stalinist economy
Significant changes occurred after Stalin's death in 1953. Greater priority was given to housing and rural development and state terror was gradually abandoned as a tool of economic policy. At first these changes were welcomed by Soviet citizens, since they brought with them a higher standard of living. In the long term, however, they exposed weaknesses in the economic system. With state terror removed, the people lacked an incentive to work. Innovation was stifled and the Soviet Union failed to keep pace with developments in the capitalist world, particularly in high technology. The transportation system was increasingly inefficient, while the economy suffered under the military budget maintaining the Soviet Union as a superpower. By the early 1980s the economy was threatening to stall. A major crisis was looming.

THE EMPIRE STRIKES BACK

As discontent and criticism of the Soviet regime reached a peak in the late 1980s, the weaknesses of the state-run economy became common knowledge both at home and abroad. The Soviet economic system resembled a giant corporation with an overbureaucratized center. In Moscow the state planning agency (Gosplan) and the economic ministries controlled the economy of the entire Soviet Union. Their Five Year Plans made decisions for factories thousands of miles away, specifying which items should be manufactured and the precise quantities to be produced. Little attention was paid to how much public demand existed, nor to the actual factory costs of production. Consequently goods were often manufactured at a loss, while the absence of any kind of quality control encouraged waste. The highly centralized system also stifled local initiatives to improve the product or the system as the crucial decisions were made by officials too distant to comprehend local issues.

The economy functioned best when organizing prestigious priority projects in which the leadership showed personal interest, such as weapons production or channeling investment to exploit the oil and gas resources of western Siberia. Lower-profile manufacturing and production of consumer goods including clothes, furniture and foodstuffs were dogged by poor workmanship and inefficient distribution, causing shortages. It was clear that the economic system was in urgent need of reform, yet change from within proved difficult to achieve, especially as the ideology of the system allowed little in the way of objective self-assessment or admission of failure. During the late

1950s Soviet Premier, Nikita Khrushchev (1949–1971), tried to tackle the overcentralized planning system but his efforts came to nothing. Only a generation later, when total national production had actually begun to shrink, was a thorough and radical effort made to regenerate the economic system.

Attempted restructuring

Mikhail Gorbachev, who assumed power in March 1985, initiated a program of perestroika or economic restructuring. One strand of this policy was to modernize factory equipment, much of which had not been updated since the 1930s. At the same time, smallscale private enter-

prise was encouraged in the form of cooperatives, especially in the service sector which had never functioned well under the old Soviet system. An effort was also made to decentralize, with local factory managers given greater control over production. Industrial plants were encouraged to be financially independent, while the more efficient among them were to be rewarded with greater government investment and higher pay for workers. This last measure introduced a kind of state-controlled profit motive.

Income distribution in the Eurasian republics
Incomes are higher in the Baltics – Latvia, Estonia and Lithuania – which broke away early from the Soviet Union. The southern republics are very poor.

Exports

9%
8%
6%
20.5%
56.5%

Trading partners
- CIS
- Ukraine
- Germany
- United States
- other countries

39.1%
6%
11%
14%
29.9%

Imports

Figures for the following countries are not available: Armenia, Azerbaijan, Georgia, Uzbekistan

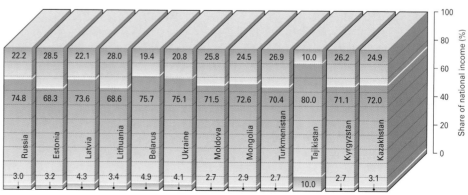

	Russia	Estonia	Latvia	Lithuania	Belarus	Ukraine	Moldova	Mongolia	Turkmenistan	Tajikistan	Kyrgyzstan	Kazakhstan
	22.2	28.5	22.1	28.0	19.4	20.8	25.8	24.5	26.9	10.0	26.2	24.9
	74.8	68.3	73.6	68.6	75.7	75.1	71.5	72.6	70.4	80.0	71.1	72.0
	3.0	3.2	4.3	3.4	4.9	4.1	2.7	2.9	2.7	10.0	2.7	3.1

Share of national income (%): 100, 80, 60, 40, 20, 0

OPENING THE DOOR TO TRADE

Nearly 70 years of isolation from the capitalist world economy ended in 1987 when Mikhail Gorbachev opened the Soviet Union to trade with Western companies. He hoped that numerous joint-venture schemes would develop between foreign and local enterprises. Western companies would be invited to contribute vital management skills and high technology in exchange for access to the Soviet Union's wealth of resources and to its market of 280 million people. In spite of these high hopes, joint ventures were slow to develop.

After the collapse of the Soviet Union the independent republics opened the door to Western trade even wider. Restrictions on where Western companies could operate were lifted and there were moves toward creating free-enterprise zones. Russia's Pacific coast, for example, was designated as an area open to Japanese investment.

These initiatives encouraged foreign investment, but enthusiasm was dampened by the world recession of the early 1990s and by Russia's financial crisis in 1998 when the rouble was devalued and Russia defaulted on its international debt. Recently, closer ties have been made within the region by the formation of economic zones such as that between Kazakhstan, Kyrgyzstan and Uzbekistan and between members of the Black Sea Economic Cooperation Group (BSEC) or the Council of Baltic Sea States. Trade agreements have also been made with the European Union.

Turning culture into cash (*left*) Hand-painted trinkets are for sale at an artist's shop in Astana, capital of Kazakhstan. Small enterprises such as this are already flourishing, and may serve a future tourist trade.

The Trans-Siberian express market (*below*) Passengers traveling from Mongolia sell goods from the train to local people along the journey to Moscow. Some foods and other products are available in China, across the southern border, but not in Russia.

tige led to obstruction and sabotage within the administration, and this combined with corruption to impede change. Production fell and the transport system deteriorated, adding to widespread shortages of food and essential goods. As the situation worsened, the government acknowledged that the budget deficit had increased from 15 to 200 billion roubles between 1985 and 1991.

An uncertain future

As the dissolution of the USSR took effect in late 1991, President Yeltsin announced an economic program aimed at creating a healthy mixed economy with a powerful private sector. A state program of privatization was inaugurated, but the initial effect was chaos: industrial and agricultural production fell; unemployment, prices and inflation rose, food supply was affected, and both real incomes and the value of the ruble plummeted. IMF loans and even food aid from the US in 1992 and 1993 went some way towards stabilizing the economy, but progress was slow and hindered by entrenched political and administrative bureaucracies. As Russia suffered in the global economic crisis of 1997–99, national income and foreign investments fell sharply. The ruble lost two thirds of its value in 1998 while inflation rose to 30 percent and at least 30 percent of Russians were estimated to have an income below the poverty line. In 1999, a rise in international oil prices and a small growth in GDP gave some hope for the future, but with inflation rising to over 80 percent it was clearly going to be some time before conditions improved.

Lastly, the Soviet Union was opened up to the world economy. Until the mid 1980s more than half of Soviet trade had been with the socialist states and military allies that made up the COMECON bloc. From 1987 most Soviet enterprises were prompted to enter into joint ventures with capitalist investors. These changes, it was hoped, would bring the region into the modern market economy, with enhanced efficiency, improved technology and greater commitment from the workforce.

Dissent and fragmentation

Perestroika failed in its attempt at economic regeneration because the Soviet Union's bureaucracy hampered the independence of the cooperatives and the managers of state factories. A burgeoning black market was the main area of economic growth and centralized economic decision-making remained largely unaltered. As perestroika continued, the attempted reforms began to have a destructive effect on the economy. Resentment at the loss of power and pres-

THE NORTH-SOUTH DIVIDE

One of the main aims of the founders of the Soviet Union was to create an equal and just society and to ensure the well-being of the population. During three generations of Soviet state rule, average living standards certainly improved, helped by the growing urbanization and industrialization of the country. At the same time, free healthcare and education became available to all Soviet citizens, irrespective of social or ethnic background. Improved healthcare caused a leap in average life expectancy from 32 years before the 1917 revolution to as much as 70 years in the 1970s.

By the late 1980s illiteracy had largely been eradicated and the region could boast greater numbers of students entering higher education than probably any

other region in the world. Unemployment was virtually nonexistent, as the state placed a premium on the right of every worker to have a job. At the same time the centrally controlled wage structure ensured that income differentials between professions remained much smaller than in market-economy states.

Spreading power around

Soviet leaders also strove to create social equality between different regions of the country, and between the cities and the countryside. The economic planners in Moscow were particularly concerned with the five mainly Muslim republics of central Asia (Turkmenistan, Uzbekistan, Tajikistan, Kyrgyzstan and Kazakhstan), which lagged behind the European part of the country in terms of development. Largescale investment was made in these republics in an effort to give them a

Learning to dance (*above*) Ballet was part of the curriculum for kindergarten children such as these in Khabarovsk, eastern Russia in 1988. Generous state-funding for the arts, assured under the Communist system, is now threatened.

manufacturing base; they were also allowed to retain most of their contributions to the federal budget. Local people were promoted to key positions within their republics so as to create upward mobility into the local Communist Party, government administration and the professions.

These measures had some limited success, but the north-south economic divide proved an enduring one. Central Asians did begin to rise through their republics' hierarchies – but Russians continued to hold numerous key posts. At the same time poverty remained more common in central Asia than in European republics. In 1991, on the eve of the collapse of the Soviet Union, it was estimated that 11 percent of the country's total population lived below the poverty line while in the five central Asian republics the proportion was 40 percent. Despite the efforts of the country's rulers huge economic disparities also existed between the towns and the countryside. In central Asia, as throughout the Soviet Union, rural areas remained significantly poorer than the cities.

Disadvantaged farmers

One reason for the enduring north–south divide was the government's policy of paying more to industrial workers than to agricultural laborers, reflecting an ideological preference for the work of the proletariat. In spite of the investment program designed to create an industrial base, the economy of central Asia remained overwhelmingly agricultural. Consequently its population enjoyed none of the favorable treatment which, in some northern industrial complexes, extended to providing workers with public services ranging from housing to kindergartens. The five central Asian republics also suffered from high birthrates, which meant a greater proportion of their populations were too young to contribute to the economy. In 1989 the average birth rate in the whole Soviet Union was 10 births per thousand, while in central Asia the proportion varied from 23 per thousand in Kazakhstan to as many as 38.7 per thousand in Tajikistan.

Nor was it possible for central Asians to migrate to wealthier areas, which would happen in Western economies. The Soviet state's commitment to full employment tended to keep them within their republics. Indeed, for some decades central Asia was a recipient of labor, as Russians and other European nationalities were sent south to provide managerial and administrative

THE BLACK ECONOMY

The Soviet system always included a mainly private "second economy" that existed alongside the state sector and provided the products that it was largely unable to deliver. Some aspects of this parallel economy, such as private agriculture, were only tolerated by the regime, while others, ranging from car repairs to dentistry, were accepted as forming an integral part of the system. In all, the "second economy" contributed a staggering 10 percent of total national production throughout the Soviet era.

Since the collapse of the Soviet Union in 1991 the "second economy" has expanded rapidly, until it is well on the way to displacing the first economy. At the same time, however, illegal black market enterprises have also flourished. These range from trade in sought-after foreign goods (jeans, video-recorders) to organized crime, including prostitution, drug-trading and selling goods pilfered from state factories. The "Mafia type" black-market sector was estimated to be worth as much as 500 billion rubles in the early 1990s, and to have spawned no fewer than 150,000 ruble millionaires. It quickly became a major problem for the region's post-Soviet leaders. The challenge in all the republics is to find a way of replacing the discredited planned economy with the advantages of a market system, while avoiding the worst excesses of capitalism.

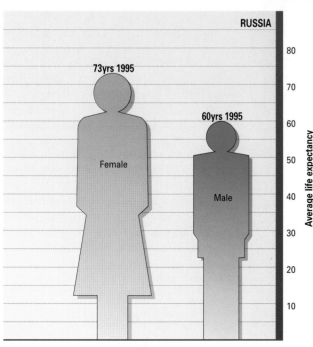

RUSSIA

73yrs 1995

Female

60yrs 1995

Male

Average life expectancy

Black market in a suitcase (*above*) A speculator sells vodka illegally to a passerby at a figure far above the market price. Huge profits can be made by street vendors as they try to meet the demand for alcohol and other goods in short supply. Foreign-made clothes, shoes, electronics, and drugs are all commonly sold from suitcases.

Life expectancy (*left*) At the end of the 1980s, life expectancy in the former Soviet Union was slightly lower than the average for Europe and North America, with women living almost a decade longer than men. In the 1990s, the collapse of the Soviet Union resulted in economic struggle for almost all the countries involved, leading to reductions in health care and subsequent worsening in life expectancy. In Russia, life expectancy for men reduced from 64 to 60.6 years. In common with most developed countries, Russia has steadily increasing numbers of elderly people.

skills. Only from the mid 1970s did this migration become reversed. Between 1976 and 1988 as many as 1.6 million Russians and other Europeans left central Asia, with the exodus considerably increasing after the five republics became independent in 1991.

The collapse of the Soviet Union was destabilizing for the central Asian states, who were forced to restructure their economies without Moscow's generous investment in employment and education. Azerbaijan, Turkmenistan and Kazakhstan looked to have the most promising futures in the 21st century following the discovery of potentially huge reserves of natural gas and oil in each country. However, the future stability would depend on the successful transformation to market-based economies and a peaceful resolution to the tangled ethnic and political rivalries that divide this troubled area.

Economic sovereignty and its limits

The rejection of communism that followed the failed coup of August 1991 dissolved the glue holding together the last of Europe's multiethnic empires. The leaders of the 15 independent republics that emerged from the ruins of the Soviet Union abruptly found themselves in control of their countries' economies. A wealth of new possibilities blossomed, followed closely by a host of new problems.

Governments all across the region began exploring how to use their new economic sovereignty. Setting up new financial institutions was a priority, including banking and tax systems, national currencies, and border controls that brought the possibility of protectionist tariffs. Each republic sought to find a niche for itself within the global economy, and to foster new trade partnerships across previously closed frontiers. The republics of central Asia began developing ties with Turkey, China and Iran, while Latvia, Lithuania and Estonia looked toward the Nordic countries and the European Community. All across the region there was a move to the free market, though individual states soon began to follow different paths toward this end.

Unpicking the network

Soviet rule had encouraged specialization in different parts of the region. For example, Uzbekistan became the Soviet Union's main source of cotton, while Azerbijan produced equipment for the oil industry, and Georgia grew citrus fruits. Such a system entailed considerable internal trade and created extensive economic interdependency between republics that would not be easy to escape. This was true even of a large republic such as Ukraine, which had a significant manufacturing base and a population of 52 million. Before 1991, almost 40 percent of Ukraine's total industrial and agricultural production was exported to other republics.

Even where economic change was embarked on with enthusiasm, it was dogged by the existing bureaucracy, subverted by the unscrupulous and sometimes hindered by deliberate obstruction when those in power could see their status and income threatened. For instance, in

The cost of perestroika An old man in Tallinn, Estonia, counts his money carefully before making a purchase. The end of state price controls caused enormous increases in the cost of basic necessities. Old people were particularly badly affected.

1992, Russia implemented a privatization program, part of which involved issuing each Russian citizen with vouchers that could be used to purchase shares in firms that were being privatized. These were frequently sold for cash and accumulated by entrepreneurs. With price controls removed, inflation escalated; unemployment increased, as did food shortages and crime, making the economic reforms deeply unpopular with Russian citizens.

Ukraine's market-centered reforms were dogged by a reluctant Supreme Council and by ex-communist apparatchiks in the administration. In 1998, a large number of factory bosses were detained in a civil defense camp for failing to declare financial interests. The problems presented by lowered production levels, rampant inflation and failing currency were exacerbated by dependence on Russia for oil supplies. By the late 1990s, Ukraine had expanded its trading network, but almost 41 percent of exports and 60 percent of imports were still with CIS countries and Russia remained the largest trading partner.

The Baltic States, in common with the other former Soviet states, found the transition to a market-based economy fraught with difficulties. Estonia, Latvia and Lithuania all suffered severe economic downturns in the early 1990s, but made good progress in initiating free trade agreements between themselves and with the European Union (EU). By the late 1990s Estonia and Latvia were conducting most of their trade with the Nordic countries or countries of the EU. All three were keen to join the EU early in the 2000s.

The future of the three countries of the Caucasus – Georgia, Armenia and Azerbaijan – remains tied up with that of the central Asian states of Turkmenistan, Uzbekistan, Kazakhstan, Tajikistan and Kyrgyzstan, all troubled by civil wars and ethnic strife. Azerbaijan, Kazakhstan and Turkmenistan have the resources to become major energy suppliers, but they are landlocked. Successful export of oil and gas to the West or east to China depends on agreements with neighboring countries and is subject to pressures from major oil consumers who have their own preferred routes for new pipelines.

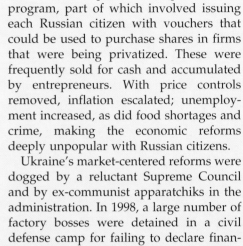

"Lenin is a cheater" (*right*) One of Russia's new homeless underclass makes his opinions known outside a shack not far from the Kremlin. Outspoken criticism of the early Soviet thinkers has become common, but poverty and upheaval makes those trying to manage the transition unpopular as well.

The consumer-goods revolution

All across the former Soviet Union industrial plants that used to make a single product are attempting to transform into market-sensitive businesses to serve the region's new consumers.

A large number of public-sector firms are being turned over to local management teams and these enterprises are expected to run at a profit and to sell their goods in markets which are no longer guaranteed by the state. In the long run this should encourage such factories to diversify their production bases and to improve the quality of the goods that they are trying to sell.

Some engineering plants are already beginning to manufacture components for automobiles, refrigerators, televisions and washing machines. New forms of contract are developing to link such enterprises together and turn them into efficient producers of components for new consumer-goods industries. In the short-term, however, the re-equipping of deregulated public-sector factories is proving very difficult. The new managers of such factories often lack the managerial skills that would be taken for granted in Europe, Japan and the United States and the cost of retooling factories can sometimes be prohibitive. Survival in the new world of the postsocialist economy is by no means guaranteed. The risk of failure is high, and an emerging private sector is offering them stiff competition.

Heating elements for washing machines, part of the new product range at the Tselinogradselmash industrial plant in Akmola, Kazakhstan. The plant was formally a single-product manufacturer of agricultural machinery.

PEOPLES AND CULTURES

A PATTERN OF PEOPLES · CREATING A NEW SOCIETY · LIVING WITH THE SYSTEM

Most of the numerous ethnic groups within the Soviet Union as it existed before 1991 came together through a gradual process of conquest by the Russian people, who expanded southward and eastward from their power base in Moscow between the 15th and the 19th centuries. These disparate peoples were held together by the autocratic power of the tsar. In 1917 this was exchanged for the rule of the Moscow-dominated Communist Party, which attempted to create a unifying Soviet character that would transcend linguistic, religious and cultural differences. National groups were effectively denied self-determination, cultural traditions were forbidden, and opposition suppressed. With the collapse of communism, differences of nationality assumed even greater significance.

COUNTRIES IN THE REGION

Armenia, Azerbaijan, Belarus, Estonia, Georgia, Kazakhstan, Kyrgyzstan, Latvia, Lithuania, Moldova, Mongolia, Russia, Tajikistan, Turkmenistan, Ukraine, Uzbekistan

POPULATION

Over 148 million Russia

10 million to 52 million Belarus, Kazakhstan, Ukraine, Uzbekistan

1 million to 10 million Armenia, Azerbaijan, Estonia, Georgia, Kyrgyzstan, Latvia, Lithuania, Moldova, Mongolia, Tajikistan, Turkmenistan

LANGUAGE

Countries with one official language (Armenian) Armenia, (Azeri) Azerbaijan, (Belarusian) Belarus, (Estonian) Estonia, (Georgian) Georgia, (Kazakh) Kazakhstan, (Kyrgyzian) Kyrgyzstan, (Latvian) Latvia, (Lithuanian) Lithuania, (Moldovan) Moldova, (Khalka Mongolian) Mongolia, (Russian) Russia, (Tajik) Tajikistan, (Turkmen) Turkmenistan, (Ukrainian) Ukraine, (Uzbek) Uzbekistan

Over 200 languages are spoken in the republics of the former Soviet Union. Russian is the second language in all the non-Russian republics. Other languages include Bashkir, Chuvash, German, Mordvian, Polish and Tatar

RELIGION

Countries with one major religion (AAC) Armenia; (G) Georgia; (M) Azerbaijan, Kazakhstan, Kyrgyzstan, Tajikistan, Turkmenistan, Uzbekistan; (EO) Moldova; (B) Mongolia

Countries with more than one major religion (EO,RC) Belarus, Ukraine; (L,RO,P) Estonia, Latvia; (RC,L,RO) Lithuania; (RO,RC,P,M,J,B) Russia

Key: AAC–Armenian Apostolic Church, B–Buddhism, EO–Eastern Orthodox, GO–Georgian Orthodox, J–Jewish, L–Lutheran, M–Muslim, P–other Protestant, RC–Roman Catholic, RO–Russian Orthodox

---

A PATTERN OF PEOPLES

The multi-ethnic character of the peoples of the region is immediately apparent in their enormous variety of languages, cultural traditions and religions. A diversity of traditional lifestyles reflects the broad range of physical environments; small groups within the Arctic Circle still practice a hunting-gathering way of life, and nomadic pastoralists range the grasslands of the central steppes. But since earliest times these Central Asian plains have acted as a corridor for successive migrations of people westward and southward, and the Soviet Union's cultural complexity was also the legacy of its long history of invasion and conquest.

Cultural diversity

The former Soviet government officially recognized the existence of almost 100 different nationalities, distinguished by language and locality, and further divided into hundreds of subgroups. The nationalities ranged in size of population from the 500 Aleuts living on the Pacific fringe of Siberia to 140 million Russians. Of the 93 nationalities listed in the 1979 census, only 23 were attributed with more than 1 million people.

Slavs are the largest linguistic and cultural group of nationalities within the region, both in numbers (they make up over 70 percent of the total population) and in political and economic influence. Originating in the Carpathian Mountains of Eastern Europe, they had moved into the western part of the region by the 7th century AD, and include peoples from the former Soviet Union such as the Russians, Belarusians (White Russians) and Ukrainians. In spite of close linguistic, cultural and historical ties, deep-seated rivalries continue to exist between these nationalities.

The Russians, the largest of the Slavic nationalities, began to move eastward to fill a vacuum left by the collapse of the Mongol empire in the 14th century, into what came to be the Russian Republic, by far the largest of the constituent republics of the Soviet Union. During the early years of communist rule, under the Five-Year Plans inaugurated by Joseph Stalin (1879–1953), millions more Russians (as well as Belarusians and Ukrainians) were transplanted to the new industrial cities east of the Urals. As a result, the Russian population today is found concentrated in cities rather than rural areas throughout the region.

Central Asia is populated by a number of Turkic-speaking peoples, originally from Mongolia, who spread into the area they occupy today during the 6th century. They are the second largest group in the former Soviet Union, though coming some way behind the Slavs. They include Kazakhs, Kirghiz, Turkmen and Uzbeks.

The Caucasus Mountains, between the Black and Caspian Seas, are particularly rich in contrasting cultures and languages. Protected by the remoteness of the mountain terrain they inhabit, these different peoples have resisted cultural assimilation by their neighbors. Some of them, such as the Georgians and the Armenians, have been settled in this area for thousands of years, and their written history can be traced back at least as far as Greek and Roman times. Armenia is the original homeland of a nation that once extended into large areas of Turkey and Iran, and the Armenian Orthodox church claims to be the oldest organized Christian church in the world. Other groups in this area belong to larger nations now divided by international boundaries. The Azerbaijanis are also found in northeastern Iran, and the Kurds in Iran, Iraq, Syria and Turkey. The people of Tajikistan speak Tajik, an Indo-European language that is closely related to Farsi, the language of neighboring Iran and Afghanistan.

Recent migrations

Very few of the the former Soviet republics have homogeneous populations – in most of them Russians have come to form a substantial minority. This was partly the result of a deliberate policy at the end of World War II to weaken the ethnic minorities who were felt to have been disloyal to the Soviet Union during the German occupation – thus Germans in central Russia and Tatars in Crimea, remnants of the Mongol horde that overran Asia from China to the Black Sea in the 13th century, were transplanted to Central Asia. Among those who suffered most were the people of Latvia, Estonia and Lithuania who were only incorporated into the Soviet Union in 1940. Thousands of people were deported to labor camps or dispersed throughout the Soviet Union, and were replaced by Russian emigrants.

ARCTIC OCEAN

Language families

Indo-European

Belarusian

Russian

Ukrainian

other Indo-European

Armenian

Latvian, Lithuanian

Moldovan

Tajik

Altaic (Turkic branch)

Azeri, Turkmen, Yakut

Bashkir, Tatar

Karakalpak, Kyrgyz, Uzbek

Kazakh

other Altaic

Manchu, Mongol

Caucasian

Abkhazo-Adyghian

Georgian

Nakho-Dagestanian

Uralic (Finno-Ugric and Samoyedic branches)

Estonian, Karelian, Komi, Lapp, Nenets

Paleo-Siberian

Chukchi, Gilyak, Koryak

Language diversity (*above*) The numerous languages that are spoken throughout the vast region of the Soviet Union fall into several families, the largest of which are the Slavic and the Turkic.

Strong traditions (*right*) Two elderly Muslim inhabitants of Bukhara in traditional costume. Bukhara was, with neighboring Samarkand, once a leading intellectual and cultural center of the Islamic world.

CREATING A NEW SOCIETY

From 1917 to 1990 the Communist Party was the Soviet Union's sole political party. According to communist ideology, individuals left on their own cannot be trusted to act in the best interests of society. To be most productive, they need to be organized and controlled. The goal of the Party was to create a new Soviet citizen who favored the collective over the individual good, and worked in the interest of the state. Members of the party (among whom Russians were in the vast majority) were not supposed just to provide leadership, but were expected to embody Party standards of morality and behavior, setting an example to their fellow citizens.

Creating a Soviet society was thought to necessitate making the non-Russian nationalities, particularly those of Central Asia, catch up with the developed areas of western and central Russia by ensuring they become secularized, urbanized and Russified. Nomads were settled, peasants were collectivized and people were moved into the cities. Each nationality was to become part of this new Soviet culture, discarding customs that did not fit the Soviet way of life. To this end, literature, theater and the arts were rigidly controlled and national traditions and motifs eliminated.

A policy of Russianization

For the Party authorities, advancement of the nationalities often meant cultural assimilation by the dominant group. Russian, the language of the dominant Slavic group, was the lingua franca and became the language of higher education and research. Although many nationalities developed a written language for the first time only under Soviet rule, and literacy levels rose (before 1917 only one in 500 Kirghiz could read or write), the non-Russian languages were reformed by introducing Russian words. In Uzbekistan, for example, the number of Russian words used in newspapers rose from 2 to 15 percent between 1923 and 1940. The Cyrillic alphabet of the Slavs replaced Latin and Arabic script in most regions. However, Georgia and Armenia were able to retain their distinctive alphabets, and Latin script is still used in the Baltic republics and, since 1990, in Moldova in the southwest.

Many smaller minorities were completely Russianized by these policies, and are separate nationalities in name only. They use the Russian language and have adopted Russian traditions. For many non-Russians, the only means of personal advancement was to join the Communist Party and conform to Russian cultural standards.

Russians and other Slavs were encouraged to migrate to the non-Russian republics. Today over one-third of the people of Latvia are Russian. Only one half are Latvians. In Kazakhstan, Russians account for two-fifths of the population, which also contains substantial numbers of Germans and Ukrainians. Kazakhs comprise less than 40 percent.

The religious dimension

Before 1917, in the tsarist empire, church and state were closely intertwined. In the Soviet state, religion was considered reactionary, and was actively discouraged. Religious ceremonies for marriages and funerals were replaced by new Soviet rituals. Religious holidays were replaced by secular ones. Religious groups were persecuted and driven underground. As attitudes changed with *glasnost*, the state came to permit recognized religions to function, but determined what church

buildings they could occupy and how many priests they could maintain.

There are today at least 40 million Russian Orthodox faithful. They hold the beliefs and rituals of the eastern (Orthodox) branch of Christianity, which became the accepted faith of the Russian Slavs in the 10th century. Moldovans, Armenians and Georgians are also Orthodox Christians. Like the Russians, each of these peoples has its own self-governing national church, and jealously guards its distinct ceremonies.

Most Latvians and Estonians are Protestant Christians, reflecting past links with their Scandinavian neighbors. Lithuania and the western Ukraine, both incorporated within neighboring Poland for a long period of their history, share that country's predominantly Roman Catholic faith. In both Lithuania and Latvia the expression of nationalist feeling frequently led to antagonism with the Russian Orthodox church.

Among the Turkic-speaking peoples of Central Asia, Islam is the majority religion, having entered the region in the 7th century. Azerbaijanis are also Muslims. Although all outward signs of Islam were made illegal – traditional Muslim wedding ceremonies, for example, were forbidden – most Muslims continue to practice their faith, which is an inseparable part of their cultural tradition. Distinctive forms of dress were retained, along with traditional customs.

With the collapse of communism, many underground religious institutions were able to come into the open. Nowhere was

MINORITY PROBLEMS

The republics of the former Soviet Union were officially organized around one dominant national group. However, most of them contain sizeable foreign minorities; in the case of Kazakhstan, for example, less than two in five citizens are Kazakh. In most cases, Russians constitute the leading minority group. However, other nationalities, including Germans and Ukrainians, also form substantial minorities in countries outside their own. Some groups, such as Germans and Tatars, have no regional base.

Minorities are easy to identify. Under communist rule, nationality was based not on place of residence, but on parentage, and an individual's nationality was recorded in his or her internal

passport. After the collapse of the Soviet Union and the end of communist rule, the newly independent republic governments had to come to terms with the foreigners in their midst.

In Estonia, for example, 35 percent of the population is Russian. Non-Estonians have been denied the right to vote for five years, and have been forced not only to learn the Estonian language, but to pass official government examinations in it. The more important their job, the more difficult the examination. Estonians defend this as a way of safeguarding their language, culture, and national identity. Russians, many of whom were born and raised in Estonia, and are now raising their own families, disagree.

this more evident than in Central Asia, where the rediscovery of national identities and religious values were inextricably linked. Muslim schools, called madressa, began to offer religious instruction. Old mosques were returned to the religious authorities and refurbished for worship. Copies of the Qu'ran, formerly unavailable, were supplied by donors in neighboring Islamic countries.

The religion that suffered most from repression by the authorities under the Soviet regime was Judaism. Jews were recognized as a nationality, but not as a religious group. They were allowed to have their own alphabet, but synagogues and rabbinical schools were closed and religious observances were proscribed. Added to this was a pervasive anti-Semitism, often supported by state policies, that created quotas for Jews in universities and the professions. Millions of Soviet Jews were exterminated by the Nazi occupation forces during World War II.

Today, most people in the region who are classified as Jewish have no experience of practicing their religion. However, it has become easier for those who wish to do so to emigrate to the West, particularly to Israel and the United States.

A living faith (*above*) Young girls in colorful dresses and headscarves are given instruction in a Qu'ranic school. Attempts by the Communist Party to suppress Islam were largely ineffective; most Soviet Muslims continued to practice their faith.

Reemergence of religion (*above right*) Russian Orthodox monks at the historic monastery of Saint Sergius in Sergiyev Posad. The Orthodox church suffered greatly after the Russian revolution, but the ending of state restraints on religion revived its fortunes.

Sign of identity (*left*) A Moldovan activist affixes a placard announcing a political protest meeting in both Latin and Cyrillic script. The reintroduction of Moldova's Latin script in 1990 reflected the upsurge of nationalist feeling taking place within the Soviet Union.

LIVING WITH THE SYSTEM

In the drive to create a Soviet culture, an independent legal system – the foundation of a civil society – vanished. Laws, seen as just one tool in the development of a socialist culture and morality, were enforced selectively, ignored, or reinterpreted, officially for the benefit of the Party and the state, but more usually to suit the purposes of individual bureaucrats and local leaders. Under Stalin, the autocratic methods used to eliminate opposition drifted into arbitrary terror.

The Party and the state had not only the right, but also the obligation, to make sure that all art, sculpture, music, and literature embodied a properly socialist attitude. At times, national leaders intervened personally in cultural affairs. Stalin, for example, told the world-renowned composer Dmitry Shostakovich (1906–75) to make radical changes to his style of music.

In the words of Mikhail Kalinin (1875–1946), first president of the Soviet Union, the aim of the Soviet leadership was "to teach the people of the Kirghiz steppe, the small Uzbek cotton grower,

and the Turkmenian gardener to accept the ideals of the Leningrad worker". It was in this spirit that the major nationalist epics of Azerbaijan, Kazakhstan, Uzbekistan and Turkmenistan were denounced by local communist leaders as works of religious fanaticism, Mongol epics were attacked as pro-feudal, and a Kirghiz epic was rewritten to remove all passages considered reactionary.

The histories of the nationalities were rewritten to show Russia in a favorable light. For example, a history of the Lithuanian Soviet Republic was denounced in 1961 for, among other faults, minimizing the struggle of the Russian people against the Mongols and for failing to stress Lithuania's pro-Soviet feelings between 1919 and 1940, when it was then an independent state. Non-Russian writers were expected to produce literary works that expressed the leading role of the Russian people: to do otherwise was unpatriotic to the Soviet Union.

As a consequence of these policies literature, music and the arts became very bland, and conformity became more important than originality. Artistic life was organized on the basis of professional

unions, membership of which was mandatory. Artists and writers who did not conform to the offical line were unable to have their work produced.

A Soviet outlook

Although the Soviet leadership largely failed in its attempt to replace ethnic and cultural identities with a new Soviet culture, it succeeded in creating a distinctive Soviet outlook. The terror imposed by Stalin's methods of coercion left lasting scars on the national consciousness. People learned to mistrust the state and the organs of the state, particularly the police. Their mistrust was sharpened by chronic food shortages, exacerbated by laws forbidding private trading.

As a result, virtually every Soviet citizen, from a housewife to a factory manager, had to break the law. A culture with a double set of standards thus developed: one consisting of the public display of officially sanctioned opinions and attitudes, and another – shared among close friends and family – consisting of personal beliefs. Others found a different escape route – alcoholism became widespread in the Soviet Union.

A more open society (*above*) Young Muscovites, wearing fashionable jeans and leather jackets like their peers in Europe and the United States, joke with a soldier. Before *glasnost*, it would have been impossible to imagine this scene taking place.

Unruffled by change (*left*) Turkish influences are clear to see as community elders in Tajikistan discuss the future of local schools while drinking tea. All the vicissitudes of Soviet politics failed to alter this traditional way of life.

Catching up on the news (*right*) Three supporters eagerly scan a sports newspaper for the latest results. Sports reporting was always an area of the news that was politically uncontroversial enough to escape heavy censorship by the authorities.

All aspects of daily life came to be controlled by a bureaucratic system, characterized by paperwork, that created a network reaching to every district, blanketing town and country. Forms and passes became necessary to accomplish even the simplest tasks, and everyone had to carry an internal passport on their person at all times giving exhaustive details about their personal history.

Reform and collapse

After 1956, when Stalin's methods were publicly denounced by the Soviet leadership, the Soviet Union tried to come to terms with its recent past. However, it was not until the late 1980s that the Soviet Union began a move toward the creation of a civil society based on rule by law and an independent judicial system; in the new climate of glasnost, free speech was legalized, restrictions on religions eased and, in 1991, free market trading allowed.

These changes released a surge of popular feeling and there was much questioning of formerly accepted values and standards. The shift to free market trading and private ownership, for example, angered many people who saw it not only as a betrayal of socialist principles, but as the legalization of criminal activity. Others were led to reevaluate their life styles in the light of the growing influence of the church.

The final collapse of the communist state in 1991 made it possible for many nationalities to rediscover their past and to negotiate with each other independently of Moscow. Almost all the republics demanded greater autonomy, while Leningrad's citizens voted to return to the city's former name, St Petersburg. The newly independent Baltic states restored cultural links with the Nordic Countries, but remained economically tied to the Soviet Republics. They faced demands for autonomy from enclaves of Russians and Poles within their own borders, particularly in Lithuania.

Separatist demands led to a number of civil wars in the 1990s – armed revolt in Abkhazia led to the declaration of an independent republic which both Georgia and Russia refused to recognize; South Ossetia in Georgia also attempted armed rebellion. Armenia fought a war against Azerbaijan for the ethnic enclave of Nagorno-Karabakh, a territorial dispute which was unresolved in the early 2000s. In 1992, the Crimea, homeland of the Tatar people, attempted to secede from the Ukraine. At the same time, Tatarstan, an ethnic enclave within Russia of 3.6 million people was demanding greater cultural independence, In 1994, Russia invaded the breakaway republic of Chechnya which had, until 1992, been part of the autonomous republic of Checheno-Ingush. Despite Russian claims to be in control, violence continued into the 2000s. Early in the 21st century it appeared as though the legacy of Soviet policy was strife and tension as the various ethnic groups of the former USSR struggled to resolve their reawakened desire for cultural and political autonomy.

A HIGH RATE OF DIVORCE

Two thirds of marriages in the region end in divorce – among the highest rates in the world. There are variations in the pattern of divorce – the rate is highest in Belarus and Russia and among urban populations in the larger cities. Rates are lowest in Azerbaijan, Kyrgyrzstan, Uzbekistan and Turkmenistan where the influence of religion and rural customs remains strongest. Divorce tends to occur early in the marriage – in Moscow, for example, one in ten marriages lasts under a year.

Alcoholism is blamed in almost half the cases of divorce, but stress is also a factor. Most women work full time and are financially independent. They are also usually responsible for domestic chores and childcare. Housing shortages cause strain since couples must often live in a hostel or share a small apartment with their parents until they find a home of their own.

People wishing to move to Moscow and other major cities require a permit. Often, temporary marriage to a resident provides a short cut to obtaining one. Similarly, since single people can rarely obtain an apartment, a marriage of convenience may be the best way of finding one. Finally, although no official stigma attaches to illegitimacy, or to abortion, which is the main form of birth control available, many women who are unable to obtain an abortion may get married for the birth of the child, and divorce later.

Art in the service of the state

Massive buildings in a neoclassical style, sculptures of men and women in heroic poses, and larger than life paintings glorifying the achievements of socialism sum up the official art of the Soviet Union. However, this monumentalist approach also existed in pre-Revolutionary Russia – nowhere were the imperialist aspirations of the tsarist state better symbolized than in the ornate palaces and classical buildings of St Petersburg, renamed Leningrad by the communists.

After the Revolution, Soviet architects and artists began to search for styles that could represent the life and achievements of the new state. Initially they turned to the avant-garde ideas of the Futurists and Constructivists, then in vogue among Russian artists, especially those that had trained and worked in Paris. Although they used a modern idiom, they thought in monumental terms, hoping to surpass the creativity of other countries.

They argued that in the ferment of new ideas and enthusiasms that the Revolution excited, the stale, outmoded images of the old order should be replaced by new socialist forms. Soviet architects began to formulate new, sometimes impracticable schemes, of which the most notorious was the tower designed by Vladimir Tatlin (1885–1953) as a monument to the Third Communist International. A model was exhibited in 1919, showing a striking design consisting of a leaning iron framework supporting a glass cylinder, a glass cone and a glass cube, each of which could be rotated at different speeds. The final structure, never built, was to be more than 480 m (1,300 ft) high. Frequently the state lacked the technology to build the projects. More often it lacked the money. Despite this, many international architects offered their services to the Soviet Union, planning factories, flats, offices and entire towns. They included the Swiss-born Le Corbusier (1887–1965), then just beginning to formulate his influential ideas on architecture, who designed the Tsentrosoyuz building in Moscow. In turn the innovative ideas of Soviet architects and artists such as the Vesnin brothers, Moses Ginsberg and Tatlin, won international renown, helping to establish the credentials of the new state.

A change of direction
In the late 1920s Stalin achieved a position of unopposed power. His taste in art and

Excitement of the new (*above*) An architect's fantasy of domed palaces captures the post-Revolutionary spirit of innovation and experimentation.

Tatlin's Tower (*left*) A model of the giant iron and glass tower designed by the internationally renowned architect Vladimir Tatlin to commemorate the Third Communist International. The tower – like the International's dream of world communist revolution – was destined never to become a reality.

Monument to a dictator (*right*) Soviet architecture returned to more traditional monumentalist forms as Stalin's power increased. Moscow University, for example, was the largest of seven huge buildings built in the city during his lifetime. The connection between monumentalist architecture and dictatorship is well known; in the late 20th century Kim Il Sung in North Korea, Nicolae Ceausescu (1918–89) in Romania and Saddam Hussein in Iraq all conceived grandiose schemes that were intended to glorify and legitimize their power.

sculpture was conventional, and he also had a preference for neoclassical architecture. Modernism and experimentation were consequently declared anti-Soviet. They were replaced by socialist realism, approved by Stalin as the proper style to express the heroic goals and aspirations of socialism. Works of art and architecture were to be built as inspirational monuments to the socialist future, not just replacing, but dwarfing and outlasting,

monuments from the capitalist past.

Moscow, the Soviet capital, became a showcase for the achievements of Stalin's rule. It was rebuilt in an imperial style with new, broad streets lined with monumental buildings. When Moscow's metro, or subway, was first opened in 1935, each station was an underground palace: corridors were lined with marble and mosaics, and platforms were paved with polished stone.

As Stalin's power grew, the scale of Soviet architecture increased. After World War II the rebuilding of the country's major cities, destroyed by the Germans, was planned on monumental lines, to symbolize the extent and nature of the Soviet victory. Prison labor was used extensively. Seven massive tower blocks were built in Moscow, the largest of which – Moscow University – is 240 m (800 ft) high and 480 m (1,600 ft) long.

Plans were made for a new Palace of the Soviets, which it was hoped would be the world's tallest and largest building, and would be topped by a colossal statue of Lenin, the Soviet Union's founding father. A cathedral was demolished to provide a site for the building, but the scheme was dropped after Stalin's death, when it was discovered that the site was too near a river for the deep foundations required. The excavated foundations

were transformed instead into a vast outdoor swimming pool.

Monumentalist architecture came to typify Soviet life, its grandiose details and often gimcrack construction repeated in Party headquarters, regional congress buildings and factories throughout the country. Although such schemes are now a thing of the past, in many ways they remain Stalin's most enduring legacy, now that his statues have been toppled.

CITIES

A HISTORY OF CENTRAL CONTROL · PLANNING THE SETTLEMENT SYSTEM · CITIES FOR THE PEOPLE

Before the momentous political events of 1991 that witnessed its demise, the Soviet Union, with just over 290 million people, was ranked third in population after China and India. Given the history of Russian and Soviet territorial expansion, the population was far from homogenous. However, Russians were the single largest nationality group, and the most dominant. During the 70 years of communist rule there were numerous attempts to plan cities and settlement systems across the whole region, including Mongolia. The Soviet settlement system was supposed to evolve according to socialist planning principles. The size of cities was to be limited, and urban and rural settlement systems were to develop in harmony. These policies failed to stem the growth of large cities and urban agglomerations.

COUNTRIES IN THE REGION
Armenia, Azerbaijan, Belarus, Estonia, Georgia, Kazakhstan, Kyrgyzstan, Latvia, Lithuania, Moldova, Mongolia, Russia, Tajikistan, Turkmenistan, Ukraine, Uzbekistan

POPULATION

Total population of region (millions)			293.3
	Russia	**Latvia**	**Uzbekistan**
Population density (persons per sq km)	9	38	52.5
Population change (average annual percent 1960–1990)			
Urban	+3%	−1.47%	+0.72%
Rural	−1.68%	−1.47%	+2.09%

URBAN POPULATION

As percentage of total population 1995–2000	78%	69%	37%

TEN LARGEST CITIES

	Country	Population
Moscow †	Russia	9,389,700
St Petersburg (Leningrad)	Russia	4,169,400
Kiev †	Ukraine	2,616,800
Tashkent †	Uzbekistan	2,079,000
Minsk †	Belarus	1,751,300
Kharkov	Ukraine	1,477,000
Novosibirsk	Russia	1,402,000
Nizhniy Novgorod (Gorky)	Russia	1,418,000
Yekaterinburg (Sverdlovsk)	Russia	1,367,000
Tbilisi †	Georgia	1,344,100

† *denotes capital city*

City population figures are for the city proper.

A HISTORY OF CENTRAL CONTROL

The traditional power base both of Russia and the Soviet Union has always been the European part of the country. Climatic conditions east of the Ural mountains are generally harsh, with either too much heat or cold and too much or too little water for agriculture. Thus, most of the agricultural activity, and most of the population, were located in European Russia. The paradox is that most of the resources for a modern industrial economy were, and are, found in the vast area east of the Ural mountains.

Cities played an important role in the early political and economic history of European Russia. Most developed at strategic locations along trade routes inland, or as ports. From the late 10th to the 12th century, the most important city was Kiev, now the capital of Ukraine. It was succeeded by the town of Vladimir, located to the northeast between the Volga and Oka rivers. In the 14th century the Prince of Muscovy assumed control, and Moscow became the capital city of the rapidly expanding Russian Empire.

Peter the Great (1672–1725) emerged as the first Russian tsar to leave an indelible impression on the landscape in terms of city development. In order to demonstrate the importance of Europe to Russia he embarked on a longterm project to build a new city, St Petersburg, at the mouth of the Neva river. It was symbolically Russia's "window on the west", and in architecture and design reflected the best of European talent. Construction began in 1703, and in 1713 the new city was made the capital in place of Moscow.

In the 18th and 19th centuries, the expanding empire brought the predominately Islamic regions of Central Asia under the administrative control of European Russia. Cities here, such as Tashkent, Bukhara and Samarkand, had developed as great Islamic trading centers on the overland route from China to Europe. These new territories were occupied by peoples having very different cultural, religious and language backgrounds from the ruling Russians. Many Russian bureaucrats were brought into these regions to administer and keep effective control. Garrison towns were built anew or alongside existing towns, and government and military buildings were raised in city centers – bringing Russian architecture and planning to traditional Islamic and Asian cities.

After the Russian Revolution of 1917 most of the old empire eventually became the Union of Soviet Socialist Republics. The Communist system was maintained throughout the country by the strong leadership and control imposed by Moscow through the central bureaucracy and the Party system. For the republics outside Russia, central control from Moscow

A view of the past The Kremlin of Rostov the Great, northeast of Moscow, was built in the 17th century in a spirit of nostalgic anachronism – its fortified ramparts enclosing a palace and onion-domed cathedral were already outdated when built for its ecclesiastical patron. It is a perfect replica of a medieval Russian fortress town. Today its buildings are preserved as a museum piece.

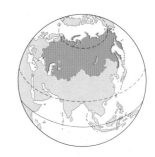

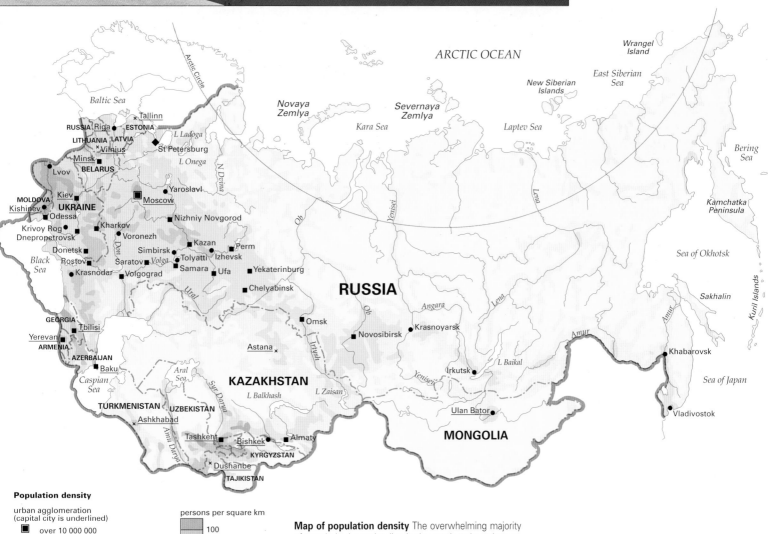

Population density

urban agglomeration
(capital city is underlined)

■	over 10 000 000
◆	5 000 000–10 000 000
■	1 000 000–4 999 999
●	600 000–999 999
×	capital city less than 600 000

persons per square km

	100
	50
	10
	1

Map of population density The overwhelming majority of people in the region live in the south and southwest where fertile soils supported early urban development. The eastward shift of population after the Revolution followed the lines of the river valleys.

meant that regional cultures, languages and religions were subordinated or in some cases even eliminated.

Shifting eastward

The Soviet experience changed traditional settlement patterns. Vast new collective farms and villages were created as well as industrial cities. Before the Revolution, most of the population lived west of the Urals. To fulfill the economic Five Year Plans, new industrial and mining towns were built in resource-rich Siberia and Central Asia. Between 1959 and 1970, Kazakhstan and Central Asia received over 1.5 million new migrants, while the Urals, Upper Volga and European regions saw their populations drop by nearly 3 million. People were not able to choose where they wanted to live but were directed to where there was work.

The legacy of the Soviet Union to the newly independent republics was a highly urbanized society – despite the administrative barriers, the attractions of urban life have been compelling.

PLANNING THE SETTLEMENT SYSTEM

Rapid urbanization, in association with industrial development, is a recent phenomenon in the region, initiated by Soviet economic planners in the late 1920s. At the beginning of the Soviet regime, barely one-sixth of the population was urban, and even as late as 1960 the majority of the population was still classified as rural. By 1990 barely one-third of the population was rural. For a great many urbanites, therefore, village life, culture and values are very much a part of living memory.

Soviet cities did not develop autonomously: planning norms were established in Moscow without regard for local needs and customs, and were implemented at republic level by regional agencies. Urbanization, particularly in Central Asia, was fueled by largescale migration of Slavs from other republics. The local populations in Central Asia had for cen-

turies lived an agricultural life with strong ties to the land, ties made stronger by limited or no ability to speak Russian and little or no training in technical, non-farming occupations. In addition, there was perhaps some preference by the central authorities to create Soviet urban enclaves in non-Slavic areas. As a result, the growing Central Asian cities such as Alma Ata, Tashkent and Dushanbe were, almost without exception, dominated by Slavs and other non-indigenous peoples.

The gap between theory and reality

In theory, the development of the urban system was to be guided by precepts and principles to ensure the rational growth of particular places and their harmonious integration into a new settlement system. Many Soviet government agencies were set up to oversee the urban development process, to coordinate design and formulate and implement planning norms.

There was a notable absence of specific policies to achieve the long-standing objective of a planned development of a

The grim legacy of Soviet planning (*left*) is all too evident in this Moscow scene. To help achieve production targets, residential blocks to house factory workers were built in industry's backyard.

Huddled against the Siberian winter (*above*) The wooden houses in this Siberian village have been built close together to conserve energy. Roofs are designed to withstand the weight of snow.

SIBERIAN BOOMTOWN

Like a great many urban settlements in Siberia, Bratsk, located on the Angara river downstream from Lake Baikal, reflects both the positive and negative features of the Soviet town planning process. Founded in 1954 in virtually a frontier location, Bratsk's existence as a new town was inextricably tied to the construction of what was then one of the world's largest hydroelectric power stations capable of generating huge blocks of seemingly inexpensive electricity. Energy-intensive industries were planned for development at Bratsk in order to take advantage of low-cost power. Thus, a largescale aluminum refining plant was built, as were several wood products and wood hydrolysis plants using local forest resources.

From the outset several different ministries were involved in the construction of factories and the urban settlement. It was to be a model new town. However, the industrial ministries involved built separate settlements for their own workers. The net result is an administrative area with 250,000 inhabitants, which consist of several physically separate settlement components. Most are modern complexes of apartments with some cultural and consumer services, but far fewer than the planning norms dictate.

On balance, the failure of central planning to bring about a single unified urban infrastructure has resulted in a lack of consumer and cultural facilities for the town's inhabitants. Schools run on three shifts daily, day care and hospital facilities are insufficient and so on. In short, Bratsk new town was not constructed according to the long-standing planning principles for urban development, and the population suffers accordingly.

settlement system. After 1933 when a decree was issued stating that cities were not to be created without due regard to their role within the evolving settlement system, close on 1,200 new towns were added to the map. Some were former rural settlements that were simply reclassified because of changes in size and economic role. Hundreds of others were literally new towns, built to house industrial workers where resource development schemes had been established.

In the last years of the Soviet Union, most new development took place in the shadow of existing large cities or urban agglomerations. Government agencies endeavored to locate new production facilities in cities or near to them, or expand existing facilities where this was feasible. Soviet town planning traditionally focused on the development of a particular city itself without regard for the surrounding area and its relationship with the other settlements within it. As a result, there was little planning of the settlement system as a whole and this favored the emergence of large urban agglomerations. The vast majority of Soviet urbanites now live within urban developments of this kind.

Individual cities grew at rates far in excess of what the planners had intended. In a non-market, planned urban environment where all the necessary resources and facilities, including housing, were to be provided in accordance with planned population growth, shortages of all kinds were the inevitable consequence.

Disintegrating control

With the passing of the Soviet Union and centralized urban planning, the independent republics have assumed responsibility for urban and rural development. There are, however, some new problems. The inter-nationality conflicts in the Caucasus and Central Asia have produced massive internal migration.

In the late 1990s, at least 2 million people could quite legitimately be described as internal refugees. Not all were non-Russian minorities such as the Azeris or Armenians of the troubled Caucasus region. Many Slavs, especially Russians, who had migrated to the cities of Central Asia and the Caucasus were forced to flee situations that had become unsafe. These migrants frequently descended upon already overcrowded and under-provisioned cities in European Russia. The concerted efforts of the newly independent states to adopt the attributes of a free market system, including the privatization of the state housing stock and a market valuation system for the allocation of land to users, presented additional difficulties to those on the move.

CITIES FOR THE PEOPLE

The Russian Revolution of 1917 ushered in a new era of socialism, and expectations of what the state could deliver to its people were very high. Putting these expectations into practice, however, proved to be difficult – in improving social conditions in the cities, as in other areas of life. The struggle to consolidate the Revolution was the main concern of government planners in the first decade of the new Union, and little happened to change the urban scene until the adoption of the Plan for the Reconstruction of Moscow in 1935, which finally laid down Soviet principles for urban development. Because of the highly centralized state planning system and the continuous pressure to achieve conformity throughout the country, the Moscow Plan became the basis for overall city development.

Unattainable goals
Guidelines in the Moscow Plan called for limited city size, ideological rather than "business" functions for city centers, state control and allocation of housing, equality in the distribution of consumer and cultural services, and a limited journey to work. Planned urban development and limited city size assumed that population growth could be controlled. To ensure population control, a number of measures limiting citizens' right to free movement were introduced. These included internal passports, residence permits – required before housing could be allocated – and the surveillance of people's movements.

Despite these measures, urban growth regularly exceeded what the planners expected and housing was in short supply. Instead of the official one family per apartment, by the early 1950s a family per room was more often than not the reality of urban life for the masses. The devolution of the Soviet Union left its successors with continuing housing shortage problems, though the extreme problems of 40 years ago had been eased.

Over the years urban development principles were translated into hundreds of specific planning norms. For example, 9 sq m (96 sq ft) of living space was to be the minimum amount for each urban inhabitant to satisfy basic sanitary requirements. This norm, set in 1923, is still not satisfied in many former Soviet cities, especially in the smaller, more remote centers. These norms were intended to ensure an equal allocation of consumer services, cultural facilities and housing – all at a nominal cost. The reality however was that privilege always existed within Soviet society and manifested itself in elite groups having more of whatever was available, often at the cost of denying the same service or facility to the masses.

Privileged elites
Like society itself, the Soviet cities were riven with paradoxes and contradictions. Private housing has always existed. Cooperatives were legalized again in 1962 after almost 25 years of proscription. These sectors now comprise about 22 and 8 percent respectively of the total urban housing stock. Although residential areas

City of Central Asia (*right*) Samarkand in Uzbekistan was already an established city when Alexander the Great captured it in 329 BC. On the Silk Road from China to Europe, it flourished as an Islamic trading center and became a Russian city in 1868. Today monotonous apartment blocks, developed in accordance with the Moscow Plan, surround the city center. But as this view shows, mosques have survived amidst the modern city.

Clearing city streets (*below*) The socialist policies of the former Soviet Union guaranteed its people employment and a minimum standard of living. Menial tasks were often carried out by women. With economic reform and the ending of communist control, unemployment soared in the cities, and earnings fell to levels well below the official subsistence wage.

period of Mikhail Gorbachev's presidency (1985–91). But the promotion of private sector activity created a new class of wealthy Soviet citizens who had access to large amounts of money, often in the form of hard currency, which they could exchange, often on the black market, for scarce commodities or services.

Urban governments before Gorbachev's period in office had been increasingly hard-pressed to provide adequately for the needs of the cities' inhabitants. In the late 1980s many began actively to promote private sector activities in the hope that this would improve life for all. But the Soviet system meant that the transition from socialist to market principles was difficult and remained so even after the demise of communism. Moves to sell municipally owned apartments to individuals continued. Smallscale, privately owned businesses aimed at meeting the enormous but unsatisfied demand for consumer goods and services began to spring up everywhere, but were most in evidence in the larger cities.

However, with the privatization of housing and the promotion of private sector business activities, the existence of social inequalities will not only continue in the future but will be exaggerated. It remains to be seen what changes this will bring to the physical form of the region's cities, which still bear mute testimony, in their architecture and design, to decades of planning based upon the Soviet theory of equality.

were not socially segregated to the degree that they are in many European or American cities, there were still some obvious signs of privilege. Cooperative apartments were often occupied by the middle, not working, class and spacious accommodation (at least by prevailing Soviet standards) in the state housing sector was made available to favored groups such as members of the Party hierarchy.

Traditionally, privilege also brought access to consumer services, including more predictable and higher quality food supplies provided through special stores not open to the general public. Most of these privileges were removed during the

THE THREE FACES OF TASHKENT

Tashkent is the capital of Uzbekistan. Home to more than 2 million people, it is Central Asia's largest urban center and one of the oldest – dating back to about the 2nd century BC. The city has long been predominately Islamic, but the arrival of new ethnic groups and ideas that came with its absorption into the Russian empire (in 1865) and later into the Soviet Union has transformed Tashkent into a city with three separate urban identities.

Tashkent was the administrative capital of the Central Asian part of the tsarist empire. The colonial period is still visible in the 19th-century European townscape of radial thoroughfares, broad intersecting streets and government buildings reflecting the Russian architecture of the period. The bulk of the population lived apart in the

old Muslim town – a world of caravansaries and mosques, narrow streets and winding pathways. The character of the colonial city derived from the integrity of the street plan and the architectural conformity of the buildings. In the traditional Muslim quarter the intensity of human interaction, of bustle and noise, defined the old town's separate identity.

The Soviet contribution to Tashkent's urban landscape was vast, sprawling housing districts. With the break up of the Soviet Union, many native Tashkentis are returning from government and military service and swelling the population dramatically. Although the huge, drab and poorly built complexes are necessary to house the city's rapidly growing population, they add little character to the urban scene.

St Petersburg – a planned city

St Petersburg arose from the inhospitable and marshy delta of the Neva river in the early 1700s as a result of Peter the Great's determination to modernize the Russian empire. Tens of thousands of workers were forcibly transported to the western-most border of the empire to build the new city. While this was made possible by the existence of serfdom, it scarcely matched the forms of social organization in the European countries whose moder-nity Peter the Great wished Russia to emulate. Still, a city did develop, and one that contained most of the best that European (particularly French) town planning and architecture could offer. By 1713 St Petersburg had been designated capital of the Russian empire. For two centuries its plan served as a model for new town development elsewhere in Rus-sia, including Helsinki annexed in 1809.

While the principal emphasis in the city's development was on external form, the fascination with the geometry and symmetry of the town plan tended to mask the fact that it was more than simply a technical working document, but a social one as well. Land-use segregation went far beyond controlling the location of smoke-emitting industries to include provisions for the physical separation of social classes. The town plan was intend-ed to reinforce the existing social order and the values of the autocracy. Indus-trialization, which came late to Russia but had profound consequences for all cities in the region including St Petersburg, put paid to such goals.

The Revolution and beyond

St Petersburg housed barely half a million people in 1850. A substantial share lived there on a transient basis as they were serfs on leave from the village. By 1914 the capital of the Russian empire was one of the largest cities in Europe with over 2 million inhabitants. While superficially a city of palaces and grand thoroughfares and squares, life for most people was arduous in the extreme. Industrialization and a rapid increase in population had brought unprecedented pressures to bear. The city was increasingly decried by Russians and foreigners as backward, unplanned and insalubrious. Vast sprawl-ing suburbs with overcrowded, largely unserviced housing had emerged. Condi-tions were ripe for grassroots political activity. In 1917 the autocracy to the tsars collapsed and revolution took place. St Petersburg was the stage upon which these events were played out.

What emerged from the Revolution was a new political system, in which Moscow replaced St Petersburg, renamed Lenin-grad, as the capital. Vast resources were allocated to assist its industrial develop-ment and – following the siege of the city during World War II – to rebuild its historic core according to the original plans and architectural design. This in-cidentally removed some of the worst impacts that industrialization and com-mercialization had on the central city during the late imperial era.

Under the Soviet system St Petersburg was developed, like other cities, in accor-dance with the Moscow Plan of 1935. The city's housing stock expanded enormous-ly. Vast stretches of apartment blocks, 15 to 25 storeys high, signal the beginning of the city from the north and east. There is very little that suggests a rural-urban fringe. Yet, despite the huge sums in-vested, housing remains one of the city's most pressing needs. With a population of over 4 million in the late 1990s, St Peters-burg is the second largest city in Russia.

Under the Soviet planned economy, the city quickly emerged as one of the coun-try's main centers of scientific and ad-vanced manufacturing, particularly in shipbuilding, machine construction, pre-cision instrument manufacture, and defense-related electronic industries. St Petersburg's industrial managers and ur-ban administrators were unusually inno-vative in their efforts to link the city's industrial enterprises with local scientific organizations. As a result, levels of indus-trial output and – more significant in the Soviet context – quality of output achiev-ed very high standards in national terms. Entrepreneurship in its various guises played, and continues to play, an impor-tant role in boosting the city's economic development.

St Petersburg was notable in its resist-ance to the abortive hardline Communist Party coup in August 1991. Just as in 1917, events in the city played a critical role in bringing change to society at large. Its citizens remain committed to the preser-vation of the splendid urban fabric that is the legacy of imperial Russia, and to improving the poor conditions of daily labor and life that are the direct legacy of the Soviet era. With its highly skilled, educated labor force and its industrial production that is potentially competitive in the international market economy, the city's longterm prospects look good.

Treasurehouse of the tsars (*above*) The Winter Palace, seen here from across the Neva river, is among the architectural riches of St Petersburg. The former principal residence of the tsars, it was destroyed by fire in 1837 but rebuilt in identical style two years later. The adjoining Hermitage houses an unparalleled art collection.

Looking for a place to live (*left*) A street hoarding is covered with slips of paper advertising available rooms or asking for accommodation, an indication of the city's acute housing shortage.

Window on the west (*right*) Peter the Great built his city on the Gulf of Finland to give his fleets access to Europe. The city was built on land between the sea and the river Neva, with dockyards and other industrial sites strictly segregated from residential areas.

Land use

- • important site
- —— major road
- ◆— major railroad (with terminus)
- ▨ central district
- ▢ commercial and mixed
- ▨ industrial
- ▢ residential
- ▨ parks and open spaces
- ▢ other

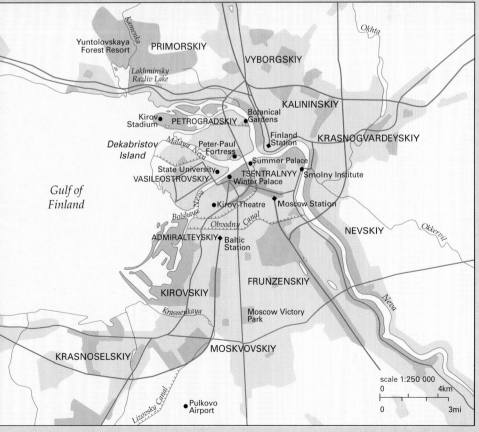

Yuntolovskaya Forest Resort
Kamenka
Okhta
PRIMORSKIY
VYBORGSKIY
Lakhminsky Razliv Lake
KALININSKIY
Kirov Stadium
PETROGRADSKIY
Botanical Gardens
Finland Station
KRASNOGVARDEYSKIY
Dekabristov Island
Malaya Neva
Peter-Paul Fortress
Summer Palace
State University
TSENTRALNYY
Smolny Institute
VASILEOSTROVSKIY
Winter Palace
Gulf of Finland
Neva
Kirov Theatre
Moscow Station
Bolshaya
Obvodny Canal
NEVSKIY
Okkervil
ADMIRALTEYSKIY
Baltic Station
FRUNZENSKIY
KIROVSKIY
Krasnenkaya
Moscow Victory Park
Neva
KRASNOSELSKIY
MOSKVOVSKIY
scale 1:250 000
0   4km
0   3mi
Lizovsky Canal
Pulkovo Airport

Power center

The most important part of any Russian medieval city was the kremlin, or citadel, usually located at a strategic point along a river and encircled both by a moat and a fortified wall. The kremlin contained both military and religious buildings, and was the center and symbol of ruling power and authority over the immediate neighborhood and other settlements. In times of war or siege, the inhabitants of the city would take refuge within its walls.

The Kremlin in Moscow is the most famous of these city forts. First built in 1156 on the left bank of the Moskva river, its original wooden palisade and buildings were replaced by stone and brick in the 14th century. Strong ramparts, 2.5 km (1.5 mi) long and topped by seven towers, surround a triangular-shaped fortification. The buildings inside were built at different times over the centuries, and encompass a range of styles and influences, including Byzantine, Russian baroque and classical.

The Kremlin has many churches, including the Blagoveshchenski (Annunciation) Cathedral where the tsars were baptized and married. It lost its military importance in the 17th century, but remained the center of Russian political power until the capital moved to St Petersburg in 1712. After an interval of 200 years, the Kremlin became the focus of power again in October 1917 when V.I. Lenin (1870–1924), the first head of the Soviet state, moved the new Soviet government to the historic citadel. As such it became the symbol of the ruling power of the Communist Party for 70 years, housing the Council of Ministers, the Presidium of the Supreme Soviet and the Palace of Congresses. With the breakup of the Soviet Union, the Kremlin became the home of the Russian parliament. So its role as a center of government continues.

Gilded domes and towers at the heart of Moscow. Among its many churches and palaces the Kremlin contains three cathedrals, built in the 15th and 16th centuries.

GOVERNMENT

COLLECTIVIZATION TO REFORM · THE MACHINERY OF COMMUNIST RULE · RETHINKING SUPERPOWER STRATEGIES

For nearly 70 years, from 1923 to 1991, the Union of Soviet Socialist Republics (USSR) was the dominant power in the region. It came into being after the 1917 communist revolution in Russia. In the ensuing civil war the communists extended their power over the Ukraine and reannexed the non-Russian territories of the former tsarist empire east of the Black Sea and in Central Asia to create the Soviet Union in 1923. Estonia, Latvia and Lithuania were annexed in 1940. In 1990 these Baltic states withdrew from the Soviet Union and were recognized internationally as independent states. The Soviet Union was dissolved the following year, to be replaced by the Commonwealth of Independent States. Mongolia, which declared itself a People's Republic in 1924, was governed along Soviet lines until 1990.

COLLECTIVIZATION TO REFORM

The head of the new Soviet government that came to power in Russia in 1917, V. I. Lenin (1870–1924), laid down the framework of communist rule in the constitution of 1918. Land was redistributed and property and banks nationalized. Three years of civil war, however, had a devastating economic effect, and the New Economic Policy (NEP) partially restored private enterprise. After Lenin's death a struggle for political power took place in the government, from which Joseph Stalin (1879–1953) emerged as leader.

For nearly 30 years of unchallenged rule, Stalin's autocratic policies were to transform the Soviet Union. Peasant agriculture was drastically reorganized into "collective" state-owned farms, and a program of rapid industrialization was undertaken. It is estimated that some 6 million peasants died as a result of collectivization. Countless more citizens were to perish in the penal labor camps and in the purges of 1936–38 that were the twin pillars, with the secret police, of Stalin's brutal regime. The legacy of the Stalin years was a socialist economy geared toward heavy industry and defense and a highly centralized one-party state dominated by a large and increasingly cumbersome bureaucracy.

Nevertheless, Stalin's total control of Soviet life may have enabled the Soviet people to withstand the German invasion of 1941. Some 20 million Soviet citizens died in the fighting and devastation of World War II, hundreds of cities lay in ruins and the economy was destroyed.

COUNTRIES IN THE REGION

Armenia, Azerbaijan, Belarus, Estonia, Georgia, Kazakhstan, Kyrgyzstan, Latvia, Lithuania, Moldova, Mongolia, Russia, Tajikistan, Turkmenistan, Ukraine, Uzbekistan

Disputed border Russia/China (Ussuri river)

Disputed territory Armenia/Azerbaijan (Nagorno-Karabakh), Moldova/Romania (Bessarabia and Bukovina), Russia/Japan (Kuri Islands and south Sakhalin island)

STYLES OF GOVERNMENT

Republics All the countries in the region

Multi-party states All the countries in the region

One-chamber assembly Armenia, Azerbaijan, Belarus, Estonia, Georgia, Kazakhstan, Latvia, Lithuania, Mongolia, Moldova, Tajikistan, Ukraine, Uzbekistan

Two-chamber assembly Kyrgyzstan, Russia, Turkmenistan

CONFLICTS (since 1945)

Nationalist movements Azerbaijan (Armenians); Georgia (Ossetians); Kyrgyzstan (Uzbeks); Moldova (Russians in Dniestr region); (Tatars, Karachai, Ingush, Volga Germans); Uzbekistan (Meskhetian Turks); Russia (Chechens)

Internal conflicts Armenia 1988–89; Azerbaijan 1988–90; Latvia 1991; Georgia 1989; Lithuania 1990, 1991; Moldova 1989–90; Russia 1990s

Civil wars Georgia 1991–2; Moldova 1992; Tajikistan 1992–97

Interstate conflicts Armenia/Azerbaijan 1990s; USSR/Hungary 1956; USSR/Czechoslovakia 1968; USSR/China 1969; USSR/Afghanistan 1979–89

MEMBERSHIP OF INTERNATIONAL ORGANIZATIONS

Commonwealth of Independent States (CIS) Armenia, Azerbaijan, Belarus, Georgia, Kazakhstan, Kyrgyzstan, Moldova, Russia, Tajikistan, Turkmenistan, Ukraine, Uzbekistan

Council of Europe Estonia, Lithuania, Latvia, Moldova, Ukraine, Georgia, Russia

Council of Baltic Sea States Estonia, Latvia, Lithuania, Russia

States of Northern Eurasia

- ● conflict
- ● civil unrest

Dwarfing its neighbors Russia accounted for more than 75 percent of the land area of the former Soviet Union. When it broke up, a mosaic of tiny states was created in the west and south.

Decline and fall In August 1991, a huge statue of Lenin, founding father of the Soviet state, was lowered unceremonially from its pedestal in a clear expression of anticommunist popular feeling. Within months, the surge of nationalist opinion in the republics had brought about the collapse of the Soviet Union.

The legacy of war The devastating experience of World War II had a dominating influence on Soviet life and ideas. This striking war memorial in St Petersburg (Leningrad) is one of thousands witnessing to the sacrifice of countless Soviet citizens.

However, the Soviet Union emerged as the victor and dominant power in Eastern Europe, with political hegemony over a series of satellite states. Its territorial gains included the three Baltic states of Estonia, Latvia and Lithuania, part of Poland's eastern territories and Moldova. Although it had declared war on Japan only three weeks before Japan's surrender, it also acquired south Sakhalin island and the Kuril Islands in the Sea of Okhotsk.

The Soviet Union after Stalin

In the years following Stalin's death in 1953, Nikita Khrushchev (1894–1971) emerged as first secretary of the CPSU. In a historic speech at the 20th Party Congress in 1956 he denounced Stalin's abuses and introduced important economic and political reforms, including the devolution of economic power to the regions (the *sovnarkhoz* experiment) and the extension of cultural freedoms. However, these changes were shortlived. The more conservative leadership of

Leonid Brezhnev (1906–82), first secretary for nearly 20 years from 1964, resulted in economic stagnation.

It was in response to the growing economic crisis that Mikhail Gorbachev, who became first secretary in March 1985, set in motion the twin policies of *perestroika* ("reconstruction") and *glasnost* ("openness"). *Perestroika* referred to a program of measures designed to reform the economic system, including the expansion of private enterprise and greater economic self-management. *Glasnost* represented a determination to democratize the social and political system.

The opening up of Soviet society to self-examination unleashed a storm of nationalist discontent. Once the system of rigid central control was relaxed, the much vaunted "friendship of the Soviet peoples" was revealed to have been little more than a policy enforced from above, and long-buried grievances emerged with frightening force. The Tatars, for example, transported from the Crimea in

1944 and resettled in Russia, staged a public demonstration in 1987 for the return of their homeland; in many of the non-Russian republics resentment of the influence wielded by Russian incomers was more and more openly expressed. In the Baltic republics (annexed by the Soviet Union in 1940) the demand for national self-determination grew rapidly in the late 1980s, and there were nationalist protests in Armenia, Belarus, Moldova, Georgia and the Ukraine. Ethnic violence was especially strong in Nagorno-Karabakh, an Armenian enclave within Azerbaijan.

The "leading role" of the CPSU came more and more into question, and in February 1990 official recognition was given to other parties. Following elections to many republic and local soviets later that year, the CPSU lost power in the Baltic republics, Armenia, Moldova and Georgia, and in Moscow and Leningrad. Mikhail Gorbachev, elected to the new role of president in March, attempted to steer a course between reformers and conservative elements in the CPSU, but satisfied neither. In August 1991 hardline communists launched an unsuccessful coup. In the immediate aftermath of this turmoil the activities of the CPSU were suppressed, and by the end of the year the Soviet Union had passed into the history books.

THE MACHINERY OF COMMUNIST RULE

As the official name (Union of Soviet Socialist Republics) suggested, power in the Soviet Union was supposed to operate through the soviets (or people's councils), which were the formal organs of state power. However, in practice, the real power always resided exclusively with the Communist Party through its control of all political activity.

Parallel systems of government

The soviets, elected by the citizenry, were intended by Lenin to form a pivotal role in the process described in his notion of "democratic centralism". This holds that democratization prevails through the election of all state bodies of government, which are accountable to the people. In turn, power is centralized through control from above, lower bodies being obliged to obey the directives of higher ones.

At the lowest level of the state apparatus were the 50,000 local soviets. Above them were the regional soviets. Each of the 15 republics of the Union had its own supreme soviet, and above them was the supreme soviet of the Soviet Union, based in Moscow.

Over the decades democratic centralism resulted in the CPSU becoming the only

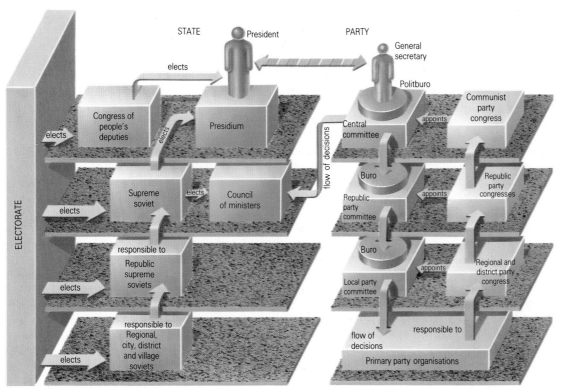

The statue of Lenin dominates the proceedings of the 27th Party Congress in 1986, which was the launching pad for the *perestroika* reforms. The party congresses, held every five years, were the forum for the CPSU to announce new directives and rubber stamp decisions. Day-to-day power lay with the politburo, the inner cabinet of the CPSU's ruling central committee.

The highest state legislative body (*left*) in the Soviet Union was the two-chamber supreme soviet, which met only for two or three days each year – between sessions the presidium acted as the supreme state authority. The council of ministers was the highest executive body, but it was the CPSU that dictated policy decisions. The Congress of People's Deputies was established in 1989 as a working legislature. In 1990 it elected Mikhail Gorbachev, general secretary of the CPSU, as the first and last president of the Soviet Union. The congress's power was to be shortlived – the political structure of the Soviet Union collapsed in 1991.

THE COUP THAT FAILED

The overthrow of Eastern Europe's communist regimes at the end of 1989 threw the Soviet Union's policy-makers into confusion. Many welcomed the changes as signaling the need for greater democratic reform and argued that the country's worsening economic situation called for a speeding up of moves toward a market economy. The loss of a "buffer zone" of satellite states on the Soviet Union's western flank, however, led hardliners within the CPSU to call for controls to be tightened rather than loosened.

Gorbachev was forced to follow a delicate path between these opposing camps. After his failure to condemn the revolutions in Eastern Europe was criticized at the 28th Party Congress in July 1990 he took steps to weaken the power of the CPSU, and pushed through a series of measures including recognition of the unification of Germany and the abolition of press censorship. But by late 1990 he appeared to be bowing to conservative pressure when he failed to implement promised economic change.

By the summer of 1991 there was a swing back toward reform. Steps were taken to allow the sale of state-owned enterprises, and on 24 July agreement was reached with 9 of the 15 republics on a draft Union Treaty decentralizing power in the Soviet Union.

All of this was too much for the old guard. Two days before the Union Treaty was due to be signed on 20 August an ultimatum was delivered to Gorbachev, on holiday in the Crimea, demanding that he resign and declare a state of emergency. On refusing to do so he was placed under house arrest. In Moscow a self-proclaimed State Committee for the State of Emergency (SCSE) assumed power.

The overthrow of the coup came through the efforts of Boris Yeltsin, president of the Russian Federation since 1990. From his position in the Russian government building ("the White House") he organized opposition on the streets and as columns of tanks entered Moscow on 20 August tens of thousands of people gathered to defend the building. Three people were killed, but the coup quickly collapsed. The leaders were arrested and Gorbachev returned to Moscow.

It was, however, Yeltsin who emerged as the clear winner. In the days after the coup the Russian government took over the functions of the all-Union government. In a showdown on television on 23 August Yeltsin signed a decree suspending the activities of the Russian Communist Party, which took Gorbachev completely by surprise. The ultimate result of the failed coup was the collapse of the Soviet Union.

---

dominant political force in the Soviet Union. Proclaiming itself the "leading and guiding force in Soviet society", it was charged both with making policies and ensuring that decisions were carried out promptly and efficiently.

At the apex of the CPSU was the central committee and its "inner cabinet", the politburo. Made up of between 11 and 15 members and 6 and 8 non-voting (candidate) members, the politburo, headed by the general secretary, exercised power over both policy making and day-to-day decisions.

The hierarchical nature of the CPSU's organization stretched through all levels of Soviet society down to the primary party organizations which existed in every farm, factory and enterprise and which reported on problems of inefficiency and mismanagement. The CPSU also took responsibility for general political education and, through its "party list" system, had the power to make appointments to all positions in economic and social life.

The end of Soviet rule

The political superstructure of the Soviet Union collapsed after a conservative coup in August 1991 failed. After Boris Yeltsin suspended the Russian Communist Party, Gorbachev resigned as general secretary of the CPSU and nationalized all its assets. More than 70 years of communist government were at an end. The State Council (President Gorbachev and the heads of the participating republics) assumed executive control and recognized the independence of Latvia, Lithuania and Estonia.

In December 1991 the leaders of Russia, Ukraine and Belarus met to set up a Commonwealth of Independent States (CIS), based on voluntary ties and cooperation in economic and foreign policy. Eight of the other new republics – Moldova, Tajikistan, Armenia, Azerbaijan, Turkmenistan, Kazakhstan, Kyrgyzstan and Uzbekistan – joined in 1992, and Georgia in 1994. The CIS has no formal political institutions but uses summits to formulate joint policy.

By the late 1990s, most of the republics had new constitutions and were nominally democratic, but political strife continued due to complex ethnic rivalries and resistance to change by ex-communist officials and administrators. In Russia, President Yeltsin, who had emerged victorious from an armed rebellion in 1993, received an endorsement of extended presidential power by referendum. He was re-elected as president in 1996 despite his obvious ill health. Yeltsin sacked the entire government in 1998 as the financial situation worsened and economic reform was blocked by the Duma. There were sustained allegations of corruption against state officials, including the embezzlement of IMF funds amounting to US$50 billion by Central Bank staff.

At the end of 1999, Yeltsin appointed as prime minister Vladimir Putin, a former KGB officer. He then resigned the presidency, nominating Putin as his successor; the nomination was confirmed in the presidential election of March 2000.

RETHINKING SUPERPOWER
STRATEGIES

The Soviet Union rapidly emerged as a global superpower after World War II, rivaled only by the United States in its military and political influence. The Soviet troops remaining in Eastern Europe after its liberation in 1945 helped to establish socialist states under Soviet control in Bulgaria, Czechoslovakia, Hungary, Poland and Romania, as well as the eastern half of Germany (the German Democratic Republic).

Formal treaties – the Council for Mutual Economic Assistance (COMECON) and the Warsaw Pact (a defensive agreement to counter the North Atlantic Treaty Organization, NATO) – bound these countries economically and militarily to Moscow, and completed the Soviet Union's domination of the region. The Soviet Union also assumed political leadership of a numerically powerful bloc of socialist states in Asia, including Mongolia, North Korea (1948), China (1949) and North Vietnam (1954). In 1961 Cuba joined the Soviet bloc.

During the "Cold War" years of extreme political hostility – which reached its height with the Cuban missile crisis of 1962 – the Soviet Union and the United States embarked upon a nuclear arms race that came to dominate global politics for the next two decades.

The Brezhnev doctrine

By the early 1960s the Soviet Union was finding it increasingly difficult to maintain control over the geographically fragmented bloc of socialist states. Even within Eastern Europe tensions erupted. On two notable occasions – Hungary (1956) and Czechoslovakia (1968) – Soviet troops were sent in to restore order. Explicit justification for such intervention was spelt out in 1968 in the so-called Brezhnev doctrine, whereby Moscow claimed a right to intervene in the internal affairs of socialist countries wherever socialism was deemed to be threatened.

Relations between China and the Soviet Union had become very strained. Under the leadership of Mao Zedong (1893–1976), China chose to follow an increasingly independent socialist path, and by 1960 all the Soviet Union's advisors and technicians in China had been withdrawn.

The signing of the 1972 Strategic Arms

A grim display of military might Rockets are paraded through Red Square at the height of the Cold War. Next to Khrushchev on the viewing platform, in the soft hat, is the bearded figure of Cuba's Fidel Castro.

Grozny ablaze The capital of Chechnya was bombed intensively by Russia, beginning in 1994. Russia's conduct in the war has aroused criticism abroad but is painted in patriotic colors at home.

Limitation Treaty (SALT I) marked a thaw in relations between the Soviet Union and the United States, improved further by the withdrawal of United States troops from Vietnam after 1973. But detente did not prevent the Soviet Union from increasing its supply of arms to Third World countries, or from sending military advisors to wars in Angola and the Horn of Africa. The Soviet invasion of Afghanistan in December 1979 brought a revival of Cold War attitudes.

End of a superpower

By the mid-1980s the Soviet Union was spending 15 percent of its GNP on defense (compared with the United States' 6 percent). The burden on its domestic economy became increasingly unacceptable. The election of Mikhail Gorbachev as general secretary in 1985 heralded a new era in East–West relations, with new emphasis on reducing military and nuclear commitments, and a call for all countries to cooperate to resolve the world's problems.

The signing of the Intermediate Range Nuclear Force (INF) treaty in December 1987 was the first step in reversing the arms race. It was followed by Soviet withdrawal from Afghanistan, the scaling down of its presence in Mongolia and the reduction of aid to socialist movements in the Third World. As the communist regimes of Eastern Europe fell in 1989, the Soviet Union chose not to assert the Brezhnev doctrine. In November 1990 Gorbachev attended a meeting of the Conference of Security and Cooperation in Europe (CSCE) in Paris ending the 40-year ideological division in Europe. That same year he won the Nobel peace prize.

The collapse of the Soviet Union inevitably changed regional security. The CIS initially tried to establish unified defenses, but this collapsed in 1993 and was replaced by a committee responsible for co-ordinating military defense between the states. The CIS was active in negotiating ceasefires in Abkhazia and Nagorno-Karabakh and discussed a united air-defense system in the late 1990s, but relations were marred by arguments over Russia's continued domination. In 1993 Russia and the US signed the START II and in March 1997 agreed to begin drafting START III, which would reduce the nuclear arsenals of each country further. The Black Sea Fleet, however, remained contested between Russia and Ukraine.

Russia's relationship with NATO became increasingly strained in the late 1990s. Russia joined NATO's Partnership for Peace program of military co-operation in 1994 and signed a "Fundamental Act on Relations, Co-operation and Mutual Security" in 1997. Following this, Russia agreed to Poland, Hungary and the Czech Republic joining NATO. However, in 1998, Russia was angry not to be informed about NATO air exercises in the Balkans, and when NATO began an offensive against Yugoslavia in 1999, Russia suspended its relations with the alliance. Prior to this, Russia had mediated in the conflict with Yugoslavia and also between the UN and Iraq.

Russia's relationships with China and India improved dramatically in the late 1990s with resolution of territorial disputes and signature of agreements relating to gas pipelines and the provision of nuclear generating equipment. As the 20th century came to a close it was far from clear how relations in this part of the world would ultimately be resolved.

CHECHNYA

The Russian Federation's handling of Chechnya has echoes of the Soviet military failure in Afghanistan in the 1980s. The autonomous district of Checheno-Ingush refused to sign the federal treaty of 1992 and declared itself an independent republic. This declaration was never accepted by Russia, and after several years of terrorism by Chechen rebels, Russia invaded the region in 1994. Its forces met with fierce resistance. The capital Grozny was bombed indiscriminately, with many civilian casualties. Russia's conduct of the war was criticized at home and abroad and the invasion had little success in subduing the region, although up to 80,000 people may have died. In 1995, a ceasefire granted autonomy to Chechnya, but fighting continued until mid-1996.

A constant campaign of terrorism was waged by Chechen guerrillas over the next three years, including bomb attacks in Moscow. In August 1999, rebels attacked the neighboring republic of Dagestan, hoping to create a unified Islamic state. Russia responded with air strikes and a ground invasion. In May 2000 Russia imposed direct rule, ousting the democratically elected incumbent president Aslan Maskhadov. The conflict displaced up to half a million people and killed thousands more. Russia was criticized abroad for human rights abuses, but public support at home remained high. Russia insisted that its domestic troubles in Chechnya did not concern outsiders. It did, however, allow a Council of Europe fact-finding mission in Chechnya in 2000.

The conflict was far from settled in the early 2000s. Violence continued with the guerrillas resorting to suicide bombs and lightning raids. Russia remained determined to assert its right to hang on to Chechnya and to ensure that any new government of the republic would be firmly pro-Russian in stance.

The Baltic States: return to sovereignty

The Baltic states of Estonia, Latvia and Lithuania were part of the tsarist Russian empire until its collapse in 1917. On 3 March 1918 the new revolutionary Bolshevik government in Moscow concluded the Treaty of Brest-Litovsk with Germany and relinquished control of the old empire's Baltic provinces. With the end of World War I in November, the provisions of this treaty lapsed, leaving the Baltic provinces with an uncertain future. Revolutionary forces in Estonia set up a workers' commune on German withdrawal, but this was overthrown in the ensuing civil war with the assistance of British naval forces operating in the Baltic. A democratic republic was proclaimed in May 1919. Democratic republics were set up in the same year in Latvia and Lithuania. But these regimes did not survive the difficult interwar years. The first regime to be toppled by a coup was in Lithuania in December 1926, followed by Estonia in March 1934 and Latvia in May 1934.

World War II signalled the end of independence for all three states. In a secret protocol of the Soviet-German agreement signed on 23 August 1939, the Baltic republics were assigned to the Soviet sphere of interest. In June 1940 a Soviet ultimatum forced the governments

Incident in Lithuania Thousands of mourners gather for the funerals of 15 civilians killed when Soviet special troops (the Black Berets) stormed the TV tower in Vilnius in January 1991 and fired on a crowd of peaceful demonstrators.

State of emergency Following the Soviet assault, Lithuanian nationalists form an armed blockade to defend the parliament building against possible attack, while a line of Red Cross volunteers stand by to attend the wounded.

of all three to resign, to be replaced by those acceptable to Stalin. A month later these puppet governments declared themselves Soviet Socialist Republics and applied to join the Soviet Union, which they duly did in August. Less than a year later all three were invaded by German forces, but in the withdrawal of the occupying armies in 1944 they returned to the Soviet Union.

From Soviet republic to independence

During the Cold War, the Baltic Soviet republics, which have direct access to the North Atlantic, were of stragetic importance to the Soviet Union, and were firmly entrenched as an integral part of its war machine. An important naval base was built at Liepaja (Latvia). In the redrawing of the political boundaries after World War II the former German Baltic port of Königsburg, renamed Kaliningrad, was made an enclave of the Russian republic and crucial communication lines across Lithuania linked this high security zone with the rest of Russia.

Glasnost opened the way to a new assertion of national identity among the Baltic peoples. In the Soviet Union's first open elections to the Congress of People's Deputies in March 1989, "people power" in the Baltic region was expressed by throwing out the CPSU's nominees, including the prime ministers of both Latvia and Lithuania, and electing a new national leadership. From this point on the movement toward regaining independence was swift but by no means smooth.

In February and March 1990 multiparty elections to the republics' supreme soviets resulted in total victory for the nationalists in Lithuania. Sajudis, the nationalist movement, won by a large majority and on 11 March it became the first union republic to declare its independence from the Soviet Union. On 30 March the Estonian soviet voted 70 to 0

(3 abstensions) to proclaim the 1940 Soviet occupation of their country illegal. In May it renamed itself simply the "Republic of Estonia" and restored the pre-1940 flag and national anthem. The Latvians too voted the 1940 occupation illegal and resolved to return to their 1922 constitution.

International recognition of the Baltic states was not forthcoming, and the concentration of Soviet armed forces in the

Baltic states was a barrier to progress toward independence. On 10 January 1991 President Gorbachev told Lithuania that it must accept Soviet central control. This precipitated popular demonstrations in the capital Vilnius, and on 13 January Soviet paratroopers fired on an unarmed crowd killing 15 people and injuring 140. As international opinion turned against Gorbachev, Lithuania responded by voting to secede from the Soviet Union and organized a plebiscite on the question. Gorbachev declared the plebiscite illegal but it went ahead nonetheless, with over 90 percent voting for independence. Similar ballots in Latvia and Estonia in March recorded large majorities for independence. Stalemate had been reached.

The Soviet coup of August 1991 totally transformed the situation. The international discrediting of the communist regime gave the Baltic republics the chance they had been looking for. Within days of Gorbachev's return to Moscow, the European Community had taken the lead in recognizing the independence of the three republics on 27 August. Two weeks later the Soviet State Council accepted the inevitable and finally recognized the independence of Estonia, Latvia and Lithuania on 6 September. All three countries were granted membership of the United Nations in the same year.

ENVIRONMENTAL ISSUES

MISMANAGED RESOURCES · FAR-FLUNG POLLUTION · A SLOW, COSTLY CLEAN-UP

Many of the environmental problems of the republics that comprised the former Soviet Union stem from the rapid industrialization that began after the Bolshevik Revolution of 1917. From then until the breakup of the Soviet Union in 1991 resources were exploited on a gigantic scale, controlled by a communist regime desperate to catch up economically with the West. Ecological destruction is now widespread: in Central Asia, the Aral Sea has shrunk because of excessive water extraction for irrigation from the rivers that feed it; Siberia's Lake Baikal is being fouled by industrial effluent; air pollution levels in Ukrainian and Russian industrial centers are often above the official limit; while radioactive fallout from the 1986 Chernobyl nuclear accident still blights lives and land.

COUNTRIES IN THE REGION

Armenia, Azerbaijan, Belarus, Estonia, Georgia, Kazakhstan, Kyrgyzstan, Latvia, Lithuania, Moldova, Mongolia, Russia, Tajikistan, Turkmenistan, Ukraine, Uzbekistan

POPULATION AND WEALTH

	Highest	Middle	Lowest
Population (millions)	146.001 (Russia)	16.733 (Kazakh.)	1.431 (Estonia)
Population increase (% 1990–95)	1.6% (Mongolia)	−0.2% (Russia)	−1.2% (Estonia)
Energy use (kg/year per person of oil equivalent)	4,009 (Russia)	1,833 (Uzbek.)	448 (Georgia)
Purchasing power (Int$/per year)	4,363 (Russia)	2,518 (Armenia)	1,115 (Tajikistan)

ENVIRONMENTAL INDICATORS

CO_2 emissions ('000 tonnes year)	1,818,011 (Russia)	438,211 (Ukraine)	3,649 (Armenia)
Car ownership (% of population)	19% (Lithuania)	10% (Georgia)	4% (Moldova)
Protected territory including marine areas	13% (Latvia)	7% (Armenia)	1.5% (Moldova)
Forests as a % of original forest	69% (Russia)	27% (Belarus)	4% (Turkmen.)
Artificial fertilizer use (kg/ha/year)	157% (Belarus)	82% (Turkmen.)	2% (Mongolia)
Access to safe drinking water (% population; rural/urban)	88/99% (Uzbekistan)	49/82% (Tajikistan)	3/73% (Mongolia)

MAJOR ENVIRONMENTAL PROBLEMS AND SOURCES

Air pollution: generally high, urban very high; acid rain prevalent; high greenhouse gas emissions
River/lake pollution: high; *sources*: industry, agriculture, sewage, acid deposition, nuclear, forestry
Land pollution: high; *sources*: industry, agriculture, urban/household, nuclear
Land degradation: *types*: desertification, soil erosion, salinization, deforestation; *causes*: agriculture, industry
Waste disposal issues: domestic; industrial; nuclear
Major events: Chernobyl (1986) and Sosnovyy Bor (1992), nuclear accidents; Kyshtym (1957) hazardous waste spill; Novosibirsk (1979) catastrophic industrial accident; oil spills in Arctic (1994)

MISMANAGED RESOURCES

The critical environmental situation of the former Soviet Union has its roots in the complex interplay of political, economic and social factors that has marked the region since the formation of the communist state in 1922. Long before the fall of Tsar Nicholas II (1868–1918), Russia had already opened up its Siberian territories – and the vast mineral wealth there – with the start of the Trans-Siberian railroad in 1891. On the overpopulated land to the west, agricultural techniques were backward, the soil was exhausted and there were frequent crop failures.

From 1924 onward, under the dictatorship of Joseph Stalin (1879–1953), a series of Five-Year Plans aimed to industrialize and modernize the Soviet Union. This included the building of gigantic new dams, power stations, industrial plants and huge factories. But the decisions of an overcentralized, bureaucratic government were made without thought for their environmental impact. The state's Central Planning Committee – influenced by the underlying Marxist ideology and the vast size of the country – believed that the Soviet Union's resources were inexhaustible. In most of the industrialized world, the volume of mineral and fuel extracted doubles every 15 to 18 years, but in the Soviet Union it doubled every 8 to 10 years.

Before the breakup of the Soviet Union – and with it the centralized bureaucracies – no one took responsibility for environmental problems. Ministries and institutions protected their own interests. Environmental control was either ignored or responsibility for it was shifted up and down the chain of command. Management was mainly interested in obtaining raw materials for their specific industry and meeting production targets, often regardless of cost and in the shortest time.

Unlimited exploitation

Irrigated areas were expanded on a vast scale, and there has been massive overuse of mineral fertilizers. Excess is also a characteristic of the region's many hydroelectric power (HEP) schemes. The harnessing of rivers for HEP provided a cheap means of increasing energy supplies. As a result of extensive dam building – in the 1990s the number of reservoirs exceeded 3,500 – the former Soviet Union has lost 21 million ha (50.5 million acres) of arable land through flooding.

Burned out (*left*) Desolation reigns after a fire in a taiga forest in the northwest of the Ural Mountains in Russia. As many as 30,000 fires may rage through the forests of the former Soviet Union every year, contributing to pollution and destroying habitats.

Map of environmental problems (*below*) Air and water pollution are worst in the west of the region; 103 cities exceed by 10 times the air pollution limits set by the former Soviet Union. Even in the relatively cleaner east, industrial waste from pulp and paper mills is polluting Lake Baikal's freshwater. In the Russian Arctic, leaking oil pipelines have caused massive damage to the tundra environment.

The timber industry, too, reflects resource mismanagement. Although the former Soviet Union still has over 800 million ha (over 2 billion acres) of forested land – 91.6 percent of it in Russia – it regarded these as inexhaustible. Loggers exceeded the permitted cutting quotas in many areas, and replanted too little. Since 1970 cedar forests in the far east of Russia have been reduced by 21.8 percent. For the Ministry of Timber Industry, the increased logging was a goal in itself, necessary for fulfilling the state plan, even though each year 85,000 cu m (3 million cu ft) of cut timber sank while being floated illegally down the rivers.

Key environmental issues

- major town or city
- heavily polluted town or city
- major pollution event
- heavily polluted river

area affected by permafrost

dead lake

annual air pollution (tonnes per square km)

	20
	10
	5
	2

FAR-FLUNG POLLUTION

Northern Eurasia must urgently address the issues of air, water and land pollution, radioactive contamination, excessive logging, and the slow death of rivers through salinization and stagnation. In Siberia and Russia's far east, destruction of permafrost (permanently frozen ground) is a growing problem. Although many of the causes of pollution declined when economies in the region collapsed in the early 90s, economic recovery is likely to cause their recurrence.

The energy industry is the main polluter of air. Coal-fired power stations, which produce about 20 percent of the region's electricity, are the chief source of sulfur dioxide, nitrogen oxides and dust emissions. Other sources of air pollution are factories producing metals, chemicals and pulp and paper. Levels of air pollution 10 times above the legal limit have been recorded in 103 cities – with a total population of nearly 40 million – across the region. The worst levels are in industrialized areas such as Donetsk-Dnieper in Ukraine, some 250 km (200 mi) north of the Black Sea; in the Kuznetsk coal basin (Kuzbas) of southwestern Siberia; and in Norilsk in eastern Siberia, where sulfurous smoke pours out from smelters processing nickel, cobalt and copper. Some 97.5 percent of pollutants are either solid particles or sulfur dioxide, carbon monoxide, nitrogen oxides and hydrocarbons.

Local pollution can be horrendous. In Nizhniy Tagil, a Russian town in the Ural Mountains, one industrial plant was releasing 700,000 tonnes of poisonous fumes annually – the equivalent of 2 tonnes for each of the town's inhabitants. Pollution from vehicles is likely to increase as private transport increases. Even in the recession from 1990 to 1994, the number of private cars increased by 143 percent in Russia, 130 percent in Ukraine and 123 percent in Kazakhstan.

The region is still a major contributor to global air pollution problems. Russia produces 1.8 billion tonnes of carbon dioxide a year, equivalent to 12 tonnes per person. This increases the "greenhouse effect" (atmospheric warming caused by so-called greenhouse gases absorbing heat radiated from the Earth). However, Moldova produces only the equivalent of 2.5 tonnes per person. For comparison, the United States produces 20.5 tonnes per person and the world average is 4 tonnes per person. The

Extent of radiation dispersal (*below*) seven days after the explosion at Chernobyl. The release of radioactive material lasted for 10 days in all, its distribution varying as the winds changed. Initially southeasterly winds blew it over Poland, Ukraine, Belarus, Latvia, Lithuania, Finland and across Norway and Sweden. The winds then changed, leaving fallout over most of Europe. The extent of the fallout was determined by whether or not rain washed the contamination from the atmosphere, sometimes creating higher than expected levels as in the central British Isles. One of the most dangerous contaminants was caesium-137, which contaminated livestock that ate grass on which the chemical had settled. Restrictions on livestock movement and slaughter were introduced in the United Kingdom and the Nordic Countries and lasted many years.

Cause of the Chernobyl disaster (*right*) Prior to testing a generator's capacity to power emergency systems, engineers shut off the emergency core-cooling systems so as not to affect the test results. In a further breach of safety standards, almost all the neutron-absorbing control rods were removed from the core to increase power output. However, coolant water was unable to reach the reactor as power output was too low. When the test started, power generation went out of control and an explosion of steam tore the reactor apart.

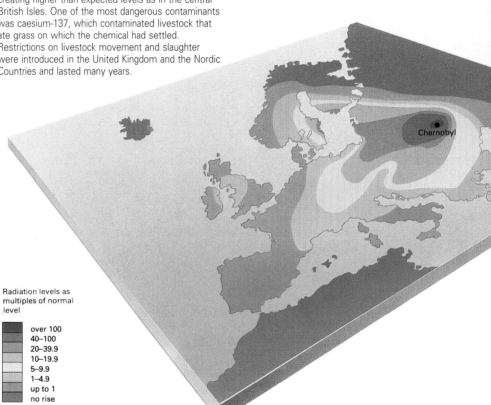

Radiation levels as multiples of normal level

- over 100
- 40–100
- 20–39.9
- 10–19.9
- 5–9.9
- 1–4.9
- up to 1
- no rise

burning of fossil fuels also causes acidification, although sulfur dioxide emissions have generally decreased since the mid-1980s as a result of a regional agreement. Russia agreed to phase out the production of CFCs (chlorofluorocarbons) during 2000. CFCs deplete the stratosphere's ozone layer that blocks harmful ultra-violet radiation from the Sun.

Troubled waters

Bodies of water throughout the region are abused and mismanaged. One of the most critical concerns is Lake Baikal, in southern Siberia. With a depth of 1,620 m (5,315 ft), it is the world's oldest and deepest freshwater lake. It has 20 percent of the world's freshwater supply. Its unique plants and aquatic animals – including freshwater seals – are seriously threatened by wastes, including dioxin, pumped into it by pulp and paper mills on its shores. In addition, sewage is pumped into the lake.

Such practices are not unique to Lake Baikal. Throughout the region untreated industrial effluent and raw sewage are pumped directly into rivers and lakes, killing fishes and poisoning water supplies. The river Volga, flowing 3,690 km (2,293 mi) from northern Russia into the Caspian Sea was chosen as an industrial, energy and transportation artery for the Soviet Union in the 1930s. Its extensive system of dams and irrigation channels and pollution from chemical factories, oil refineries, sewage and agriculture have brought the sturgeon that produces caviar close to extinction. Attempts are being made to protect areas in the lower Volga.

Grass roots pollution

The land and its people are also under attack from pollution. Across Northern Eurasia, the overcutting of forests has led to severe soil erosion, the loss of animal habitats and soil fertility, and the silting of

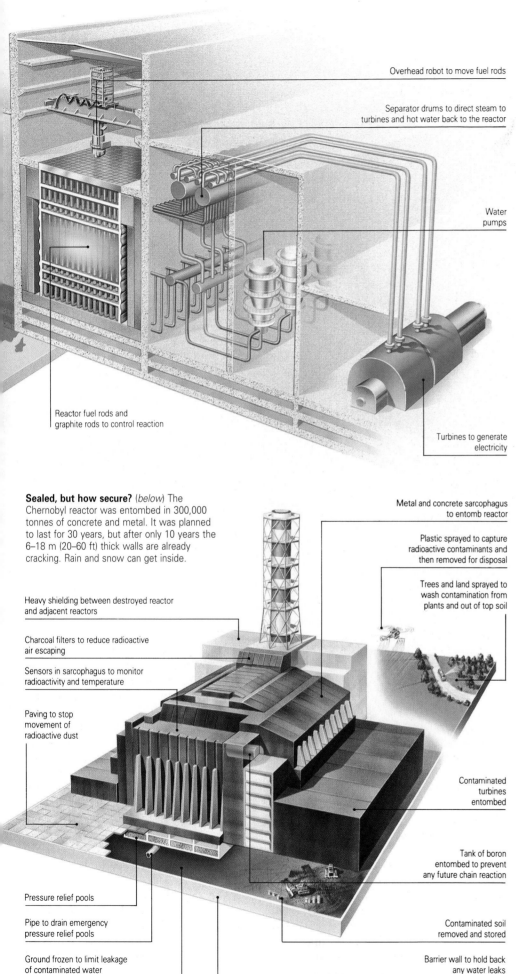

Overhead robot to move fuel rods

Separator drums to direct steam to turbines and hot water back to the reactor

Water pumps

Reactor fuel rods and graphite rods to control reaction

Turbines to generate electricity

Sealed, but how secure? (*below*) The Chernobyl reactor was entombed in 300,000 tonnes of concrete and metal. It was planned to last for 30 years, but after only 10 years the 6–18 m (20–60 ft) thick walls are already cracking. Rain and snow can get inside.

Heavy shielding between destroyed reactor and adjacent reactors

Charcoal filters to reduce radioactive air escaping

Sensors in sarcophagus to monitor radioactivity and temperature

Paving to stop movement of radioactive dust

Pressure relief pools

Pipe to drain emergency pressure relief pools

Ground frozen to limit leakage of contaminated water

Metal and concrete sarcophagus to entomb reactor

Plastic sprayed to capture radioactive contaminants and then removed for disposal

Trees and land sprayed to wash contamination from plants and out of top soil

Contaminated turbines entombed

Tank of boron entombed to prevent any future chain reaction

Contaminated soil removed and stored

Barrier wall to hold back any water leaks

CHERNOBYL – A NUCLEAR DISASTER

On Saturday April 26 1986, the world's worst nuclear accident occurred in the Ukrainian town of Chernobyl, 150 km (80 mi) north of Kiev. An explosion in the No. 4 reactor of the town's nuclear power plant ripped the 1,000 tonne steel lid from the reactor's core and blasted through the concrete containment shell. The fire that followed released a cloud of highly radioactive substances, equivalent to 90 bombs of the type that destroyed Hiroshima in Japan in 1945.

For 10 days, radioactive fumes poured out of the plant, carried by winds far beyond Ukraine. The gases included iodine-131, which affects the thyroid glands, and even more hazardous cesium-137, which collects in muscle tissue. The effects of the accident will remain for a long time to come. Around 2,800 sq km (1,000 sq mi) are contaminated. A 30 km (19 mi) zone around the plant was evacuated; 135,000 people had to move and and are unlikely to be able to return. The immediate death toll was 31, but in the next five years 7,000 to 10,000 more people died, mainly those who worked on the cleanup. 150,000 registered as victims of the accident, but the real figure is more likely to be around one million. Thyroid cancers have increased significantly in the region. As people left, moose, wolves, wild boar, otters and lynx moved in and became established. There is now talk of making Chernobyl a wildlife reserve.

rivers from landslides. From Moldova to Kazakhstan an indiscriminate use of agricultural chemicals has triggered a steep rise in the incidence of cancer, mental illness and birth defects.

Nuclear contamination from leaks or open waste dumps is a major concern (in the wake of Chernobyl). In March 1992 a leak of radioactive iodine from a reactor at Sosnovyy Bor, 100 km (62 mi) west of St Petersburg, created fears of a new disaster.

Exploitation of the ecologically sensitive tundra in the far north of Russia is another worrying issue. In the ever-pressing search for natural gas and oil, not only are crystal-clear rivers and lakes being polluted, forests cut down and the lifestyles of local peoples dislocated, but also construction work is destroying the moss and lichens that insulate the permafrost below ground; the permafrost then melts, creating bogs that may have long-term effects on Siberia's ecological health.

A SLOW, COSTLY CLEAN-UP

From the early 1970s, although economic goals remained the priority, authorities in the Soviet Union began to consider the environmental costs of the Communist Party's fifty years of emphasis on industrialization, and adopted many fundamental environmental laws. These included acts relating to the protection of land, water, the geological environment, forests and the atmosphere. Almost every year, the Communist Party and Council of Ministers issued directives on nature conservation, but they made little impact on reducing pollution across the country. Cleaning up an environment that has been abused for so long is expensive, and the old systems are slow to change. The dead hand of bureaucracy still weighs heavily, even after the demise of the Soviet Union.

Until the rise of the reforming president Mikhail Gorbachev, environmental protest was regarded by the Soviet authorities as dissident behavior – a form of political agitation. In the wake of *glasnost* (the period of "openness" and reform that preceded the collapse of communism), there was considerable outspoken protest about the state of the environment. "Green" groups have proliferated. There are even green parties and protest groups.

The fight for Lake Baikal, which has been going on for 30 years, has had some successes. To prevent excessive logging, all felling of trees along the lake's shoreline was banned in 1988; this helps to stop soil erosion and landslides, which causes silt to enter nearby rivers and ultimately the lake itself. The greatest fight has been to stop untreated waste being poured into the lake from the 100 or so factories on Lake Baikal's shore and on the banks of the rivers that feed the lake. The worst pollution has come from two pulp and cellulose mills: one at Baikalsk at the lake's southern end and the other at Selenginsk on the Selenga river, near the lake's southeastern shore.

The defenders of Lake Baikal are now seeing the fruits of their efforts. In 1987, the former Soviet Union's Central Committee and Council of Ministers decided to phase out Baikalsk's hazardous operations, and ordered pollution control equipment to be installed at the Selenginsk plant. In 1989 a conservation scheme was adopted and in 1993 a Baikal Commission was established. In 1996, it

COPING AFTER COMMUNISM

The environmental troubles facing the independent states of the former Soviet union stemmed from two fundamental beliefs: that the natural resources of the region were inexhaustible; and that any environmental legislation was acceptable as long as it did not threaten economic progress.

In the early years after communism environmentalists were successful in pushing through stringent legislation, especially in Russia. Pressure groups flourished. At the same time, however, national economies were collapsing. Industrial and agricultural production dropped dramatically and as a result pollution levels dropped too. For most people, life became much worse.

Western investment, expertise and technology are helping environmental and economic recovery, but two dangers are becoming apparent. The first is auto-

matic rejection of Soviet policies, which did have some positive elements for the environment. For example, there were strong state systems for protected areas enabling huge areas to remain unspoiled. Food packaging was largely reusable, public transport systems were well developed and used, and manufactured goods needed to last a long time.

The second danger is that, ten years since the end of the USSR, official hostility to environmental protection in Russia seems to be growing. In March 2000 the offices of Greenpeace in Moscow were raided under a decision of the anti-terrorist commission of Moscow city. In July the same year, President Vladimir Putin disbanded the State Committee for Environment Protection and passed its functions to the Ministry of Natural Resources, whose priority is economic development.

Early preparation (*above*)
Kindergarten students learn what to do in case of an accident at the gas factory in Astrakhan, 8 km (5 mi) from their village school. Faulty construction at the factory has increased the risk.

Follow-up to Chernobyl (*left*)
Radiologists from Kiev take soil samples in the village of Vylgvo near Chernobyl. Many of the 247 original residents refused to leave in spite of the closure of local wells, a ban on fishing in the local river, and the contamination of 105 houses, now condemned.

became a World Heritage Site. The future of the lake is looking brighter. Pollution from the Selenginsk complex and the damaging practice of transporting logs on the lake have ceased.

The Caspian fiasco
The Caspian Sea is the largest water body on Earth that is not connected to the oceans. Its water level is subject to regular and dramatic changes: from 1933–1941 its level fell by 1.7m (5.5 ft). Evaporation from the bay was high. State planners decided to dam the Kara-Bogaz-Gol, a large shallow bay adjoining the Caspian Sea in Turkmenistan. By cutting it off, the planners intended to reduce evaporation from the Caspian.

The dam was completed in 1980, coinciding with a period of rising water level; between 1978 and 1994 the level rose by 2.25 m (7.25 ft). In 1992 the dam was

breached to allow water back in again, but not before residual salt from the dried out bay had blown onto farmland and contaminated it. The rising sea level has flooded fishing villages, oil installations, recreational facilities and other low-lying facilities. All the newly independent republics surrounding the Caspian are now working together to study the resulting environmental problems and plan solutions.

Chernobyl: still not safe
The 1986 Chernobyl nuclear accident deeply affected the Soviet government's approach to nuclear power, which – before the USSR's disintegration – met about 3.3 percent of the country's electricity needs. After the accident, a massive surge of environmental protest forced the Soviet authorities to stop the construction of a number of nuclear reactors, and plans for 10 nuclear-powered district heating stations

in major cities were cancelled. In addition, the region's nuclear industry was opened up, for the first time, to international scrutiny.

In the aftermath of Chernobyl, the state had to build new settlements for over 100,000 evacuees from the area, buy up condemned meat from local livestock, and introduce new safety features and training at other nuclear reactors – all at vast expense. And Chernobyl is still not safe. To try to contain the radioactivity, the reactor that exploded was entombed in concrete walls 60 m (197 ft) high, 60 m long and 6–18 m (20–60 ft) thick. Nevertheless, the concrete has become brittle from the continuous irradiation and the difference of temperature between the inner and outer walls. An earthquake of 6 or more on the Richter scale could cause it to collapse. An earthquake of that magnitude is estimated to happen in the region once every 100 years. If that happens, yet more radioactivity will be released.

Chernobyl is not the only radiation danger zone. In Kazakhstan, the region once favored by the Soviet Union for testing nuclear weapons, deformities among people who were living close to the test sites have been passed on to their children. Eighty kilometers (50 mi) north of Chelyabinsk is an atomic weapons complex whose existence has only recently been admitted by the Russian authorities. Western scientists who have inspected the site have described it as the most dangerously polluted spot on Earth.

The Aral Sea crisis

The most obvious environmental disaster to strike Northern Eurasia – even worse, many say, than the Chernobyl nuclear accident – is the drying up of the Aral Sea. This vast salty lake lies some 400 km (250 mi) east of the Caspian Sea and was once the Earth's fourth largest inland water body. In the early 1960s, a decision was taken by the former Soviet Union's central planning authorities to increase cotton production dramatically in Kazakhstan and the Central Asian republic of Uzbekistan bordering the Aral Sea. Water for irrigation was to be drawn from the two main rivers feeding the Aral, the Syr Darya and Amu Darya. In the years that followed, 90 percent of water was drained from these rivers by irrigation canals for cotton, as well as other crops, and only 10 percent remained to replenish the Aral and counteract evaporation. The scale of the problem prompted the Soviet Union's ruling body, the Supreme Soviet, to declare the Aral Sea basin an ecological disaster area "beyond human control".

In 1960 the Aral's water level was just over 53 m (175 ft) and its area 66,820 sq km (25,800 sq mi). By 1987 the sea level had fallen 13 m (43 ft), and its area decreased by 40 percent – in other words, 27,000 sq km (10,424 sq mi) of the Aral's surface area had dried up, an area roughly the size of Belgium. The water is still receding, and at such a steady pace that, unless drastic action is taken, the Aral Sea could disappear by 2020. The consequences of the disappearing water have already been disastrous.

Fatal results

Each year, winds sweeping across the exposed, salt-encrusted seabed carry 75 million tonnes of salt, dust, sand and the residue of pesticides and other agricultural chemicals back onto the surrounding cottonfields to kill crops and the natural vegetation. The combination of this lethal, wind-blown brew and the huge quantities of pesticides and herbicides sprayed onto the cotton crops each year has taken a terrible toll on human health – especially of children. Infant mortality among the local Kara-kalpak people is four times the national average, and more than one in ten babies die before their first birthday. In the Central Asian cottonfields, some 83 percent of the

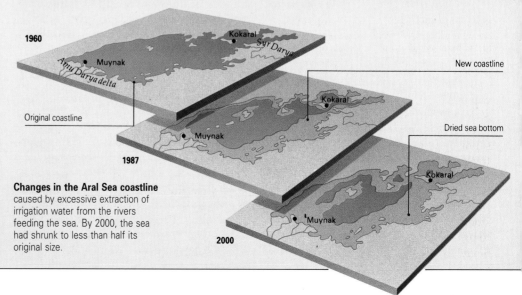

Changes in the Aral Sea coastline caused by excessive extraction of irrigation water from the rivers feeding the sea. By 2000, the sea had shrunk to less than half its original size.

Ships of the desert (*above*) The rusty hulk of a boat litters the salty bed of what was once the world's fourth largest inland sea, but is now terrain more suitable for camels than ships. The fishing industry – formerly a major employer – has been decimated.

children who survive longer suffer from serious illnesses.

With so much of the Aral Sea gone, the salinity of the remaining water has nearly tripled. Twenty species of fish have been killed off, and with them the sea's fishing industry, which once employed 60,000 people. The port of Muynak, which once stood on the Aral's southern shore, used to produce more than a tenth of the former Soviet Union's fish catch. This once-bustling city is now virtually a ghost town standing 48 km (30 mi) from the receding water.

The death of the Aral Sea has had other effects, too: the water once moderated the area's climate, but extreme temperatures are now more common. Ironically, it was the sea's influence on the climate that made it possible to grow cotton so far north in the first place. The industry now suffers from shorter growing seasons and harsher conditions. Since gaining independence in 1991, responsibility for decisions about water management in Central Asia has passed to Kazakhstan, Kyrgyzstan, Tajikistan, Turkmenistan and Uzbekistan.

In 1993 the governments and peoples of the republics established the International Aral Sea Rehabilitation Fund. Experts agree it is not possible to restore fully the Aral Sea. Cutting back on cotton production or modernizing the irrigation systems to be less wasteful of water would help, but at a very high cost. Progress will only be made with international support. A United Nations sponsored conference in 1995 addressed the problems and there is growing international support for individual projects, although there has been criticism that the international community is not coordinating its activities sufficiently.

GLOSSARY

Acid rain Rain or any other form of PRECIPITATION that has become more acid by absorbing waste gases (for example, sulfur dioxide and nitrogen oxides) discharged into the ATMOSPHERE.

Acid soil Soil that has a pH of less than 7; it is often PEATY.

Added value A higher price fetched by an article or RESOURCE after it has been processed, such as crude oil after refining.

Agricultural economy An economy where most people work as cultivators or PASTORALISTS.

AIDS Acquired Immune Deficiency Syndrome, a disease that damages the body's immune system, making people more susceptible to disease. Human Immunodeficiency Virus (HIV) is one of the viruses that can lead to AIDS.

Air pollution The presence of gases and suspended particles in the air in high enough concentrations to harm humans, other animals, vegetation or materials. Human activity is the source of most pollution.

Alkaline soil Soil that has a pH of more than 7; chalk or limestone soils.

Alpine (1) A treeless ENVIRONMENT found on a mountain above the tree line but beneath the limit of permanent snow. (2) A plant that is adapted to grow in the TUNDRA-like environment of mountain areas.

Amphibian An animal that lives on land but whose life cycle requires some time in water.

Apartheid A way of organizing society to keep different racial groups apart. Introduced in South Africa by the National Party after 1948 as a means of ensuring continued white political dominance, it was dismantled in the 1990s.

Aquifer An underground layer of permeable rock, sand or gravel that absorbs and holds GROUNDWATER.

Arctic The northern POLAR region. In biological terms it also refers to the northern region of the globe where the mean temperature of the warmest month does not exceed 10°C (50°F).

Arid (climate) Dry and usually hot. Arid areas generally have less than 250 mm (10 inches) of rain a year.

Atmosphere The gaseous layer surrounding the Earth. It consists of nitrogen (78 percent), oxygen (21 percent), argon (1 percent), tiny amounts of carbon dioxide, neon, ozone, hydrogen and krypton, and varying amounts of water vapor.

Atoll A circular chain of CORAL reefs enclosing a lagoon. Atolls form as coral reefs fringing a volcanic island; as sea levels rise or the island sinks a lagoon is formed.

Autonomy The condition of being self-governing, usually granted to a subdivision of a larger STATE or to a territory belonging to it.

Balance of payments A statement of a country's transactions with all other countries over a given period.

Balance of power A theory of political stability based upon an even distribution of power among the leading STATES.

Basalt A fine-grained IGNEOUS ROCK. It has a dark color and contains little silica. Ninety percent of lavas are basaltic.

Bible The book of scriptures of CHRISTIANITY and JUDAISM. The Jewish Bible contains many books in common with the Christian version describing historical events and prophetic teachings, but the latter also includes accounts of the life and teachings of Jesus Christ.

Biodegradable (of a substance) easily broken down into simpler substances by bacteria or other decomposers. Products made of organic materials such as paper, woolens, leather and wood are biodegradable; many plastics are not.

Biodiversity The number of different species of plants and animals found in a given area. In general, the greater the number of species, the more stable and robust the ECOSYSTEM is.

Biomass The total mass of all the living organisms in a defined area or ECOSYSTEM.

Biosphere The thin layer of the Earth that contains all living organisms and the ENVIRONMENT that supports them.

Biotechnology Technology applied to biological processes, including genetic engineering, the manipulation of the genetic makeup of living organisms.

Birthrate The number of births expressed as a proportion of a population. Usually given as the annual number of live births per 1,000 population (also known as the crude birth rate).

Black economy The sector of the economy that avoids paying tax.

Bloc A group of countries closely bound by economic and/or political ties.

Boreal Typical of the northern climates lying between the ARCTIC and latitude 50°N, characterized by long cold winters and short summers. Vegetation in these regions is dominated by BOREAL FOREST.

Boreal forest The name given to the CONIFEROUS FORESTS or TAIGA of the northern hemisphere.

Brown coal A peat-like material, also known as lignite, which has a lower energy value than more mature forms of coal.

Buddhism A religion founded in the 6th and 5th centuries BC and based on the teachings of Siddhartha Gautama; it is widely observed in southern and southeast Asia.

Bureaucracy The body of STATE officials that carry out the day-to-day running of government. It may also refer to a system of a ministration marked by the inflexible application of rules.

Capital Machinery, investment funds or an employment relationship involving waged labor.

Capitalism A political and economic system based on the production of goods and services for profitable exchange in which labor is bought and sold for wages. Capitalist economies can be more or less regulated by governments. In a capitalist mixed economy the government owns some of the country's utilities and industries and also acts as a major employer.

Cash crop A crop grown for sale rather than for SUBSISTENCE.

Caste A system of rigid hereditary social divisions, normally associated with the Hindu caste system in India, where an individual is born into the caste of his or her parents, must marry within it, and cannot leave it.

Caucasian (1) A racial classification based on white or light skin color. (2) An inhabitant of the Caucasus region or the Indo-European language of this people.

Cereal A cultivated grass that has been bred selectively to produce high yields of edible grain for consumption by humans and livestock. The most important are wheat (*Triticum* sp.), rice (*Oryza sativa*) and maize (*Zea mays*).

CFCs (chlorofluorocarbons) Organic compounds made up of atoms of carbon, chlorine and fluorine. Gaseous CFCs used as aerosol propellants, refrigerant gases and solvent cleaners are known to cause depletion of the OZONE LAYER.

Christianity A religion based on the teachings of Jesus Christ and originating in the 1st century AD from JUDAISM; its main beliefs are found in the BIBLE. The Roman Catholic, Orthodox and Protestant churches are its major branches.

CITES (Convention on International Trade in Endangered Species) An international agreement signed by over 90 countries since 1973. SPECIES (FAUNA and FLORA) placed in Appendix I are considered to be in danger of EXTINCTION, and trade is prohibited without an export permit. Signatory countries must supply data to the World Conservation Union, which monitors IMPORTS and EXPORTS. Appendix II species may be threatened with extinction if trade is unregulated.

City-state An independent STATE consisting of a single city and the surrounding countryside needed to support it. Singapore is an example of a modern city-state.

Class (1) A group of people sharing a common economic position, for example large landowners, waged laborers or owners of small businesses. (2) (in zoology and botany) A rank in the taxonomic hierarchy coming between phylum and order. *See* CLASSIFICATION.

Classification A system of arranging the different types of living organisms according to the degree of similarity of their inherited characteristics. The classification system enables organisms to be identified and may also reveal the relationships between different groups. The internationally accepted classification hierarchy groups organisms first into divisions, then phyla, CLASSES, orders, FAMILIES, GENERA, SPECIES and SUBSPECIES.

Collectivization The organization of an economy (typically communist) by collective control through agencies of the state. *See* COMMUNISM.

Colonialism The political practice of occupying a foreign country for settlement and economic exploitation.

Colony A territory under the sovereignty of a foreign power.

COMECON The Council for Mutual Economic Assistance, formed in 1947 as an organization to further trade and economic cooperation between communist countries. It had 10 members before its collapse in 1989: the Soviet Union, Bulgaria, Czechoslovakia, Hungary, Poland, Romania, East Germany, Mongolia, Cuba, and Vietnam.

Commonwealth A loose association of STATES that were members of the former British EMPIRE, with the British monarch at its head.

Communism A social and economic system based on the communal ownership of property. It usually refers to the state-controlled social and economic systems in the former Soviet Union and Soviet-bloc countries and in the People's Republic of China. *See* SOCIALISM.

Coniferous forest A forest of mainly coniferous, or cone-bearing trees, frequently with evergreen needle-shaped leaves and found principally in the TEMPERATE ZONES and BOREAL regions.

Conservation The use, management and protection of NATURAL RESOURCES so that they are not degraded, depleted or wasted. *See also* SUSTAINABILITY.

Constitution The written statement of laws that defines the way in which a country is governed.

Consumer goods Goods that are acquired for immediate use, such as foodstuffs, radios, televisions and washing machines.

Continental climate The type of climate associated with the interior of continents. It is characterized by wide daily and seasonal ranges of temperature, especially outside the TROPICS, and by low rainfall.

Continental drift The theory that today's continents, formed by the breakup of prehistoric supercontinents, have slowly drifted to their present positions. The theory was first proposed by Alfred Wegener in 1912.

Continental shelf An extension of a continent, forming a shallow, sloping shelf covered by sea.

Coral A group of animals related to sea anemones and living in warm seas. Individuals, called polyps, combine to form a COLONY.

Culture (1) The beliefs, customs and social relations of a people. (2) The assumptions that a people make in interpreting their world.

Cyclone A center of low atmospheric pressure. Tropical cyclones are known as HURRICANES or typhoons.

Dead lake (or Dead river) An area of water in which dissolved oxygen levels have fallen as a result of acidification, overgrowth of plants or high levels of pollution, to the extent that few or no living things are able to survive.

Debt The financial obligations owed by a country to the rest of the world, usually repayable in US dollars. Total external debt includes public, publicly guaranteed, and private long-term debt.

Decolonization The transfer of government from a colonial power to the people of the COLONY at the time of political independence.

Deforestation The felling of trees and clearing of forested land to be put to other uses.

Delta A large accumulation of sediment, often fan-shaped, deposited where a river enters the sea or a lake.

Democracy A form of government in which policy is made by the people (direct democracy) or on their behalf (indirect democracy). Indirect democracy usually takes the form of competition among political parties at elections.

Desert A very ARID area with less than 25 cm (10 in) rainfall a year. In hot deserts the rate of evaporation is greater than the rate of PRECIPITATION, and there is little vegetation.

Desertification The creation of desert-like conditions usually caused by a combination of overgrazing, soil EROSION, prolonged DROUGHT and climate change.

Devaluation A deliberate reduction by a government in the exchange value of its own currency in gold, or in relation to the value of another currency.

Developed country Any country with high standards of living and a sophisticated economy, in contrast to DEVELOPING COUNTRIES. Various indicators are used to measure a country's wealth and material well-being: the GROSS NATIONAL PRODUCT, the PER CAPITA consumption of energy, the number of doctors per head of population and the average life expectancy, for example.

Developing country Any country that is characterized by low standards of living and a SUBSISTENCE economy. Sometimes called THIRD WORLD countries, they include most of Africa, Asia and Central and South America.

Dictator A leader who concentrates the power of the STATE in his or her own hands.

Divide see WATERSHED.

Dominant species The most numerous or prevailing SPECIES in a community of plants or animals.

Dormancy A period during which the metabolic activity of a plant or animal is reduced to such an extent that it can withstand difficult environmental conditions such as cold or DROUGHT.

Drought An extended period in which rainfall is substantially lower than average and the water supply is insufficient to meet demand.

EC *See* EUROPEAN COMMUNITY.

Ecology (1) The study of the interactions of living organisms with each other and with their ENVIRONMENT. (2) The study of the structure and functions of nature.

Ecosystem A community of plants and animals and the ENVIRONMENT in which they live and react with each other.

Effluent Any liquid waste discharged into the ENVIRONMENT as a byproduct of industry, agriculture or sewage treatment.

Emission A substance discharged into the air in the form of gases and suspended particles, from automobile engines and industrial smokestacks, for example.

Empire (1) A political organization of STATES and territories in which one dominates the rest. (2) The territory that constitutes such a group of states.

Endangered species A SPECIES whose population has dropped to such low levels that its continued survival is threatened.

Endemic species A SPECIES that is native to one specific area, and is therefore often said to be characteristic of that area.

Environment (1) The external conditions – climate, geology and other living things – that influence the life of individual organisms or ECOSYSTEMS. (2) The surroundings in which animals and plants live and interact.

Erosion The process by which exposed land surfaces are broken down into smaller particles or worn away by water, wind or ice.

Ethnic group A group of people sharing a social identity or **culture** based on language, religion, customs and/or common descent or kinship.

Euro The common currency of the EUROPEAN UNION, introduced in 1999. The euro operates at a fixed rate alongside the national currencies of member states until 2002, when it will supersede them. To enter the euro trading zone countries needed to meet financial convergence criteria set out in the Maastricht Treaty of 1992. Eleven countries did so: Austria, Belgium, Finland, France, Germany, Ireland, Italy, Luxembourg, the Netherlands, Portugal and Spain. Membership in the euro zone involves ceding control of monetary policy to the European Central Bank, which some countries – notably Britain – remain reluctant to do.

European Community (EC) An alliance of western European nations formed to agree common policies on trade, aid, agriculture and economics. The founder members in 1957 were France, West Germany, Belgium, Holland, Luxembourg and Italy. Britain, Ireland and Denmark joined in 1973, Greece in 1981 and Spain and Portugal in 1986. East Germany became a member when it was reunited with West Germany in 1990. It became the EUROPEAN UNION with the Maastricht Treaty of 1992.

European Union (EU) The former EUROPEAN COMMUNITY, created by the Maastricht Treaty, which was signed in 1992 and implemented from 1993. The treaty gave the European parliament wider powers, setting the agenda for achieving full monetary and political union. Austria, Finland and Sweden joined the EU in 1995.

Evolution The process by which SPECIES develop their appearance, form and behavior through the process of NATURAL SELECTION, and by which new species or varieties are formed.

Exotic (animal or plant) Not native to an area but established after being introduced from elsewhere, often for commercial or decorative use.

Exports Goods and services sold to other countries, bringing in foreign exchange.

Extinction The loss of a local population of a articular SPECIES or even the entire species. It may be natural or be caused by human activity.

Family A taxonomic term for a group of related plants or animals. For example, the family Felidae (cat family) includes the lion, the tiger and all the smaller cats. Most families contain several GENERA, and families are grouped together into orders. *See* CLASSIFICATION.

Famine An acute shortage of food leading to widespread malnutrition and starvation.

Fault A fracture or crack in the Earth along which there has been movement of the rock masses.

Fauna The general term for the animals that live in a particular region.

Feudalism (1) A type of society in which landlords collect dues from the agricultural producers in return for military protection. (2) A hierarchical society of mutual obligations that preceded CAPITALISM in Europe.

First World A term sometimes used to describe the advanced industrial or DEVELOPED COUNTRIES.

Fjord A steep-sided inlet formed when the sea floods and covers a glaciated U-shaped valley. *See* GLACIATION.

Flora The plant life of a particular region.

Fossil fuel Any fuel, such as coal, oil and NATURAL GAS, formed beneath the Earth's surface under conditions of heat and pressure from organisms that died millions of years ago.

Free trade A system of international trade in which goods and services are exchanged without TARIFFS, QUOTAS or other restrictions.

GATT The General Agreement on Tariffs and Trade, a treaty that governs world imports and exports. Its aim is to promote FREE TRADE, but many countries impose TARIFF barriers to favor their own industries and agricultural produce.

GDP *See* GROSS DOMESTIC PRODUCT.

Genus (pl. genera) A level of biological CLASSIFICATION of organisms in which closely related SPECIES are grouped. For example, dogs, wolves, jackals and coyotes are all grouped together in the genus *Canis*.

Ghetto A slum area in a city that is occupied by an ETHNIC minority. The word originally referred to the area of medieval European cities to which Jews were restricted by law.

Glaciation The process of GLACIER and ice sheet growth, and their effect on the landscape.

Glacier A mass of ice formed by the compaction

and freezing of snow and which shows evidence of past or present movement.

Global warming The increase in the average temperature of the Earth that is believed to be caused by the GREENHOUSE EFFECT.

GNP *See* GROSS NATIONAL PRODUCT.

Greenhouse effect The effect of certain gases in the ATMOSPHERE, such as carbon dioxide and METHANE, in absorbing solar heat radiated back from the surface of the Earth and preventing its escape into space. Without these gases the Earth would be too cold for living things, but the burning of FOSSIL FUELS for industry and transportation has caused atmospheric levels of these gases to increase, and this is believed to be a cause of GLOBAL WARMING.

Green Revolution The introduction of high-yielding varieties of seeds (especially rice and wheat) and modern agricultural techniques to increase agricultural production in DEVELOPING COUNTRIES. It began in the early 1960s.

Gross Domestic Product (GDP) The total value of a country's annual output of goods and services, with allowances being made for depreciation. Growth in GDP is usually expressed in constant prices to offset the effects of inflation. GDP is a useful guide to the level of economic activity in a country.

Gross National Product (GNP) A country's GROSS DOMESTIC PRODUCT plus income from abroad.

Groundwater Water that has percolated into the ground from the Earth's surface, filling pores, cracks and fissures. An impermeable layer of rock prevents it from moving deeper so that the lower levels become saturate . The upper limit of saturation is known as the WATER TABLE.

Growing season The period of the year when the average temperature is high enough for plants to grow. It is longest at low altitudes and latitudes. Most plants can grow when the temperature exceeds 5°C (42°F).

Habitat The external ENVIRONMENT to which an animal or plant is adapted and in which it prefers to live, usually defined in terms of vegetation, climate or altitude – eg grassland habitat.

Hard currency A currency used by international traders because they think it is safe from DEVALUATION.

Hinduism A body of religious practices, originating in India in the 2nd millennium BC, that emphasizes ways of living rather than ways of thought. Its beliefs and practices are based on the Vedas and other scriptures and are closely intertwined with the culture of India's people.

HIV (Human Immunodeficiency Virus) *See* AIDS.

Hunter-gatherers People who obtain their food requirements by hunting wild animals and gathering the berries and fruits from wild plants.

Hurricane A tropical CYCLONE, usually found in the Caribbean and western North Atlantic.

Hybrid An animal or plant that is the offspring of two genetically different individuals. Hybrid crops are often grown because they give higher yields and are more resistant to disease.

Ice age A long period of geological time in which the temperature of the Earth falls, and snow and ice sheets are present throughout the year in mid and high latitudes.

Igneous rock Rock formed when magma (molten material in the Earth's crust) cools and solidifies.

Imperialism The process whereby one country forces its rule on another country, frequently in order to establish an EMPIRE.

Imports Goods and services purchased from other countries.

Import substitution industry Any industry that has been set up (mainly in DEVELOPING COUNTRIES) to manufacture products that used to be imported. Import substitution industries are normally simple ones with an immediate local market, such as the manufacture of cigarettes, soap and textiles. They are protected during their start-up phase by high TARIFFS on foreign rivals.

Indigenous peoples The original inhabitants of a region, generally leading a traditional way of life.

Inflation The general rise in prices when the supply of money and credit in an economy is increasing faster than the availability of goods and services.

Islam A religion based on the revelations of God to the prophet Muhammed in the 7th century AD, which are contained in the Qu'ran. Islam is widely practiced throughout North Africa, the Indian subcontinent, the Middle East and parts of Southeast Asia.

Judaism A religion founded in 2000 BC among the ancient Hebrews and practiced by Jews; its main beliefs are contained in the BIBLE.

Labor force The economically active population of a country or region, including the armed forces and the unemployed. Full-time homemakers and unpaid caregivers are not included.

Leaching The process by which water washes nutrients and minerals downward from one layer of soil to another, or into streams.

Legislature The branch of government responsible for enacting laws.

Mammal A vertebrate animal of the CLASS Mammalia, with a four-chambered heart, fur or hair, and mammae (nipples) for feeding its young on milk. Except for monotremes, mammals do not lay eggs but give birth to live young.

Mangrove A dense forest of shrubs and trees growing on tidal coastal mudflats and estuaries throughout the tropics.

Maquis The typical vegetation of the Mediterranean coast, consisting of aromatic shrubs, laurel, myrtle, rock rose, broom and small trees such as olive, fig and holm oak.

Maritime climate A generally moist climate close to the sea, whose slow cooling and heating reduces variations in temperature.

Market economy An economy in which most activities are transacted by private individuals and firms in largely unregulated markets.

Marxism The system of thought derived from the 19th-century political theorist Karl Marx, in which politics is interpreted as a struggle between economic CLASSES. It promotes communal ownership of property when it is practiced, so is popularly known as COMMUNISM.

Methane A gas produced by decomposing organic matter that burns without releasing pollutants and can be used as an energy source. Excessive methane production from vast amounts of animal manure is believed to contribute to the GREENHOUSE EFFECT.

Migrant workers Part of the LABOR FORCE which has come from another region or country, looking for temporary employment.

Monetarism An economic philosophy that sees INFLATION as the main menace to economic growth and proposes a direct relationship between the rate of growth of the money supply of a country and its subsequent rate of inflation.

Monsoon (1) The wind systems in the TROPICS that reverse their direction according to the seasons. (2) The rain caused by these winds.

Montane The zone at middle altitudes on the slopes of mountains, below the ALPINE zone.

NAFTA The North American Free Trade Agreement, signed by Canada, Mexico and the United States, and implemented on 1 January 1994, lowering trade barriers between them, though many in the US and Canada feared the massive loss of jobs to less expensive Mexico.

Nation A community that believes it consists of a single people, based upon historical and cultural criteria and sharing a common territory. Sometimes used interchangeably with STATE.

Nationalism An ideology that assumes all NATIONS should have their own STATE, a NATION-STATE, in their own territory, the national homeland.

Nation-state A STATE in which the inhabitants all belong to one NATION. Most states claim to be nation-states; in practice almost all of them include minority groups.

Natural gas A FOSSIL FUEL in the form of a flammable gas that occurs naturally in the Earth. It is often found with deposits of petroleum.

Natural resources REOURCES created by the Earth's natural processes including mineral deposits, FOSSIL FUELS, soil, air, water, plants and animals. Most natural resources are harvested by people for use in agriculture, industry and economic activities.

Natural selection The process by which organisms not well suited to their ENVIRONMENT are eliminated by predation, parasitism, competition, etc, and those that are well suited survive, breed and pass on their genes.

Nomad A member of a (usually pastoral) people that moves seasonally from one place to another in search of food, water or pasture for their animals. *See* PASTORALIST.

Nonrenewable resource A NATURAL RESOURCE that is present in the Earth's makeup in finite amounts (coal, oil etc) and cannot be replaced once reserves are exhausted.

OECD (Organization for Economic Cooperation and Development) An international organization set up in 1961 to promote the economic growth of its (now 24) member countries.

One-party system A political system in which there is no competition to the government PARTY at elections (eg communist and military regimes) and all but the government party is banned.

OPEC The Organization of Petroleum Exporting Countries, an 11-member cartel that is able to exercise a degree of control over the price of oil.

Ozone layer A band of enriched oxygen or ozone found in the upper ATMOSPHERE. It absorbs harmful ultraviolet radiation from the Sun. The heat this creates provides a cap for the Earth's weather systems.

Pangea The supercontinent that was composed of all the present-day continents and therefore included both Gondwanaland and Laurasia. It existed between 250 and 200 million years ago. *See also* CONTINENTAL DRIFT.

Parliamentary democracy A political system in which the LEGISLATURE (parliament) is elected by all the adult members of the population and the government is formed by the PARTY that commands a majority in the parliament.

Party An organized group seeking political power to implement an agreed set of policies.

Pastoralism A way of life based on tending herds

of animals such as sheep, cattle, goats or camels; often NOMADIC, it involves moving the herds as the seasons change.

Peat Soil formed by an accumulation of plant material incompletely decomposed due to low temperature and lack of oxygen, usually as a result of waterlogging.

Per capita Per head of population.

Permafrost Soil and rock that remains permanently frozen, typically in the POLAR REGIONS. A layer of soil at the surface may melt in summer, but refreezes in colder conditions.

Pesticide Any chemical substance used to control the pests that can damage crops, such as insects and rodents. Often used as a general term for herbicides, insecticides and fungicides.

pH A measurement on the scale 0–14 of the acidity or alkalinity of a substance.

Plateau A large area of level, elevated land. When bordered by steep slopes it is called a tableland.

Polar regions The regions that lie within the lines of latitude known as the ARCTIC and Antarctic circles, respectively 66°32′ north and south of the Equator. At this latitude the sun does not set in midsummer nor rise in midwinter.

Polder An area of level land at or below sea level obtained by land reclamation. It is normally used for agriculture.

Poverty line A measure of deprivation that varies from country to country. In low-income economies a certain percentage of the population lacks sufficient food and shelter. In the industrial world people are considered to be poor if they earn less than 60 percent of the average wage.

PPP Purchasing power parity – a way of measuring income or GDP for different countries based on standardized dollar values, rather than the conventional method of converting different currencies according to official exchange rates. By taking away the currency exchange factor, PPP is less prone to fluctuations that may distort the comparisons between countries.

Prairie The flat grassland in the interior of North America between 30°N and 55°N, much of which has been plowed and is used to grow CEREALS.

Precipitation Moisture that reaches the Earth from the ATMOSPHERE, including mist, dew, rain, sleet, snow and hail.

Predator An animal that feeds on another animal (the PREY).

President A head of state, elected in some countries directly by the voters and in others by members of the LEGISLATURE. In some political systems the president is chief executive, in others the office is largely ceremonial.

Prey An animal that a PREDATOR hunts and kills for food.

Productivity (1) A measure of economic output in relation to the quantity of economic inputs (labor, machines, land, etc) needed for production. (2) The amount of weight (or energy) gained by an individual, a SPECIES or an ECOSYSTEM per unit of area per unit of time.

Quota A limit imposed on the amount of a product that can be imported in a given time.

Radioactivity The emission of alpha-, beta- and gamma particles from atomic nuclei. This is greatest when the atom is split, as in a nuclear reactor. Prolonged exposure to radioactive material can cause damage to living tissue, leading to cancers and ultimately death.

Rainforest Forest in which there is abundant rainfall all year long – in tropical as well as TEMPERATE ZONES. Rainforests probably contain half of all the Earth's plant and animal species.

Refuge A place where a SPECIES of plant or animal has survived after formerly occupying a much larger area.

Resource Any material, source of information or skill that is of economic value to industry and business.

Runoff Water produced by rainfall or melting snow that flows across the land surface into streams and rivers.

Salinization The accumulation of soluble salts near or at the surface of soil in an ARID climate. Salinization can also occur when water used for irrigation evaporates; the land becomes so salty that it is worthless for cultivation.

Savanna A HABITAT of open grassland with scattered trees in tropical and subtropical areas. There is a marked dry season and too little rain to support large areas of forest.

Second World A term sometimes used to describe the DEVELOPED socialist countries (including the former Soviet Union and former Soviet bloc).

Semiarid land Any area between an ARID DESERT and a more fertile region where there is sufficient moisture to support a little more vegetation than can survive in a desert. Also called semidesert.

Separatism A political movement in a STATE that supports the secession of a particular minority group, within a defined territory, from that state.

Service industries Industries that supply services to customers or to other sectors of the economy: typically banking, transport, insurance, education, healthcare, retailing and distribution.

Shanty town An area of very poor housing consisting of ramshackle huts and other simple dwellings often made from waste materials and with inadequate services.

Shifting cultivation A method of farming prevalent in tropical areas in which a piece of land is cleared and cultivated until its fertility is diminished. The farmer then abandons the land, which restores itself naturally.

Slash-and-burn farming A method of farming in tropical areas in which the vegetation cover is cut and burned to fertilize the land before crops are planted. Often a feature of SHIFTING CULTIVATION.

Socialism An economic system and political ideology based upon the principle of equality between people, the redistribution of wealth and property, and equal access to benefits such as healthcare and education.

Solar energy The radiant energy, produced by the Sun, that powers all the Earth's processes. It can be captured and used to provide domestic heating or converted to produce electrical energy.

Specialization (in natural history) The evolutionary development of a SPECIES, leading to narrow limits of tolerance and a restricted role (or niche) in the community.

Species The basic unit of CLASSIFICATION of plants and animals. Species are grouped into GENERA and variations may be categorized into SUBSPECIES in descending order of hierarchy.

State The primary political unit of the modern world, usually defined by its possession of sovereignty over a territory and its people.

Steppe An open grassy plain with few trees or shrubs, characterized by low andsporadic rainfall, with fluctuating temperatures during the year.

Subsistence A term applied to systems in which producers can supply their own needs for food, shelter, etc but have little or no surplus to trade.

Subspecies A rank in the CLASSIFICATION of plants and animals between SPECIES and variety. It often denotes a geographical variation of a species.

Subtropical The climate zone between the TROPICS and TEMPERATE ZONES. There are marked seasonal changes of temperature but it is never very cold.

Succession The development and maturation of an ECOSYSTEM, through changes in the types and abundance of SPECIES.

Sustainability The concept of using the Earth's NATURAL RESOURCES to improve people's lives without diminishing the ability of the Earth to support life today and in the future.

Taiga The CONIFEROUS FOREST and PEAT landbelt that stretches around the world in the northern hemisphere, south of the TUNDRA and north of the DECIDUOUS forests and grasslands.

Tariff A tax on imported goods or services.

Taxonomy The scientific CLASSIFICATION of organisms.

Temperate zone Any one of the climatic zones in mid latitudes, with a mild climate. They cover areas between the warm TROPICS and cold POLAR REGIONS.

Terrestrial (of a plant, animal etc) spending its entire life cycle on the land.

Third World A term first used to refer to ex-COLONIES that were neither fully capitalist (FIRST WORLD) nor fully socialist (SECOND WORLD). Now used to refer to the poorer, less industrialized countries of the developing world.

Tribe A group of people united by a common language, religion, customs and/or descent and kinship; often used to describe the social groups of peoples who have no developed STATE or government and whose social organization is based on ancestry and extended family systems.

Tropics The area of the Earth lying between the Tropic of Cancer (23°30′ N) and the Tropic of Capricorn (23°30′ S).

Tundra The level, treeless land lying in the very cold northern regions of Europe, Asia and North America, where winters are long and cold and the ground beneath the surface is permanently frozen. *See also* PERMAFROST.

Urbanization (1) The process by which city populations grow as the rural population diminishes. (2) City formation and growth.

Water table The uppermost level of underground rock that is permanently saturated with GROUNDWATER.

Watershed The boundary line dividing two river systems. It is also known as a water-parting or divide, particularly in the United States, where the word watershed refers to a river basin (the area drained by a river and its tributaries).

Welfare state A social and economic system based on STATE provision of healthcare, pensions and unemployment insurance. These services are financed by contributions from the working population, and access is intended to be available to all, free of charge.

Wetland A HABITAT that is waterlogged all or enough of the time to support vegetation adapted to these conditions.

INDEX

Page numbers in **bold** refer to extended treatment of topic; in *italics* to caption, maps or tables

Acknowledgments

CONTRIBUTORS

General Advisory Editor
Professor Peter Haggett, University of Bristol, UK

COUNTRY PROFILES

Advisory Editor
Dr Tatyana, Vlasova, Academy of Sciences, Moscow, Russia
Dr Mike Bradshaw, University of Birmingham, UK

Writers
Asgard Publishing Services:
    Philip Gardner
    Allan Scott
    Michael Scott Rohan
    Andrew Shackleton
John and Barbara Baines
Ann Furtado

REGIONAL PROFILES

Advisory Editors

Professor Ken J. Gregory, Goldsmith's College, London, UK
Physical Geography

Robert Burton, Huntingdon, UK
Habitats and their Conservation, Animal Life

Professor D.M. Moore, University of Reading, UK
Plant Life

Dr John Tarrant, University of East Anglia, UK
Agriculture

Dr Ian Hamilton, London School of Economics, UK
Industry

Dr Stuart Corbridge, University of Cambridge, UK
Economy

Dr Alisdair Rogers, University of Oxford, UK
Peoples and Cultures

Professor John Rennie Short, Syracuse University, USA
Cities

Dr Peter Taylor, University of Newcastle upon Tyne, UK
Government

Dr Michael Williams, University of Oxford, UK
Environmental Issues

Writers

Professor Leonid Serebryanny, Academy of Sciences, Moscow, Russia   *Physical Geography*

Dr Z.J. Karpowicz, World Conservation Monitoring Center, Cambridge, UK   *Habitats and their Conservation*

Linda Gamblin, Bath, UK   *Animal Life*

Charles Jeffrey, Royal Botanic Gardens, Kew, UK   *Plant Life*

Dr John Tarrant, University of East Anglia, UK   *Agriculture*

Dr Ian Hamilton, London School of Economics, UK   *Industry*

Dr Graham Smith, University of Cambridge, UK   *Economy*

Dr Andrew Ryder, University of Portsmouth, UK
Peoples and Cultures

Professor J.H. Bater, University of Waterloo, Ontario, Canada
Cities

Dr G.E. Smith, Univeristy of Cambridge, UK   *Government*

Dr Tatyana Vlasova, Academy of Sciences, Moscow, Russia
Environmental Issues

Updated edition:

Editorial Director: Graham Bateman
Project Manager: Lauren Bourque
Cartography Manager: Richard Watts
Cartography Editor: Tim Williams
Editorial Assistant: Rita Demetriou
Picture Manager: Claire Turner
Picture Research: Alison Floyd
Design: Martin Anderson
Typesetting: Brian Blackmore
Production: Clive Sparling, Nicolette Colborne

Further Reading

Bridges, O. and Bridges, J. *Losing Hope: The Environment and Health in Russia* (Ashgate Publishing, Brookfield, USA, 1996)

Chernov, Yu. I. *The Living Tundra* (Cambridge University Press, Cambridge, 1985)

Dawisha, K. and Parrott, B. *Russia and the New States of Eurasia* (Cambridge University Press, Cambridge, 1994)

Ellman, M. and Kontrovich, V. (eds.) *The Disintegration of the Soviet Economic System* (Routledge, London, 1992)

Flint, V.E., Boehme, R.L., Kostin, Y.V. and Kuznetsov, A.A. *A Field Guide to Birds of Russia and Adjacent Territories* Repr. (Princeton University Press, 1989)

Harris, D.R. (ed.) *The Origins and Spread of Agriculture and Pastoralism in Eurasia* (Smithsonian Institution Press, USA, 1996)

International Politics of Eurasia Series, 10 vols. (M.E. Sharpe, Armonk, USA, 1995)

Khazanov, A.M. *After the USSR: Ethnicity, Nationalism, and Politics in the Commonwealth of Indepedent States* (University of Wisconsin Press, Madison, 1996)

McFaul, M. *Russia's Unfinished Revolution: Political Change from Gorbachev to Putin* (Cornell University Press, Ithaca, USA, 2001)

Pryde, P.R. *Environmental Management in the Soviet Union* (Cambridge University Press, Cambridge, 1991)

Smith, G. (ed.) *The Nationalities Question in the Post-Soviet States* (Longman, London, 1995)

Sparkes, J. *Realms of the Russian Bear* (BBC, London, 1992)

Useful websites:
www.cia.gov/cia/publications/factbook
www.websites.ru
www.globalissues.org
www.whyfiles.news.wisc.edu
www.insiderussia.com

www.virtualhouse.org
www.europeaninternet.com/russia
www.igc.org
www.pacific.marine.su